THE COMPLETE STUDENT

STUDENT

ACHIEVING SUCCESS IN COLLEGE AND BEYOND

Join us on the web at

careersuccess.delmar.com

THE COMPLETE STUDENT

STUDENT

ACHIEVING SUCCESS IN COLLEGE AND BEYOND

ALAN GELB

THOMSON

DELMAR LEARNING

Australia Canada Mexico Singapore Spain United Kingdom United States

THOMSON

━━━━━━━━★━━━━━━━━ ™

DELMAR LEARNING

The Complete Student
Alan Gelb

Vice President, Career Education SBU:
Dawn Gerrain

Director of Learning Solutions:
Sherry Dickinson

Managing Editor:
Robert L. Serenka, Jr.

Acquisitions Editor:
Martine Edwards

Product Manager:
Jennifer Anderson

Editorial Assistant:
Falon Ferraro

Director of Production:
Wendy A. Troeger

Production Manager:
J.P. Henkel

Production Editor:
Rebecca Goldthwaite

Director of Marketing:
Wendy E. Mapstone

Channel Manager:
Gerard McAvey

Marketing Assistant:
Erica Conley

Cover Illustration:
©2005 James Yang, All Rights Reserved

Cover Design:
Metze Publication Design

Library of Congress Cataloging-in-Publication Data

Gelb, Alan.
  The complete student : achieving success in college and beyond / Alan Gelb.-- 1st ed.
    p. cm.
  Includes bibliographical references and index.
  ISBN-13: 978-1-4018-9565-5 (alk. paper)
  ISBN-10: 1-4018-9565-4 (alk. paper)
  1. College student orientation--United States. 2. Study skills--United States. I. Title.
  LB2343.32.G45 2006
  378.1'98--dc22

                                    2006002884

NOTICE TO THE READER

Publisher does not warrant or guarantee any of the products described herein or perform any independent analysis in connection with any of the product information contained herein. Publisher does not assume, and expressly disclaims, any obligation to obtain and include information other than that provided to it by the manufacturer.

The reader is expressly warned to consider and adopt all safety precautions that might be indicated by the activities herein and to avoid all potential hazards. By following the instructions contained herein, the reader willingly assumes all risks in connection with such instructions.

The Publisher makes no representation or warranties of any kind, including but not limited to, the warranties of fitness for particular purpose or merchantability, nor are any such representations implied with respect to the material set forth herein, and the publisher takes no responsibility with respect to such material. The publisher shall not be liable for any special, consequential, or exemplary damages resulting, in whole or part, from the readers' use of, or reliance upon, this material.

The authors and Thomson Delmar Learning affirm that the Web site URLs referenced herein were accurate at the time of printing. However, due to the fluid nature of the Internet, we cannot guarantee their accuracy for the life of the edition.

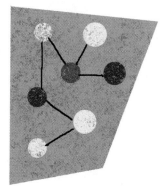

INTRODUCTION: WHY THIS BOOK?

Here you are, ready for college. It's that pivotal point in your life when the future has become the present. Whether you're a first-time college student right out of high school, an older student who has been putting off this experience, or a returning student whose progress was interrupted, the big moment has arrived. This is a time of great excitement, as you sort out all the change that is coming your way, and it can also be a time of stress. After all, there is an awful lot to sort out, isn't there?

The college years are **permeated** with myth, and it can take a while to absorb the reality of the experience. On the one hand, you recognize that college is going to be a challenge—a time for thick books, tough professors, late nights, and grinding exams. On the other hand, college has a reputation for being a time of great fun—full of varsity games, mixers, fraternities and sororities, and opportunities to experiment with many aspects of life that until now have mostly been outside your **purview**. It can be difficult to strike the right balance, both for students starting out in adult life, who may need some maturing, and for the older student, who may feel that only a portion of the entire college experience can be enjoyed at this point in life.

permeated spread through thoroughly
purview range of view, experience, or understanding

Whatever your profile may be, one thing is clear—life is going to be different now. Even if you're living at home and school is just 5 miles down the road, the landscape will be changing. The personal growth that lies ahead is not bound by geography, economy, gender, ethnicity, religion, or age. No matter how these factors play out in your life, college provides the perfect environment for making the leap onto the next plateau of your life. *The Complete Student* was created to help maximize the growth that comes with this great opportunity. Hang around with some seriously older folks for a while, and eventually you're bound to hear someone say, "Why did I waste my college years? I had no idea how valuable they were." In fact, having this time in your life to expand your worldview, to develop a broad base of knowledge, to identify an area of interest that can sustain you over the course of a career, and to develop a foundation of skills that will allow you to embark on that career (or on a relevant course of graduate studies) is absolutely invaluable.

This is a time in your life that is characterized by newfound freedom and newfound academic demands. Again, your challenge is to strike the right balance, but don't expect to master this balancing act right from the start. Few people do. Even those students who kept everything under control in high school often become a bit unfocused when they arrive at college. The feeling of freedom is **heady**. What's more, the developmental issues that you face as you move into adulthood—things like serious romantic relationships and increased economic responsibility—can seriously distract you from your academics. As for the issues that face the older student, these come with their own set of complications. But that's where *The Complete Student* comes in: to help you gain your focus and keep it.

Because It's Different...

Why, you ask, if there are any number of excellent books on the market that are designed to help college students function more effectively, should trees be cut down for yet another one?

That's an excellent question, to which we have a simple answer: *Because this book is different*.

Although *The Complete Student* offers the same kind of solid information, tips, techniques, and tools that you would find in more conventional books about student readiness and success, it doesn't

heady intoxicating

feel like those textbooks, which often envelop readers in a film of boredom. We understand that life for college students today is very busy, intense, and pressured, and that's exactly why we set out to create a feeling of accessibility here. You should be able to pick up this book whenever and wherever you can, read a chapter or two, or even just a few pages, and come away each time having learned something truly useful and valuable.

Leaf through this book and you'll find that *The Complete Student* really does look and sound different from anything else out there. We set a goal for ourselves (and you'll be reading all about goals shortly, in Chapter 2)—to create a design that would feel clean and lively and be a pleasure to look at. The dense clutter that often characterizes books of this nature simply isn't present. What's more, we've only included material that's really important. And in terms of the writing, we wanted the book to sound like one person talking to another. We want you to enjoy reading this book, and have done our best to make sure that you do.

The online companion to *The Complete Student* provides additional resources to accompany each chapter, including interactive vocabulary and chapter review quizzes, helpful tips and articles for more information, links to resources on the Web, "Case in Point" profiles and downloadable worksheets from the text. To access the companion, go to http://www.delmarlearning.com/companions/ and search by author (Gelb) or title (The Complete Student).

Because *You're* Different...

We said it once, we'll say it again, and we'll be saying it all through this book: by the time you finish college, you will not be the same person as when you started. College is truly **transformative**. The changes ahead of you will be across-the-board—academic, social, emotional, psychological, and perhaps even spiritual in nature. That's why we've conceived a book that looks at the college experience as a whole. It doesn't make sense to talk about college simply as an academic experience. It's much more than that. No matter what your age is when you enter, college is very much about mastering all the nonacademic skills that are necessary to succeed in this world: getting along with other people, honing your ability to organize your time, managing your finances, achieving the discipline that allows you to foster good personal habits and steer clear of bad ones, and more.

transformative having the power or tendency to transform or change

Throughout the book, you'll see sections labeled Open to Discussion, like this one. These **denote** topics that can lead to some stimulating classroom exchange. Let's start with this one: discuss, as a group, what "success" means. Is it only about pulling in a good income? Where do self-respect and the respect of others come in? What about the noble ideal of helping people less fortunate than yourself? Does that still have any relevance today? Has the world changed in terms of what is valued? Exchange your thoughts in small groups if you wish, and then regroup to share these ideas collectively.

With all of this in mind, we have subtitled this book "Achieving Success in College and Beyond." That sounds inviting, doesn't it? But before you can achieve success, you have to understand what success means to you.

The other **component** of our subtitle that we wanted to draw your attention to is "in College and Beyond." We see college as a start—the beginning of the road. The habits that you should be developing in college—a truly professional work ethic, an organized approach to time, a respect for the opinions of others, an appreciation of cultural diversity, and more—are habits that will sustain you throughout your life and your career. Hence, the word "beyond." Of course, if you're an adult and/or returning student, you've already been "beyond," and are coming to college with that much more in the way of valuable life skills. Older students can be very important in the classroom in helping their younger colleagues see things from another perspective.

Keep an Eye Out for These

We'll be covering a lot of material in this book—everything from budgeting money to budgeting time to dealing effectively with teachers to buying a used car and maintaining good health habits. To help keep you focused as you proceed, we have **devised** some recurring features that can work as familiar signposts. So, before we go any further, we'd like to point out and explain these recurring features:

- *Open to Discussion* (we "opened that discussion" a few pages ago, remember?)
- *Reflections.* When you see this sign, it will signify that it's time to write. As you practice your writing, you'll be practicing a form of communication that will prove important to you throughout your life. At some future point, you may find yourself writing cover letters for resumés, letters of complaint about that car radio that didn't work or that winter coat that fell apart, and letters of reference for friends and colleagues. As a matter of fact, despite all the premature obituaries in its behalf, the truth is that the written word is alive and well. Indeed, people are probably communicating by written word more in this era of e-mail than they have at any point since the 19th century. While writing is certainly an important way for people to communicate with each other, it also happens to be a perfect way for

denote point out or make known
component part
devised produced, invented

you to communicate with *yourself*. A blank sheet of paper need not be cause for alarm. Instead, regard it as an invitation to think more deeply, to reflect, and to explore and examine those thoughts that, without reflection, would tend to buzz around randomly, threatening distraction.

• *Food for Thought.* You will regularly see this heading, which signals your chance to read additional information and insights into what we've been discussing in the chapter. Research studies, news stories, and material from miscellaneous other sources will be featured in these sections.

• *In Other Words.* Often we've found that other people have said what we'd like to say in a more compelling, inventive, and profound way. When it comes to words of wisdom, we defer to people like Gandhi, Einstein, Martin Luther King, Ralph Waldo Emerson, and Mother Teresa. If thoughts that **emanate** from great minds interest you— and we can't imagine why they wouldn't—please give them your attention. (To start your own "wisdom bank," keep a file on your computer for memorable quotes. You'll be surprised how effectively these can sustain you in times of crisis or confusion.)

• *Student Talk.* Throughout the book, you'll find places where the real voices of real students speak out. These students are very much like you—people who are striving to succeed, who have hurdles to over-come, who are entering this phase of life with hope, confusion, en-thusiasm, and sometimes fear. Hearing the voices of these students makes us realize that we all have a lot to learn from each other.

• *A Case in Point.* Every now and then, we'll choose to expand on a point by exploring the history of a particular individual in some depth. These individuals may be famous or not—it really doesn't matter. Sometimes ordinary people can be absolutely extraordinary, as you will discover. These stories **exemplify** the potential that is **inherent** in each of us.

• *What Did We Learn?* Consider this a quiz—self-tested or as directed by your instructor—that will help you review and, hopefully, retain the information you learned in any given chapter.

• *Links and Bibliographies.* As we've already said, *The Complete Student* offers a great deal of information, but it cannot be all things to all people. We realize that there are certain areas in which you

emanate to flow from a source
exemplify to show by example
inherent essential to; naturally found

IN OTHER WORDS

We couldn't leave this Introduction without sharing a few good thoughts about education in general:

• "Education is not something to prepare you for life; it is a continu-ous part of life."—Henry Ford, automobile pioneer

• "At its best, schooling can be about how to make a life, which is quite different from how to make a living."—Neil Postman, educator and media critic

• "Education is learning what you didn't even know you didn't know."— Daniel J. Boorstin, historian and Librarian of Congress Emeritus

will want to gain more knowledge on your own. These links and bibliographies will direct you to other avenues of research—books, articles, and Internet sites—that may be of interest.

Oh, we almost forgot—there's one more recurrent feature. It's called *Word Smart*. Surely by now you've noticed that certain words in this book appear in bold. If you check the bottom of the page, you will find that word's definition. Some of you may find this method to be slightly annoying; we hope not. We hope, instead, that you will take it in the spirit in which it is given—a very constructive spirit that **advocates** vocabulary building. A good vocabulary along with a sturdy grasp of English grammar will distinguish you as you make your way in the world. This book provides a nice "starter set" of words that can help you move toward the head of the class. Of course, if you already have an excellent vocabulary, just read these words in bold as you normally would, and please excuse our boldness.

Time to Begin

Now that we've discussed the theories behind this book's development and have pointed out the recurring features that will help you use it effectively, it's time to roll up our sleeves and get to work. This is your opportunity to learn, and that opportunity is a basic human right that, in some parts of the world, is feverishly sought after and often denied. You're one of the lucky ones. You can learn as much as you want. You have a powerful education system to draw upon, free libraries to use, free Internet to explore, and all kinds of resources available to you. We salute you, we congratulate you, and we wish you a hearty *bon voyage* on this journey you're undertaking. See you in Chapter 1.

advocates to speak or write in favor of

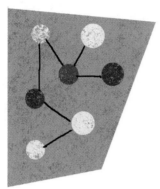

ACKNOWLEDGMENTS

Thomson Delmar Learning and the author thank the dedicated group of educators and students who reviewed this book and provided valuable suggestions for its development:

Daniel Burns
Siena College
Loudonville, New York

David L. Christensen
Lake Havasu High School
Lake Havasu City, Arizona

Janet Cutshall
Sussex County Community College
Newton, New Jersey

Mary DeBey, Ph.D.
Brooklyn College
Brooklyn, New York

Cheryl Hollatz-Wisely, M.Ed.
Portland State University
Portland, Oregon

Kevin Pugh, M.S.
University of Colorado–Boulder
Boulder, Colorado

Leo Sevigny
Lyndon State College
Lyndonville, Vermont

Anthony (Toby) J. Strianese
Schenectady County Community College
Schenectady, New York

CONTENTS

PART ONE

GETTING STARTED

LAYING THE GROUNDWORK

Different people approach school in different ways. For some students, learning comes easily. They're able to retain all kinds of information and know, for instance, where the Magna Carta, the great charter of English liberties, was signed. (In a field by the Thames River called Runnymede.) Other students not so blessed with retentive memories seem to recall that the Magna Carta was one of Columbus's ships ... wasn't it? This group of students may not be particularly gifted at retaining information, but they can have other achievements to feel good about. Perhaps they've distinguished themselves in a certain field, like sports or theater or music, and, when it comes to their studies, they're satisfied to do just "well enough." They're learning and growing, but not necessarily at an accelerated rate.

A third group are those students who float through school totally adrift. These individuals have lost their motivation, and, until they get it back, school might just as well be the state penitentiary. They feel trapped, bored, and often angry. Half the time, they're not even sure what they're angry about. They indulge in truancy and, sadly, often drop out altogether.

Finally, we have our very sizable group of adult and returning students, who have, by choice or necessity, decided against the direct route to a diploma and have put their academic aspirations on the back burner. Now, returning to school, they may feel a little rusty. Do they even remember how to take notes and study for exams?

No matter which of these groups you may belong to, it is our conviction that with the right motivation, supported by a solid set of skills, almost anyone can succeed at school. And when we refer to "skills," we're not talking about proficiency in algebra or fluency in French or knowing one's way around a lab. Those are all important *academic* skills, but, in this chapter, and throughout this book, we are going to be focusing on the life skills that we must all attempt to master to be successful in school—and beyond.

The way to begin is by understanding yourself better—and this applies to all of us, regardless of age. Where have you been and where are you going? What are your patterns and how do you wish to change? Let's cast a look backward and see what your school career has been like for you thus far.

What's Your History?

By the time students reach college age, they've compiled lengthy school histories, starting with those happy face stickers they may (or may not) have received in kindergarten and working their way through years of science fairs, art projects, research papers, group reports, reading assessments, fetal shark dissections, and so forth. For students who enter college at an older age, those memories may actually feel too remote to recall and those earlier school years exist as a kind of gray zone.

In looking backward, most people regard their school experiences with some degree of **ambivalence**. They may have done well in some subjects, but not so well in others. They might think of themselves as being "good in English" but "terrible at math" (or vice versa). There are some students who have always been at the head of the class, who know how to sit for long periods, reviewing a book, studying for an exam, and immersing themselves in the job of being a student; and then there are those who find school unbearable. In short, when it comes to school, no one is a blank slate. We all carry around the marks of our experiences.

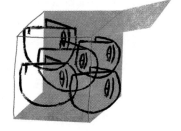

The looks we once got from a teacher or the unkind words that were said to us in second, third, or fourth grade have the power to haunt us as adults. The **stigma** we felt when we received the lowest grade in the

ambivalence contradictory emotions or ideas
stigma mark of disgrace

© Image 100 Ltd

class or when people laughed at us over a "stupid" answer can still hurt years later. On the brighter side, the sense of achievement that we enjoyed upon successfully completing a task or a project can continue to sustain us as we move forward toward bigger tasks and more far-reaching projects.

As you launch yourself on your college career—a critical juncture in your life, no matter how old you are—it is important to consider your history as a student. You'll want to understand what has motivated you in the past and what has inhibited you, what has stimulated you and what has discouraged you, what went in one ear and out the other, and what lodged so powerfully in your memory. President Harry S. Truman once said, "Those who do not read and understand history are doomed to repeat it." If you're not 100 percent satisfied with your history—and few of us are—then you definitely will want to explore the matter to discover the source of any negative thoughts and feelings.

The Time of Your Life

Once you've finished your Reflections exercise, you may find that a whole new set of questions has opened up for you. For instance, if you've never felt very good about school, then why are you here now, doing *more* of it? If what you really want is to become a hair stylist or an airline pilot or a pastry chef, then why do you need to know who signed the Declaration of Independence or how many couplets are in a sonnet? Even if you happen to be academically inclined, you may be more confused and pressured about what you should be doing and feeling right now than you've ever felt before.

This kind of confusion and pressure very typically affects incoming college students, no matter what your age. College is an exciting time,

REFLECTIONS: *YOUR HISTORY*

With this exercise, we'd like you to explore what being a student has meant to you. Jot down your thoughts prompted by the questions listed here. You do not need to use complete sentences. Right now, this is just for you ... or whomever you wish to share it with.

- Which school experiences have made you feel good?
- Which have made you feel bad?
- What was there about school that excited you, if anything?
- If you could go back in time and be a different kind of student, what would you change?
- Fill in the blank: *The first word that comes to mind when I think of school is _____.*

but it can also be overwhelming. Young adulthood—the period in life that for many people is ushered in by college—is exciting and even thrilling, but it can also be daunting. As with most of life's big transitions, there are things lost and things gained. New friendships are waiting to be made—your roommates, your classmates, your teammates, your fraternity brothers or sorority sisters—but let's not forget about those friendships that may have to be put on hold, at least for a while. Even if you're just 10 miles from home or even if you're *living* at home, you may not feel like hanging around with high school chums Bob or Bill or Sue at the Tastee Diner anymore. You may feel the need to make the break with old friends, at least for a while. You'll probably want to create some new distance as well between yourself and your family. Making these kinds of changes can be painful at first for everyone.

In fact, soon after you begin college, you'll start to realize that your life is changing in all kinds of ways. There are so many new academic choices. Did your high school offer The Films of Clint Eastwood or the History of Underground Comics—courses that are found at some of our nation's colleges? But, along with this new freedom of choice, there is more responsibility. *You're* the one picking your courses. *You're* the one choosing a career path. *You're* the one responsible for getting your work in on time. *You're* the one who must make sure that your course credits are distributed according to the curriculum requirements of your school. While your parents, teachers, guidance counselor, or significant other can greatly influence your thinking about many of your college concerns, the primary responsibility remains with you, and that can feel alternately liberating and frightening.

For the young adult going through all these changes, certain habits from adolescence have a tendency to linger. Take something like peer pressure, for instance—it doesn't simply vanish the moment you step up to the registrar's office and pay your college tuition. In fact, peer pressure—often thought of as primarily an adolescent phenomenon— can intensify in college, at least at the beginning, when people are eagerly looking to form new friendships and will do almost anything to show that they know how to have a good time. This is why issues like binge drinking have become so problematic on many college campuses. (We'll be talking about binge drinking in more depth later in this book, along with other bad habits that we hope you'll sidestep.)

So, as you launch your college career—which for many people can happen years after high school graduation, but which may still present

FOOD FOR THOUGHT:
"STICKER SHOCK"

College costs are rising faster than inflation, which is a scary prospect for most
Americans. Adjusted for inflation, tuition costs for
public colleges have grown 40 percent over the
past 10 years and have more than doubled over
the past 20 years. (At private colleges and universities, tuition has outpaced inflation by 33 percent
and 112 percent over the past 10 and 20 years,
respectively.) On the other hand, on average, a
person with a college degree earns over a *million
dollars* more over the course of a lifetime than
someone with only a high school diploma. While
there is a great deal of publicity about schools
whose tuition exceeds $40,000 a year, you should
also realize that roughly 70 percent of students
who attend 4-year colleges are actually paying
less than $10,000 a year. In fact, after factoring
in financial aid, the reality is that 29 percent of
students attending 4-year colleges *pay less than
$4,000* for tuition and fees.

Source: H & R Block Web site. Retrieved
December 7, 2005, from http://www.collegeboard
.com/article/0,3868,6-29-0-638,00.html

the same sorts of pitfalls no matter what your age—you should know
that you're starting a great adventure. And virtually every great adventure begins with a somewhat nauseating feeling in the pit of the stomach—a sensation known as "butterflies." It's perfectly understandable.
After all, there's a lot at stake. Are there commitments in your life that
make it difficult for you to be here right now? Do you have a parent or
a child or a sibling who is unwell or troubled or needs extra attention?
Do you have a significant other that will want more of your time than
you'll have to offer? What about economic concerns? If you're paying
for college yourself, we don't have to say another word, do we? But even
if your parents are paying, you may be worried about whether they can
afford it. After all, a college education is a huge investment.

As you look at this exciting new era in your life, and as you consider
the questions and feelings that are raised, your best course of action is
to tell yourself that you *can* do it and that it is worth doing. The days
and years ahead of you are going to be good ones, full of discovery and
achievement and rewards. No matter how overwhelmed you may feel at
first, remind yourself that others, just like you, have managed to succeed
in school, so why you should be any different?

The way your see yourself—your self-image—plays an important role
in your ability to succeed. For this reason, we will be spending the rest
of this chapter looking at issues like self-image, self-esteem, and one's
outlook on life. It is important for you to get a handle on these issues so
that you can be in the best possible shape for the challenges you will be
facing.

The Older Student

We have mentioned adults who return to or start college years after
they've completed high school, and this book is designed to be useful to
older as well as younger students. Obviously, it is difficult to address the
interests, needs, and concerns of 18-year-olds and 35-year-olds simul-
taneously, but we'll try our best. Allow us then to take a few moments
here to discuss some of the specific concerns of the older student.

One of the major trends of the last 25 years has been the return of
adults over the age of 25 to colleges and universities. Recent statistics
from the U.S. Department of Education show that adult students are the
fastest growing segment of the student population in the United States,
with those over the age of 25 now representing more than 41 percent
of all college students (www.back2college.com). The concerns of the
older student are very real. College is a balancing act for all students,

© Image 100 Ltd

but older students may have to be even more nimble at this balancing. Students who are parents know very well how thoroughly children
can occupy your time, and creating boundaries and working out a fair
relationship with your spouse regarding child duties is not an easy task.
As we progress through this book, we will address some of the specific
issues that face the older student, but, for now, let's just look at a few of
the broader-stroke issues and how to begin to deal with them.

Here are our "top tips" for the older student:

1) *Know why you're doing this*. Going back to school is a very big
   deal, so it helps to be clear in your motivation. Do you want to
   change careers? Increase your earning potential? Feel the sense
   of pride that comes with getting a degree? As a first step, identify
   the reason(s) why you are going back to school. This will help to
   keep you focused from the very beginning of this journey.

2) *Devise a game plan*. If you have a plan in mind, you'll be more
   likely to achieve your goals. For instance, how long do you think it
   will take you to get your degree? Be realistic about your available
   time. Do you have children? If so, you can't very well ignore them
   for the next 4 (or more) years. When formulating your plan, consider the kind of support you have available to you. Do you have
   parents or siblings who could help you with your parenting duties?
   Consider and weigh the many factors involved in going to school,
   and start figuring out ways to deal with these issues.

3) *You might want to start off slowly*. When returning to school, perhaps you'll want to dip your big toe into the water first, taking a

course or two, rather than a full load. Then, when you're feeling more confident about your ability to perform academically and your capacity to juggle the demands in your life, you can take on more.

4) *View learning as a lifelong process.* Don't feel that your education is something that you have to "get done." Sure, getting a degree is a worthy goal, but you've been out in the world already and you know that a piece of paper is ultimately not going to make or break you. Integrate learning into your life in an organic way, and enjoy it.

5) *Brush up your skills as necessary.* It may have been quite a while since you were in school. Things have changed, and even those things that haven't changed may seem foreign to you at the beginning. You'll want to learn how to use the library, and you'll want to improve your computer skills. You may want to utilize your school's Writing Center to help you organize your thoughts on paper. Don't feel that you should know all this "already." Be realistic about your needs right now, and help yourself as best you can.

6) *Understand the financial picture.* Younger college students can get themselves into all kinds of trouble taking on loans and using credit in irresponsible ways. Guess what? So can adults. Sit down with a counselor in your school's Financial Aid office and make sure you understand all that you need to know about the financial aspects of this endeavor.

Your experience going to school at an older age will have its difficulties. Juggling school with life responsibilities calls for a certain amount of fortitude and daring. If you're reading this, then you've gotten quite far with your ambitions, and for that you should be congratulated. Remember, too, that adult students have maturity on their side. They're experienced with decision making and crisis management. In other words, you have the life skills at this point to deal with almost anything that comes your way.

Self-Esteem

No matter how old you are, lack of self-esteem can be a serious problem that can inhibit you from achieving your full potential. Like peer pressure, self-esteem may sound like one of those hot button issues you've been hearing about for years, but even though you may have heard a lot about it, do you really understand its critical importance?

Self-esteem is closely connected to other issues like self-image and self-validation. Too many people look to approval from others to get their validation and boost their self-esteem—it's that "15 minutes of fame" bit. Real validation, on the other hand, comes from the recognition you give to *yourself*. It can be very overt and purposeful—looking in the mirror and saying something out loud like, "I'm a hard worker"—or it can be a quieter, deeper, and more organic sense of self-worth that you cultivate and hopefully carry around with you. If you can't honestly say that you do carry around a healthy feeling of self-esteem, don't worry. There's plenty of time to start developing the good, positive, life-affirming habits that will help you build your self-esteem.

YOU'RE NOT GOING TO WEAR *THAT*, ARE YOU?

While many people are lucky enough to have grown up in supportive homes, others have unfortunately developed low self-esteem because of insensitive or even cruel voices they have heard from their earliest years. Parents who have themselves been on the receiving end of poor parenting may carry on the tradition with their children. These are the parents that call their children "stupid," "fat," "worthless," "lazy" ... need we go on? Some parents are subtler as they give off mixed messages. "You look lovely, dear, but are you really going to wear *that*?" Or, "You're a hard worker, son, but maybe you shouldn't push yourself." Or, "It's nice that you're friends with Kyle, but I think he's only using you." These kinds of negative thoughts, often veiled by sweeter ones, can be just as damaging to children as the obvious insults that some more **resilient** youths are able to tune out after a while.

Feelings of low self-esteem can also result from the way one interacts with one's peer group. Children can be very insensitive, and if you happen to be nonathletic or if your body type doesn't match this month's teen idol or you have a "weird" name, you could be in for it. Some people who are teased have the capacity to bounce back quickly from the taunting. Others are not so strong, and, in fact, might "buy into" the game by becoming chronic victims—a role that is at least clearly defined for them.

Another way that low self-esteem can infect a child is when he or she is exposed to a teacher who is cruel. Some teachers are notorious for their cruelty, but because their reputation is already so widespread, their capacity to damage a student's ego may be somewhat diminished. After

resilient able to recover quickly

FOOD FOR THOUGHT: GAUGING YOUR SELF-ESTEEM

How do you know if your self-esteem is everything it should be? Ask yourself the following questions:

- Do you feel confident entering a room full of strangers?
- Do you see yourself as an interesting and worthwhile person?
- Do you feel as attractive and socially comfortable as others?
- Do you give yourself a chance to try new things?

If you find yourself answering "No" more than "Yes," then this is a topic that you'll want to pay close attention to.

"**W**hen did my self-esteem start to slide? It goes way back, to when I was really young. I was one of those kids who could never sit still in my seat. Teachers hated me! Then I got my diagnosis—Attention Deficit Disorder. I started on prescription drugs and they helped me a lot. But the damage was already done to my self-image, and it's taken me many years to build it back up again."

—Terry S., 18, Boise, ID.

OPEN FOR DISCUSSION:
SELF-IMAGE

As a group, spend some time thinking about how society at large affects the development of an individual's self-image.

- How do media and advertising influence the way we see ourselves and other people?
- Can you think of specific ways that certain individuals or groups are held up to ridicule in our society?
- What are some ways that you yourself buy into society's vision of what's hot and what's not?

all, if you know what to expect, you might be able to prepare yourself for it. Other teachers, however, may be subtly cruel, lacing their words with sarcasm or habitually ignoring certain students. Such techniques can have a harmful effect on a student's self-esteem that can last for years. Fortunately, however, far more of our teachers are constructive rather than destructive.

Here's a news flash: it is virtually impossible to know who among us suffers from low self-esteem. Just because a person is beautiful or seems to be popular or does well in school does not mean that he or she has a positive self-image. That beautiful girl in your French class may well have the stuff to become a supermodel, but she could also be suffering from an eating disorder. The captain of the football team may be a big man on campus, but that doesn't mean that he's immune from depression. **Conversely**, the boy with the terrible acne might feel very good about himself, having been well loved and well cared for all his life. Similarly, the girl who is 100 pounds overweight might possess a positive self-image, even though she has to cope with society's rudeness toward people who don't conform to certain standards of beauty.

Personality and Behavior

To a certain extent, your ability to feel genuine self-esteem will be dictated by the nature of your personality. There are many indicators that affect personality—everything from stress to cultural norms to gender characteristics—but, in the context of this discussion, we are going to focus on two particularly important traits: *optimism* and *pessimism*. While you may not fall neatly into either one of these camps, most people definitely feel a gravitational pull toward one or the other of these twin poles.

You've probably heard the expression that the world is divided between those who see the glass as half-full and those who see it as half-empty. The half-full folks are your optimists. They look to the bright side, which is undoubtedly an easier way to live. Pessimists tend to see the worst in any situation, and, therefore, may be reluctant to fully embrace all aspects of life. If, for instance, you're worried about an ice cream cone melting on you, you may avoid ice cream cones altogether and that would be a sad day in August, wouldn't it?

While optimism and pessimism are broad-based orientations, most of us carry around negative and positive thoughts and beliefs that we are

conversely with the terms of the relation reversed

constantly trying to balance. Some of these beliefs are drummed into us at a very early age and it can be extremely difficult to rid yourself of them. Indeed, you can be a fundamentally positive and optimistic sort of person but you can still carry around such negative self-beliefs as, "I can't do math" or "I can't carry a tune." Somewhere along the line these messages were hard-wired into your brain.

An optimistic orientation certainly makes it easier to rid oneself of negative thoughts, but steady determination and even the intervention of others may be necessary to complete the job. If the negative thought is strong enough—as in "I can't do math"—it may actually work itself up into a *self-fulfilling prophecy*. This is a belief that is so strong that it often comes true, even if the belief has no basis in reality and logic. That person who thinks he can't do math (but who actually might be perfectly capable of it) may go into a daze sitting down for a standardized math test, thus turning his conviction about himself into an absolute truth.

LEARNED OPTIMISM

In fact, people do change ... if they're really motivated. But can a person actually transform his or her basic orientation from pessimistic to optimistic? Cognitive psychologist Martin Seligman is convinced you can and that is the premise of his 1991 best seller, *Learned Optimism*.

In this thought-provoking book, Seligman ponders why some people are able to persevere in the face of great disappointment or loss while others succumb to the sadness. He believes that it is not so much a matter of will but rather of learned behavior. Those who can survive disappointment and loss do not view defeat as a permanent condition or a reflection on their basic value as human beings. Instead, they see this as a temporary state that they can find their way out of.

It is Seligman's theory that, while a pessimist may wilt in the face of disappointment, an optimist will find the resources to break through the barriers. While he acknowledges that people tend to be either more or less optimistic or pessimistic, he believes that one can learn new ways of being, and that anyone, regardless of their disappointment or difficulties, has the capacity to become an optimist. "Pessimism," states Seligman, "is escapable."

The ways to escape include: (1) adopting an "explanatory style" in which you routinely explain to yourself why things happen the way they do; (2) boosting your mood and your immune system with healthful thoughts; and (3) changing your interior dialogue, eliminating expressions like "I give up." Another powerful tool for changing the way you

STUDENT TALK: LOOKING AT THE GLASS

"My sister and I are total opposites. She's Miss Glass Half-Empty while I'm Mister Glass Half-Full. The other day, we stopped in at this bakery to get doughnuts, and I'm standing there trying to make up my mind between lemon custard and German chocolate while she's going on about how the holes have gotten bigger! That's just the way she is, and you know what? She's never going to change."

—Will L., 21, Philadelphia, PA.

react to disappointments or difficulties is *positive self-talk*. Positive self-talk along with positive thinking are superb tools for strengthening your self-esteem.

Positive Thinking and Positive Self-Talk

It is an unfortunate fact that too many people go around muttering cruel, rude, and unpleasant things to themselves.

> "Boy, were you stupid in that class!"
> "What's the matter with you?"
> "Everybody was laughing."
> "You can't do anything right."

Positive self-talk is based on the **premise** that it's just as easy to be kind and supportive to oneself as it is to be unkind and not supportive.

People who have developed positive outlooks on life clearly understand that what is happening today may not necessarily happen tomorrow. A day in which your car breaks down, you lose the paper you've worked on all night, your romantic partner tells you that he or she needs some "distance," or your child gets suspended from middle school can give way tomorrow to all kinds of good luck, satisfying achievements, ego-building feedback, and more.

A person who has the knack for positive self-talk will use a comforting inner dialogue to get through those rough patches that life **inevitably** doles out. How do you acquire that knack? The good news is that it's really not that hard. If you have the motivation to start thinking in new and different ways, then you'll soon be able to master the techniques of this form. A main characteristic of positive self-talk is that it is active. Always use the present tense when you're talking to yourself. Instead of saying, "I *will* feel better" or "I *should* feel better" or "I'm *going to* feel better," stay in the present. Tell yourself, "I'm feeling good" or "I'm feeling strong" or "I'm cruising along great now." And focusing on the "I" is important, too. No more statements like, "Is this ever going to end?" Instead, try something like, "I'm putting an end to this right now."

Beyond these practical techniques, there are certain core **precepts** that will enable you to really *believe* the positive self-talk you're dishing out. Of course, all people have to find the beliefs that work for them,

premise basis or principle
inevitably unavoidably
precepts rules of personal conduct

based on their own values and world view, but in talking with a great many people, we've found that the following precepts tend to be characteristic of happy, well-adjusted individuals:

- *Stay in the moment*. Buddhists advocate "mindfulness"—the practice of training the mind to become increasingly aware of moment-to-moment existence. If you're driving home from school, and you've had a day full of aggravation, try this mindfulness exercise: Look at what lies ahead of you and perhaps you'll see a meadow or a field or a body of water or the adorable face of a child. Using positive self-talk, you can reinforce mindfulness by taking a moment and saying something to yourself like, "Here I am, looking at the sun shining on the pond." Try this and you may find yourself situated in real time and a real place, instead of racing off with all kinds of worst-case scenarios that you probably can't do much to control anyway.

- *Stop Thought*. Sometimes bad thoughts are so powerful that they need to be dealt with strictly and forcefully before they are allowed to undermine your positive self-talk. When you feel a bad thought coming on, picture a stop sign—a nice big red hexagon—and hold it up in your mind, saying, *Stop Thought*. When you've chased that thought away—or at least wrestled it into a corner—then you can immediately bring forth a positive thought to put in its place. "I am doing fine now." "I have everything under control." "I am feeling good about myself."

- *Forget about failure*. Failure is not an operative word in the vocabulary of successful people. And, besides, what defines failure anyway? There are innumerable stories of people who have overcome truly daunting tragedies and losses to go on to success. Successful people see things in terms of good and bad *results*. When the results are bad, they make changes and look for improvement.

- *I've done my best and that's the best I can do.* Successful, well-adjusted people are confident in the fact that they have done all they can in any given situation. If things don't work out well, they do not punish themselves. They assure themselves that they did what they could and next time maybe things will work out better.

Your Life's Work

The issues that we've discussed in this chapter—self-esteem, self-validation, positive thinking, and positive self-talk—are issues that all of us have to work at throughout our lives to strengthen and improve. If you are just entering college from high school, then this pivotal moment in your development, when you are beginning to experience greater **autonomy,** should make you realize that your situation, both now and in

autonomy independence or freedom

CASE IN POINT: MAX CLELAND

There is no room for failure in the life of Max Cleland, former U. S. senator from Georgia. Cleland volunteered for duty in Vietnam in 1967 and rose to the rank of captain. In 1968, he threw himself on a grenade to save his fellow servicemen and was grievously injured. Both of his legs and one arm were amputated. Cleland's autobiography, *Strong at the Broken Places,* unflinchingly discusses his road to recovery as he came to terms, both physically and psychologically, with what had happened to him on the battlefield.

"Bitterness raged in me," Cleland wrote. "As I lay there alone, the futility of my life bore in on me. What was I living for? To get myself together every morning to go through the pain, anguish, and humiliation of therapy just to do it again the following day? Weekends were reserved for drinking and trying to forget. I wasn't living, I was existing."

Cleland had to touch bottom before he could rise up. "I sank into a deep depression. In a deep wrenching of the soul, I lay in bed, convulsed with agonizing, gut-wracking sobs. I was bitter over the past. I was afraid of the future. And the torturous present seemed unbearable ... I could live, or I could die. The choice was still up to me."

The choice that Max Cleland made was a testimony to the human spirit. He decided to dedicate his life to public service. At the age of 28, Cleland ran for the Georgia State Senate and became the youngest member of that body and its only Vietnam veteran. He wrote the state law that makes public facilities accessible to the elderly and handicapped. From the state senate he went on to another important job—as the youngest-ever administrator of the U. S. Department of Veterans Affairs. In this capacity, he managed the country's largest educational

assistance program, the GI Bill, and its largest healthcare system, the VA Hospital program. Cleland was also responsible for the Vet Center counseling program. This innovative program, which helps veterans and their families deal with post-traumatic stress disorder and other problems associated with the trauma of war, now has over 200 locations throughout the nation.

After his work with Veterans Affairs, Cleland returned to Georgia politics. He was elected to three successive terms as the secretary of state of Georgia, and became the first state official ever to garner more than a million votes. In 1996, he was elected to the United States Senate, where he served for a term.

Source: Introduction to Senator Max Cleland by David B. Gowler. Retrieved November 15, 2005, from http://www.emory.edu/EMORY_MAGAZINE/summer97/max.html

the future, will have more to do with decisions that *you* make than with decisions that are made *for* you. If you are an older or returning student, your self-esteem may have been somewhat tarnished by disappointments and frustrations you've experienced along the way, and this new chance is underlined by the reality that there is truly much at stake.

If your self-esteem occasionally droops during this challenging new time as a college student, don't despair. Remember, failure has no place in your vocabulary. Tell yourself that you're doing your very best to develop new skills, to keep everything under control, and to grow. It's a tall task, but you're up to it. Of course, when you're trying to feel good about yourself and confident, it helps to have some sense of where you're headed. We all feel better setting off on a big trip with a road map in the car. That's why it's important to start sorting out your goals now—and that is the subject of our next chapter.

What Did We Learn?

Try your hand at the following questions and exercises to see what you've retained from this chapter.

1. Give an example of one way that peer pressure still affects you at the college level.
2. True or False? Most students who attend 4-year colleges pay more than $10,000 annually in tuition and fees.
3. What are some indicators that you might be suffering from low self-esteem?
4. Define *self-fulfilling prophecy*.
5. Name three techniques for turning pessimism into optimism.
6. What are the essential characteristics of positive self-talk?
7. Define *mindfulness*.

Bibliography

Braden, N. (1988). *How to raise your self-esteem: The proven action-oriented approach to greater self-respect and self-confidence.* New York: Bantam.

Seligman, M. *Learned optimism: How to change your mind and your life.* (1998). New York: Free Press.

Sorensen, M. J. (1998). *Breaking the chain of low self-esteem.* Sherwood, OR: Wolf Publishing.

Talarico, D. (2005). *"Kids, have you seen my backpack ... ? and other inspirational stories of non-traditional students: an adult learner anthology.* (A collection of 22 essays from adult learners across the country.

Can be purchased through http://www
.adultlearnertoday.com/bookinfo.pdf.)

Links

Adults returning to school. Retrieved
November 15, 2005, from
http://www.campus.umr.edu/
counsel/selfhelp/vpl/adults.html

National Association for Self-Esteem. Retrieved
November 15, 2005, from http://www
.self-esteem-nase.org/

Positive thinking and self-talk information.
Retrieved November 15, 2005, from http://
www.selfgrowth.com/positive.html

The top ten tips for survival as a non-
traditional student. Retrieved November 15,
2005, from http://www.topten.org/public/
AB/AB2.html

Word Smart

**Let the following words from this chapter
sink into your mind. They will valuably enrich
your vocabulary.**

ambivalence

autonomy

conversely

inevitably

precept

premise

resilient

stigma

2

THE GOAL ZONE

As a general rule, sports metaphors are wildly overused in our ultra-competitive culture. In some cases, however, they're still an effective way to get a point across. That said, we're going to ask you to visualize yourself in a soccer game. There you are, poised at midfield, when suddenly one of your teammates finds you open. He passes the ball, you trap it, and then you're on your way, taking it down the line. As you move into the zone, you spot what clearly looks like an opportunity to score. You position yourself, find your balance, allow your mind and body to come together in a powerful visualization of what you hope to achieve, and then you boot the ball. As time hangs suspended, you watch the ball travel through space and then sail into the right top corner of the net. Wham! It's a goal!

Even if you've never played soccer, you can still imagine what a moment like this must feel like. The coming together of mind and body in such a powerful way is extraordinarily exciting no matter how many times you experience it. Have you ever felt that kind of coming together? Think about it.

The Psychology of Goal Setting

Here's another exercise: Think about the word "goal" and see where it leads you. Ambition. Target. Objective. Wish. Hope. Dream. When it comes to goal setting, none of the aforementioned are wrong answers. All of these words apply.

Some people grow up with clearly defined goals: *I want to be a firefighter. I want to be a doctor. I want to be a Marine.* Other people may grow up publicly acknowledging these "appropriate" goals, but, privately and internally, they don't really believe in them. Maybe the parents or grandparents of these individuals had all kinds of expectations for them and went around saying things like, "One day, when you're a doctor, we're going to be so proud of you," but meanwhile these individuals have secretly been harboring the wish to become a professional basketball player or a hip-hop artist or a racecar driver. Over time, such wishes may fade, but in some cases, the private dreams persist and prevail, even in the face of extreme familial disapproval and emotional cost.

Then there are those individuals who don't appear to have any far-reaching ambitions at all. They just "go with the flow," their wishes and desires focused on something they might be able to achieve a week or a day or an hour from now. Moment to moment, they may dream of a new stereo system or a second-hand car or even a slice of pizza. Either they can't see the big picture, or they choose not to.

The way people relate to their wishes and desires, their dreams and goals, is crucial to how they decide to live their lives. Some people are so intensely attached to their dreams that they are willing to do anything and everything in their pursuit of them. Nothing will satisfy them except achieving success as an actor, let's say, and they'll spend years waiting tables or driving a cab while going on auditions and taking acting classes on the outside chance that someday they might land a break-through role. The world is full of such stories and, unfortunately, many of them become sad portraits of frustration and disappointment. Some of these stories, however, do become extraordinary testaments to the human spirit, a spirit that honors dreams and acknowledges their central position in life. And some of these stories become wildly **improbable** fables with happy endings, where 20 years of driving a cab can segue to Broadway stardom after all.

So, how can we begin to sort out our ambitions, our dreams, and our goals? Basically this is something that needs to be done on an individual's own timetable. An understanding of the dynamics of goal setting can help with the process. This chapter will explore those dynamics and, in so doing, will offer a useful overview of a complex subject.

improbable not likely to happen

REFLECTIONS: *YOUR HISTORY*

Can you recall a time when you badly wanted something and set your sights on it? Try to remember what that felt like and, as best you can, recapture the feeling of energy you generated as your mind and body came together. Where and how did this happen for you? Going down a ski slope? Playing the cello in a recital? Winning an argument? Landing your first job? In a short piece, write about such an experience and describe what it meant to you.

The Fundamentals of Success

Goals are designed to end in achievement or success. The idea is to put the ball into the net, hit the high note on the trumpet, score at a certain level on your GREs, propose to the person you love and have that person say "yes." If we think of a goal as something that is followed by success, then it's a good idea to have a real sense of what "success" means—at least in terms of your own personal value system. First and foremost, it's important to understand that "success" does not mean the same thing to all people.

Oh, come on, you say—sure it does. Everyone wants to be Donald Trump, right? And are you telling us that the average woman wouldn't sell her soul to be Jennifer Lopez? Well, we hate to break it to you, but that's exactly what we're saying. Some people really *don't* care to be Donald Trump or Jennifer Lopez. Some people realize that, for all of his millions, Trump still relies on the old comb-over to disguise his baldness while J-Lo seems to have **inordinate** difficulty staying married, having already been to the altar three times in her relatively young life.

The fact is that all human beings are ultimately just that … human. And to be human means to be imperfect. Every one of us functions in a variety of realms—family, career, health—and we are all subject to the disappointments, mistakes, lapses of judgment, bad luck, and other shortcomings that mark us as human.

For many of us, being successful means being able to realize our goals. But even that does not necessarily constitute success in the long run. The world is full of stories of people who were wildly successful in their chosen career or pursuit, only to discover that this success was not the answer they were looking for after all. In fact, people often don't even know what they're looking for until they've gone down a few different paths. As people change, so do their goals. So, with that said, if reaching your goals does not necessarily ensure success, then what does?

Different people define success in different ways. For some, it's all about money and how much you make. These people tend to see the world in terms of winners and losers, the winners being those with the biggest pot at the end of the game. Now, we fully recognize the importance of money and the degree of pleasure and peace of mind it can **confer**. The famous comedienne Fanny Brice, on whose life the musical

inordinate excessive, beyond normal limits
confer to give or grant

STUDENT TALK: *IN THE EYE OF THE BEHOLDER*

"The most successful person I've ever known has to be my grandfather. Now understand—most people in the world would not see Grandpa Louis as successful. He owned this little barbershop in a not very good section of Toledo. He didn't stay with the styles and his business went under. 'Whose fault is it?' Louis would say. 'Nobody's but my own.' But did he allow failure to get him down? No way. He went to work for one of the big chain discounters, managing the garden shop. (He was always an awesome gardener.) Did he wind up as an executive in the front office? Hardly. He was just an ordinary guy, except in one way—he was a truly happy man. He was married to my grandmother for 62 years. His kids and his grandchildren were all crazy about him. Everybody in his church was crazy about him. His dog and two cats were crazy about him. Every morning, he got up, eager to see what the day held for him. Was Grandpa Louis a success? Absolutely. With a capital 'S'."

—José L., 29, Cleveland, OH.

Funny Girl was based, put it well: "I've been rich and I've been poor and
rich is better." In some situations, financial success is particularly prized.
For newly immigrated families, coming from famine-stricken or war-torn
parts of the world, the American dream continues to be about having
the kind of material things they haven't been able to have previously.
And for some older students who have been out in the world, perhaps
working in menial jobs, the possibility of financial success is truly a great
motivator. But, ultimately, financial success is just one form of success.
There are others and, some would argue, these others may be more
solid and satisfying in the long run.

If success isn't just about money, then what else could it be about?
For some people, success is synonymous with security. This security is
usually related to money, but it doesn't have to be a lot of money—just
regular, steady income. People who place a great emphasis on security
might choose a career as a teacher or a nurse or a social worker—professions that may not pay off in penthouses and yachts, but that can
offer stability and the ongoing opportunity for satisfying professional
fulfillment.

Then there are those who recognize the relative merits of money
and security, but who are dedicated instead to personal expression,
which they equate with success. These people may be artists—paint-
ers, writers, actors, singers, dancers, musicians—who, if they computed
their income on an hourly basis might laugh and cry at how little they
were making. But they don't care. Even if they didn't love what they do
(although most of them *do* love what they do), they cannot tamp down
their artistic ambitions.

Another example of a person who places a high value on personal
expression is the **entrepreneur**. The entrepreneur is fueled by the fantasy of realizing his or her vision and making lots of money. Others, who
dedicate themselves to personal expression, might be on a religious or
spiritual path or perhaps might choose to live their lives for the sake of
the public good.

Dedicating your life to personal expression can be an unconventional
and even risky choice—alternately exhilarating and difficult. Deciding
which route to take to success is truly one of life's big decisions. What
route do you see yourself taking?

entrepreneur one who undertakes to start and conduct an enterprise or business,
assuming full control or risk
impediments obstacles

Goal Setting

To achieve your goals, you have to be able to recognize them, but just knowing that you want to make a team or ace a test or buy a new car is not enough. You will need a method to take you where you want to go. To that end, we're going to provide you with the following "golden rules" of goal setting.

THE TEN GOLDEN RULES OF GOAL SETTING

All of the following are equally important and they all work together:

1) *Think and act positively.* You can go so much further with a positive frame of mind than you can with a negative orientation. Instead of muttering nasty comments to yourself like "Don't make any mistakes, stupid," try some kinder thoughts like "Proceed carefully and cautiously." After all, why berate yourself? The unfortunate truth is that we all encounter plenty of people in the course of our lifetimes that are more than happy to do the berating for us.

2) *Develop a game plan.* A game plan is a carefully thought-out, multifaceted blueprint intended to help you achieve your goal. It takes into account the resources you will need to succeed and shows you how to secure those resources. A game plan is to goal setting what a business plan is to a business idea.

3) *Create "goal units."* Some goals, like graduating from college, are large in scope and, generally speaking, the larger the goal, the more likely you are to be overwhelmed by it. So do yourself a favor—break your goals down into smaller "goal units." Passing a course or even passing a test may represent a much more sensible goal for you right now than earning your college degree.

4) *Own your own goals as best you can.* Ideally, goals are personal. Just because your parents want you to be a teacher is no reason why you should abandon your desire to be a fashion designer. Of course, what is ideal and what is realistic are often poles apart. While families with a long history of living in a privileged society like the United States may prize independence, newly immigrated families may not regard independence as a cultural value. It can be extremely difficult for a young person to defy cultural expectations, and, in fact, to do so can actually cause

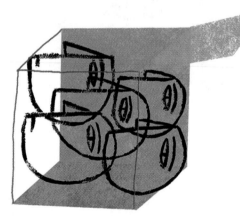

permanent rifts with one's family. There are no simple solutions to this complicated issue. Your answer has to come out of what feels right to you.

5) *Put it in writing*. You'll find that you're much more likely to realize your goals if you commit them to writing. This writing does not have to be shared with others, but the more *you* see your goals written out, the more they will be imprinted on your brain. Try writing your goals on a piece of paper the size of a business card and carry that around in your wallet. Look at it several times a day so that the message sinks in.

6) *Be specific*. Set a date by which you want to achieve your goal, and figure out how you're going to measure your progress. If, for instance, you wish to lose weight, don't state your goal simply as "Lose weight." You'll want to be able to enjoy your progress, even if the process is lengthy and frustrating at times, so set a goal like "Lose five pounds," which you know is attainable.

7) *Assess your goals to determine if they can truly be achieved.* How **viable** are your goals? Be realistic. Don't do yourself a disservice by setting up goals that you can't possibly achieve. Surely, you've watched *American Idol* and have seen completely tone-deaf people aching to become the next big rock star. If you can't carry a tune, don't dedicate yourself to being a singer. If you're 5'2" tall, professional basketball might not be the best career path, no matter how high you can jump. Dreaming is fine, but there's something to be said for realism as well.

8) *Know that all goals are not created equal.* Understand the difference between a short-term goal and a long-term goal. A short-term goal is passing that test on Friday. An intermediate goal is passing the course. A long-term goal is graduating. It usually requires more planning to achieve long-term goals than short-term ones.

9) *Have a back-up plan.* As hard as you try, you may fail to achieve your goal. If, for instance, your goal was to pass a certain course and you didn't, you'll want to be able to quickly regroup. Don't wallow in disappointment and despair. (Well, wallow if you must, but only for a day—no more.) Have a back-up plan ready. "If this doesn't work out, I'll try that."

10) *Understand that goal setting never ends.* If you look at the habits of successful people, you'll see that they don't rest on their laurels. Bill Gates didn't decide to go fishing after he made his first billion. Jimmy Carter didn't soak up the rays once his term as president ended—he went on to a whole other career as an international watchdog of human rights and won the Nobel Prize. There are many elderly people, long retired, who still give rich meaning to their lives by setting all kinds of goals for themselves, like learning how to play the piano or how to speak a second language. These people understand that goals make life worth living.

viable capable of living

This is a lot to absorb and, as our goal is to have you understand how goal setting works, we'd like to restate them in the following "Goal Setting-at-a-Glance" format:

1) Think and act positively.

2) Develop a game plan.

3) Create "goal units."

4) Own your own goals as best you can.

5) Put it in writing.

6) Be specific.

7) Assess your goals to determine if they can be truly achieved.

8) Know that all goals are not created equal.

9) Have a back-up plan.

10) Understand that goal setting never ends.

CASE IN POINT: IT'S NEVER TOO LATE

Can you imagine waiting 55 years for your novel to be published? That's what it was like for Helen Hooven Santmyer, who published a novel entitled *The Fierce Dispute* in 1928 and then waited until 1982 for the publication of her second novel. Santmyer was born in Cincinnati in 1895 and, as a young girl, fell in love with literature when she read Louisa May Alcott's *Little Women*. After graduating from college in 1918, she went to New York City, where she was a **suffragist** and held an office job at *Scribner's*, a leading literary magazine of its day. Family responsibilities soon called her back to Ohio however and, from then on, Santmyer held positions as the head of the English Department at Cedarville College and as a librarian in Dayton. Ill health forced

her to retire at the age of 64, whereupon she resumed her writing career. She published a collection of essays in 1963 and then commenced the project she had been waiting all her life to undertake: an epic novel entitled … *And Ladies of the Club*, about four generations of ordinary life in a rural Ohio town.

Santmyer began her book in 1964 at the age of 69 and finished it roughly 10 years later. Its 1,300 manuscript pages were shipped in 11 boxes to Ohio State University Press, who published it in 1982. A year later, publishing giant G. P. Putnam's Sons purchased the rights to the book and brought it to the attention of the general public. Then in her late eighties and living in a nursing home, Santmyer watched her novel rise to the top of the *New York Times* best-seller

list, where it held the #1 position for 7 weeks (37 weeks on the list altogether). The Book-of-the-Month Club chose it for its Main Selection, and it went on to sell 162,000 hardcover copies and over a million in paperback. Santmyer, a humble Midwesterner, was pleased by all this attention to her work, but was also a bit skeptical of it. "I think part of the interest is because I'm an old lady," she told the press. In 1986, at the age of 91, Santmyer died in Xenia, Ohio, where she was raised. Her life was a testament to perseverance and the belief in oneself. Santmyer kept her eye on the prize, and the prize finally came home.

Source: Helen Hooven Santmyer. Retrieved November 17, 2005, from http://www .ohioreadingroadtrip.org/santmyer/

suffragist an advocate of women's right to vote

Undermining Success

Why are some people successful and others not? Your first response to that question might be that it has to do with talent or luck or hard work. In fact, success is dependent on all those factors. And then there are the wild cards.

Different people handle success differently. Surely you've heard the expression, "Shooting yourself in the foot"? It means finding ways—often wildly creative ways—to undermine your success. The world is full of such stories. Glittering celebrities who seem to have everything—great wealth, public esteem, beauty, and more—who get caught doing what they shouldn't be doing, like shoplifting or driving under the influence or stealing from the company till. Why do people inflict such punishment on themselves (and others)? The answer is that there is no one answer.

For one reason or another, people can have very conflicted feelings about success. Perhaps they've gotten mixed messages as they were growing up. In certain cultures, it is expected that parents will make sacrifices for their children so that their children can surpass them in achievement and distinction. In other cultures, however, it is considered disrespectful for a child to surpass a parent in worldly achievement. If you've grown up in such a culture, even though you may have rationally discarded such **strictures**, you may still be psychologically bound by them.

In a whole other scenario, your fear of success may come from a deep-seated feeling of inadequacy that you've never adequately dealt with. Imagine, if you will, a person who starts out in life being distinctly overweight. As time goes on and this individual passes from childhood to adolescence and then adulthood, she loses her extra weight and emerges with the kind of beauty that society **sanctions**—in other words, she's thin. In fact, she is so thin and strikingly attractive that she becomes a model. Despite her success, however, the overweight child within her has never been left behind. She fears that this child will somehow be "exposed" and, before long, the superstar model is in the grip of an eating disorder that threatens to derail her success. Her current reality and her self-image are out of sync, and so the success she has earned is suddenly at great risk.

People who are lucky enough not to experience conflict around success enjoy a definite advantage in life. They can cut a clear path to

strictures something that checks or restricts
sanctions to approve authoritatively

OPEN FOR DISCUSSION: SELF-SABOTAGE

Why do some people sabotage themselves? Can you think of any famous people who have indulged in self-sabotaging behavior? (Clue: they're everywhere!) Why do you think successful people might engage in self-destructive behaviors like substance abuse, gambling, cheating, and so on, when they have so much to lose?

"When I was 12 years old, I spent the better part of a summer reading *Gone With the Wind*. I've always loved books. My idea of school is that you should just be left alone to read whatever you want to read. (Unfortunately, that doesn't seem to be anybody else's idea of school.) Anyway, there I was, lying on the hammock in our backyard, working my way through a box of candy and this enormous book, and when I got to the part where Scarlett O'Hara says, 'I'll think of it to-morrow, at Tara' (that was the name of her plantation, in case you haven't read the book), I said to myself, 'That's me! I'm Scarlett O'Hara without all the petticoats'."

—Linda E., 22, Arlington, VA.

© Digital Vision

their goals. Many people, however, experience considerable conflict around success, and if you think you fall into that camp, then you should be aware of certain modes of behavior that can totally derail the goal-setting process. Ultimately, you will need to deal with your ambivalence, which you may choose to do by self-examination or by talking with friends, family, a mentor, or a counselor. In the meantime, however, it certainly won't hurt to keep a lookout for unnecessary and distracting behaviors. Chief among these behaviors are the two "P's"—*procrastination* and *perfectionism*.

PROCRASTINATION

Procrastination is the fine art of putting off until tomorrow what you'd be better off doing today. Procrastination is such an effective trap that some people spend more time figuring out ways to postpone doing something that they don't want to do than they would actually spend doing the task itself.

If you think you suffer from procrastination—and the truth is that it's a habit that can afflict almost anyone—there are some practical strategies for overcoming it. These include:

- *Set a firm deadline for starting your task*. This is an actual time—not when the stars are aligned in their most advantageous position; not as soon as you've cleaned up your desk; not when you shake that headache (which you probably have on account of all the guilt and stress you're experiencing from your procrastination). What we have in mind is a time like Monday, Thursday, Saturday, or whatever works best with your schedule.

- *Start small, if necessary*. Do you remember those "goal units" we mentioned earlier? You can adapt that concept to help you resolve your procrastination issues. It's perfectly normal to be overwhelmed, at least momentarily, by the prospect of large undertakings. When it was time for us to begin work on *The Complete Student*, we hemmed and hawed and walked around in circles and then had a brilliant idea for how to begin: Sharpen some pencils! If you're confronting a job you dread, such as organizing your tax materials, start with something you *know* you can handle, like alphabetizing a list or cleaning out a file box. Completing one small job will give you a sense of achievement that will fuel you as you go on to your next task.

- *Reward yourself for a job well done*. Everyone likes rewards, so, when you've accomplished something that you've been avoiding, give yourself a treat. Did you finally launder that enormous pile of clothing that's been sitting in the corner of your room? Buy yourself a double mocha macchiato-frappuccino with a swirl. Have you completed that paper on *Romeo and Juliet* that you've been dreading? Take a nice long nap or go for a bike ride. The reward is up to you—just make sure you select something that gives you real pleasure.

PERFECTIONISM

Perfectionism is not quite as **prevalent** as procrastination but for those who are in its grip, it can be every bit as counterproductive. What is it exactly? Perfectionism is perhaps best defined as a self-defeating mode of thinking and behavior wherein one aims for excessively high and unrealistic goals. How can you identify a perfectionist? They're the sort that clean the bathroom grout with a toothbrush and turn Christmas into a frantic, pressured marathon of cookie baking and gift wrapping. How do you know if *you're* a perfectionist? Ask yourself the following questions:

- Is "good enough" not a part of your vocabulary?
- If an experience involves some aspect of performance, do you get a whopping case of stage fright?
- Do you delay turning in papers and other assignments because you're always trying to get them "just right"?

If you've answered "yes" to any of these questions, you may be suffering from this syndrome. At the same time, you may be unaware that you're suffering. Our society **tacitly** endorses perfectionism by holding up *workaholism* as a value. Workaholism is an unhealthy relationship with one's work that leaves little or no time for self-nurturing or satisfying relationships with others. If you think that sleep and leisure are a waste of time, if you can't make a move without your cell phone, your computer, and your wireless device, if you live for your work, then you are probably guilty of being a workaholic and, by extension, you most likely suffer from perfectionism. Unfortunately, our society encourages these behaviors by cutting back on vacations and leisure time. In many quarters, it is considered a desirable attribute to be working all the time. In fact, there's nothing healthy or valuable about it. Usually, workaholics with perfectionist streaks accomplish no more and often less than people who take a more balanced approach to their responsibilities.

prevalent widespread
tacitly by unexpressed agreement

Perfectionists engage in thinking that is marked by the following characteristics:

- Fear of failure.
- Fear of making mistakes.
- Fear of disapproval, rejection, and criticism.
- A tendency to use the word "should."
- Jealousy of the "ease" with which others achieve and enjoy success.

These habitual ways of thinking are there to cover up feelings of inadequacy, but what perfectionists don't realize is that mistakes are a completely normal and inevitable part of the learning process and *everyone* experiences them.

Perfectionists need to review and adjust their goal-setting processes. Keep the following pointers in mind to help you with this problem:

- Formulate goals that are realistic and attainable.
- Experiment with *not* being perfect. Aim for a "B" on an exam, for once.
- Focus on process, not product. For example, instead of being satisfied only if you lose 20 pounds, try telling yourself to feel good simply from the benefits of exercise and healthy eating.
- Check in with yourself regularly. If you're feeling anxious or depressed about your work, ask yourself if you've set impossible standards.
- Here is another question to ask yourself: What's the very worst thing that can happen? If you don't get an A on that paper, what's that really going to mean?
- Reflect on your mistakes. Ask yourself if you've learned anything from your mistakes, painful as they may be.

Remember: perfectionism is just a habit. And habits can, with work, be broken.

Surviving Setbacks

The great American poet Theodore Roethke once wrote, "In a dark time, the eye begins to see." We know exactly what he meant. Think of being in a darkened room. At first, it's almost impossible to make things out. As the eye becomes adjusted, however, greater clarity is achieved. This is a good metaphor for how to adjust to situations of disappointment and frustration. When you experience the setbacks that make for "dark" times, take a moment and let your eye adapt.

There is comfort in knowing that we all experience such setbacks. Consider a true story about Michael Jordan, perhaps the most famous athlete in the world. When Jordan was a sophomore at Laney High School in Wilmington, North Carolina, he was cut from the basketball team. Instead of giving up, Jordan let this rejection fuel his drive to succeed. "Whenever I was working out and got tired and figured I ought to stop," he recalled, "I'd close my eyes and see that list in the locker room without my name on it and that usually got me going again." You, too, can learn how to absorb your disappointments and frustrations when you fall short of your goals. Disappointments, in fact, can work like a railroad switch, sending you in a whole other direction that can actually lead to exciting new opportunities.

We like to borrow a way of thinking from the Buddhists, who ask the question, "What is the gift in this situation?" Every situation, even the direst, has its positive facets. Getting fired might allow you to stop for a moment, take yourself off the hamster run, and find satisfying dimensions in your life that you would not have been able to discover otherwise. Ending a romantic relationship might lead to a time of valuable independence and self-exploration. Being oriented toward the positive is the best way to overcome the adversity that life routinely hands out. As the Chinese proverb puts it, "A gem cannot be polished without friction, nor a man perfected without trials." Or, as the great American humorist Will Rogers once said, "The worst thing that happens to you may be the best thing for you if you don't let it get the best of you." Got that?

Student Goals

Before we leave this chapter, we would like to focus our attention on specific goals that you, as a student, will want to set for yourself. The idea of *student professionalism* is one that we will be revisiting time and again in this book. We speak of professionalism as a quality that we hope to see in the doctors, lawyers, and accountants we hire to take care of our needs. A sense of professionalism signifies an **adherence** to a code of conduct and a commitment to achieving at the highest level. A strong sense of professionalism will benefit you as a student as well.

When we think in terms of specific student goals, here are the ones at the top of our list:

- *Be the best you can be.* This is different—very different—from being perfect. If you've read this chapter carefully, you should know

adherence attachment

OPEN FOR DISCUSSION: "PROFESSIONAL" STUDENTS

What makes a student a good student? Instead of thinking in terms of things like "All A's," think in more general terms. What qualities are you hoping to develop for your college years?

that nobody's perfect. But we can all set goals that have to do with achieving excellence. Students, especially, should aim for real accomplishment as scholars, thinkers, and doers.

- *Set standards for yourself*. Make them high standards. This means turning in assignments on time and in proper order. Do not turn in papers that are stained with coffee, are missing pages, or are full of silly, sloppy mistakes.

- *Go to all of your classes and arrive on time*. Your teachers are human beings. It bothers them when people show up late or don't show up at all. Teachers are apt to regard such behavior as discourteous and may interpret those who indulge in such behavior as uninterested. Even if your teachers aren't ruffled by absences and tardiness, *you* should care. After all, going to class is your opportunity to learn, which is why you're in college in the first place. Citing a boring teacher as an excuse for not going to class doesn't work. Even if you have a boring teacher, you should be able to find ways to make the experience interesting. That's your job.

- *Conduct yourself with honor*. Here we are talking specifically about the honor system. Written or unwritten, it should be part of your college experience. Cheating and plagiarizing have no place in this

arena. These behaviors cheapen the college experience and ultimately cheat *you* out of what you are going to college for, which is more than a degree. A degree is simply a piece of paper—valuable, we suppose, but not nearly as valuable as it is when it's backed up by knowledge acquisition.

- *Be a participant.* If you were shy in high school, now is the time to outgrow it. Set a goal to become an active contributor in class. Sit up front and make yourself known. You don't have to be the smartest person in the room in order to make a valuable contribution. All you really need to do in order to contribute meaningfully is prepare for the day's lesson. And if you contribute, you will be rewarded for your efforts. Not only will you feel more interested and will the time pass more quickly, but you will also see that teachers deeply appreciate your involvement and contribution. It makes their job much easier and they will be grateful to you for it.

Now that we've looked at the mechanics of how goals and goal setting works, let's turn our attention in our next chapter to some of the specific tools you'll need to achieve your goals. As a student, it all begins with mind power.

What Did We Learn?

The goal here was to learn about goals. Let's see how we did.

1. What is a game plan and how does it relate to goal setting?
2. Define a "goal unit."
3. What does it mean "to own your own goals"?
4. Name two modes of behavior that can short circuit the achievement of your goals.
5. What are three effective ways of countering procrastination?
6. Name some useful ways of dealing with setbacks.

Bibliography

Blair, G. R. (2000). *Goal setting 101*. Tampa, FL: Blair Publishing House.

Burka, J. B., & Yuen, L. M. (2004). *Procrastination: Why you do it, what to do about it*. Jackson, TN: Da Capo Press.

Fiore, N. (1988). *The now habit*. New York: Jeremy P. Tarcher.

Goulston, M., & Goldberg, P. (1996). *Get out of your own way: Overcoming self-defeating behavior*. New York: Perigree.

Smith, A. W. (1990). *Overcoming perfectionism: The key to balanced recovery*. Deerfield Beach, FL: HCI.

Smith, D. K. (1999). *Make success measurable! A mindbook-workbook for setting goals and taking action*. New York: Wiley.

Links

Perfectionism: University of Illinois at Urbana-Champaign Counseling Center. Retrieved November 17, 2005, from http://www.couns.uiuc.edu/Brochures/perfecti.html

Procrastination. Retrieved November 17, 2005, from http://mentalhelp.net/psyhelp/chap4/chap4r.html

Word Smart

Consider the following:

- adherence
- confer
- entrepreneur
- impediment
- improbable
- inordinate
- prevalent
- sanction
- stricture
- suffragist
- tacitly
- viable

IT'S ALL IN THE MIND

Whenever you use a piece of equipment, it helps to have some sense of how it works. You can maintain a car better and even drive a car better if you understand the fundamentals of its engineering and how the gears, spark plugs, and carburetor interact. As a student, your most critical piece of equipment is your brain, and in this chapter we will look at how the brain stores information, how it retrieves information, how it thinks, how it solves problems, and more.

The Extraordinary Organ

Every part of the human body—the heart, the lungs, the liver, the kidneys—is miraculous in its own way, but the brain is perhaps the most astounding organ of them all. The human brain weighs *three pounds*. That's about the weight of your average Chihuahua and almost seven times as much as the brains of other mammals similar to our size. Perhaps that's why humans are the species that can use tools, build bridges, go to the moon, and, on the downside, create things like nuclear bombs and recreational drugs.

If you think of your body as an orchestra, imagine your brain as the conductor. Maestro Brain calls the shots, instructing the rest of the body in what to do and what to feel. Is it time to breathe, swallow, walk, sit, compute, sing, or remove your hand from the flames? Listen to the brain—it knows.

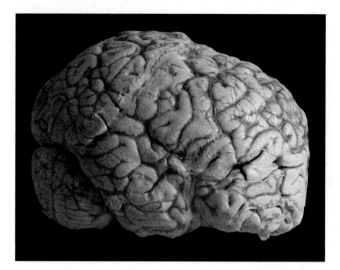

How does the brain manage to accomplish so many tasks? Through the help of about a hundred billion tiny nerve cells called *neurons*. When we say that neurons are tiny, we're not exaggerating. In fact, they're so tiny that 300,000 of them could fit on the head of a pin. The *glia*, or *neuroglia*, *are* even more populous. These are cells that support the neurons and nourish and protect the brain. There are about 10 times as many glia as there are neurons—in other words, there are *trillions* of them.

For more mind-boggling numbers, let's turn our attention to *synapses*. The synapses are specialized junctions through which the cells of the central nervous system signal to each other as well as to the non-neural cells, like those of the muscles and glands. Synapses form the circuits in which the neurons interconnect, and so they are crucial to perception, thought, movement, and all other bodily functions. The total number of possible interconnections among the synapses is said to be greater than the number of atomic particles in the entire universe. It is estimated that an average human brain holds approximately *100 trillion* synapses, or about 1,000 synapses per neuron.

Brain Function

As we can see, the brain is an incredible piece of equipment. That said, what can be done with it? The possibilities are endless. The brain operates on the principle of **synergy**. Another way of thinking of synergy is that *1 + 1 = More than 2*. Roger Sperry, who won a Nobel Prize for his research into the functioning of the left and right brain, sees this

synergy parts working together to produce an effect greater than the sum of their individual efforts

remarkable organ as a multiplying machine rather than an adding machine. The brain function that we call daydreaming is a good illustration of Sperry's point. When we daydream, it only takes a moment for our fantasies to spool off into endless variations. We might begin our fantasy by imagining ourselves landing a bit part in a movie but, before you know it, we're winning Oscars, Emmys, owning diamonds and yachts, and getting married to an equally gorgeous movie star in a sunset ceremony on a private mountaintop.

Some of you may have been accused at various points in your life of wasting your time with daydreaming, but that's really not a fair charge. In fact, daydreaming happens to be a wonderful exercise for the mind, demonstrating the ability to think with lightning speed and brilliant color and variation. How can we best harness the brain's potential? One answer is through cognition.

Cognition is a term that stands for the high-level functions that are carried out by the human brain. These functions include comprehension and the use of speech, visual perception, calculation ability, information processing, executive functions such as planning, problem solving, and self-monitoring, and memory. The ability of human beings to function cognitively is influenced by various factors, such as intelligence and environment.

For some of us, the word "intelligence" is almost enough to make us stop reading altogether. Too many of us grow up thinking that we are not intelligent "enough." But what does "enough" mean? In 1905, two French psychologists, Alfred Binet and Theodore Simon, aiming to measure intelligence, developed the first modern IQ test. Some years later, two American psychologists, Lewis M. Terman and Maud A. Merrill, both of Stanford University, adapted the work of the French psychologists to produce what is now known as the Stanford-Binet tests—the standard IQ tests that have been administered to millions of American students. These tests, once regarded as the absolute **arbiter** of intelligence, are now judged by many to be **arbitrary**. These tests can effectively assess certain cognitive abilities, but by no means all. They have been accused of confusing logic—one kind of thinking or learning skill—with overall intelligence. Worse yet, these IQ tests suggest that intelligence is fixed at birth, even though contemporary research shows quite the contrary. Intelligence is *not* fixed at birth, it *can* develop over your lifetime, and it shows itself in many different ways.

arbiter judge
arbitrary based on mere opinion or prejudice

The Theory of Multiple Intelligences

In 1983, Harvard psychologist Howard Gardner published a groundbreaking work entitled *Frames of Mind: The Theory of Multiple Intelligences*. Gardner's research challenged the idea that intelligence is just one thing, that it results from a single factor, or that it can be measured definitively by an IQ test. Instead, Gardner offered a new definition of intelligence as "the capacity to solve problems or to fashion products that are valued in one or more cultural settings" (Gardner, H. & Hatch, T. "Multiple intelligences go to school: Educational implications of the theory of multiple intelligences." *Educational Researcher*, 1989 *18* (8), 4–9). Gardner's initial list of seven intelligences included:

- *Linguistic intelligence*. People with strong linguistic intelligence are sensitive to spoken and written language. They are **adept** at learning languages and using language as a means to accomplish goals.
- *Logical-mathematical intelligence*. Those who embody this form of intelligence have the capacity to analyze problems logically, to carry out mathematical operations, and to investigate issues scientifically. They will be able to detect patterns, reason deductively, and think logically.
- *Musical intelligence*. People who possess a high level of musical intelligence are skilled at performance and/or composition, appreciate musical patterns, and are able to recognize and compose pitches, tones, and rhythms.
- *Bodily-kinesthetic intelligence*. People who demonstrate this kind of intelligence will be able to use their whole body or parts of the body to solve problems. Athletes, craftspeople, dancers, and builders typically rank high in this intelligence.
- *Visual/Spatial intelligence*. This intelligence is characterized by the ability to think in images and pictures and to excel in the creation and use of graphs, maps, charts, mazes, illustrations, art models, films, photographs, puzzles, and costumes.
- *Interpersonal intelligence*. People who possess high levels of this intelligence are exceptionally aware of the intentions, motivations, and desires of other people. Interpersonal intelligence, which allows for productive collaboration with others, is typically found in educators, salespeople, politicians, religious leaders, and counselors.

adept highly skillful

- *Intrapersonal intelligence*. This intelligence is marked by an exceptional awareness of one's own feelings and values and an orientation that is reflective and strongly **intuitive**.

Since the initial publication of *Frames of Mind*, in which these seven types of intelligences were put forth, Gardner and his colleagues have officially added an eighth type of intelligence to the list:

- *Naturalist intelligence*. The ability to recognize, categorize, and draw upon certain features in the environment. People with this intelligence can keenly observe and identify details of plants, rocks, animals, and other natural formations.

Other forms of intelligence have been considered for the list as well. Among these are:

- *Existential intelligence*. This intelligence is characterized by an interest in asking the "big" questions, like "Why do human beings exist?" (*Spiritual intelligence* is another candidate for the list, but Gardner prefers to fold that term into existential intelligence.)
- *Moral intelligence*. A particular sensitivity to the rules, behaviors, and attitudes that govern the sanctity of life are the hallmarks of this intelligence.

Gardner's theory of intelligences has had an enormous impact on educational objectives throughout the United States. Many school districts have reviewed their curricula in order to meet the interests of these varied intelligences, and are becoming increasingly sensitive to the fact that different people learn in *different* ways—not in *good*, *better*, or *best* ways.

Learn Your Own Way

Regardless of which type of intelligence most characterizes you, it is your job as a student to learn. Again, there is no right or wrong way to learn—just ways that are different. Becoming aware of how you learn best can represent a major breakthrough in your career as a student.

Many years ago, the prevailing educational philosophy in the United States was that people learned best by having information drummed into them. Usually, this was done by some kind of **rote** method. An extreme example of this would be writing out the multiplication tables 100 times—effective but deadly. Modern educators understand that rote methods will only be effective with certain kinds of material and only up to a point. The prevailing educational philosophy today recognizes that

intuitive perceived by the mind without rigorous logic or analysis
rote memorization by repetition

REFLECTIONS: *YOUR HISTORY*

Chances are you've heard the term *emotional intelligence*. This is not one of the multiple intelligences identified by Howard Gardner, but, rather, it is the title of a major best seller published in 1995 (Bantam Books) by *New York Times* science reporter Daniel Goleman. Emotional intelligence, which is closely linked to Gardner's interpersonal and intrapersonal intelligences described previously, is a form of social intelligence that allows you to "read" other people. According to researchers P. Salovey and J. D. Mayer in their article entitled "Emotional Intelligence" (*Imagination, Cognition, and Personality*, 1990 9), emotional intelligence is manifested in five major ways:

- *Self-awareness*—the ability to monitor yourself and to recognize your feelings as you experience them.
- *Managing emotions*—handling those feelings as they come up.
- *Motivating yourself*—channeling your emotions in the service of a goal.
- *Empathy*—sensitivity to the feelings and concerns of others.
- *Handling relationships*—coexisting with the emotional needs and demands of others.

How emotionally intelligent are *you* feeling these days? Explore this topic in writing. Be honest with yourself, but please—don't be harsh.

different people learn in different ways, and the way you learn best is called your *learning style*.

Currently, a good deal of valuable research is being performed on the various learning styles, and you will see these styles labeled with all kinds of different names. You might hear about active and reflective learners, intuitive learners, global learners, logicians, procedurists, communicators, experimenters, and so on. In the links section at the end of this chapter, you will find other sources of information to help you expand your knowledge of this topic, if you wish. For now, however, we would like to take a very simple, even **rudimentary** approach to the subject, and break down the three prevailing learning styles as follows:

- *Auditory*
- *Visual*
- *Kinesthetic/Tactile*

This approach may lack the **nuance** of other discussions on this subject, but it will serve as a good overall introduction to the concept of learning styles.

THE AUDITORY LEARNER

"Auditory" means related to hearing, and traditionally schools in this country have always favored the auditory learner. The traditional classroom model places the teacher at the front of the room, lecturing while students take notes. Auditory learners prefer verbal instructions when given an assignment and they like to talk out a problem with other people. They might forget a face, but they'll usually remember a name. They enjoy classroom discussion, often distinguishing themselves as active participants, and when they see a word that is unfamiliar to them, they'll try to sound it out, using a phonetic approach. One downside to being an auditory learner is that it might be difficult to tune things out. Conversations going on in the corner of the room tend to invade the brains of auditory learners who are very sensitive to any kind of noise. Auditory learners may also be overly attached to their cell phones, and may be big talkers. Their favorite part of a book is often the dialogue.

THE VISUAL LEARNER

Surely you recognize this learner—she or he sits in the classroom drawing extraordinarily elaborate and often quite beautiful doodles. Visual learners remember a word best by looking at it on the

rudimentary introductory; elementary
nuance a slight degree of difference in tone or color

STUDENT TALK:
WATCH THIS

"I guess you could say that I have a pretty high level of intrapersonal intelligence. I'm always interested in what's going on around me—maybe too interested. My mom says that when she goes out to a restaurant with me, she'd have a better chance of getting me to listen to her if she was sitting at the next table. In class, I'm often more interested in what's going on around me than in what's being said at the front of the room. Eventually, my attention goes back to the teacher—I mean, I *am* a good student—so if the teacher has reinforced what's been said by putting some notes on the board, I'm okay. I do need that visual dimension, however."

—Chloe C., 18, Colorado Springs, CO.

chalkboard. They'll never forget your face, but they might not remember your name.

Visual learners are fascinated with all kinds of graphs, maps, charts, tables, diagrams, slides, illustrations, and posters. When reading a novel, they are most likely to be drawn to descriptive passages of places and people. When reading a textbook, visual learners may see a "movie" in their minds that plays out a visual representation of the material. The downside to being a visual learner is that you can be overly attuned to your environment. The visual learner can be distracted by untidiness, for instance—particularly other people's untidiness—and can have difficulty tuning out such a distraction.

THE KINESTHETIC/TACTILE LEARNER

This type of learner is drawn to anything that has movement (kinesthesia) or anything that can be held, felt, or touched. The kinesthetic learner is the student for whom the "Touch Me" table in the museum was designed. These individuals are very active learners who enjoy diving right into any given learning situation.

The kinesthetic/tactile learner favors lessons that come with a lot of demos and props. Like auditory learners, they are subject to distraction when there is too much going on around them. (They are generally more susceptible to distraction than other kinds of learners.) They remember people not so much by their faces or their names, but by the activities they once shared. ("Oh, you were the person I met in that doubles game out on Long Island!") Sitting and reading a book is generally not this learner's idea of heaven, but, when choosing a book to read, he or she is most likely to pick something with a lot of action, rather than a character-driven story.

Let us repeat the central point here: all of these ways of learning are completely good and acceptable. One is not better than the other, and, in fact, in most individuals, there is a certain degree of overlap between the styles. What is important is to identify the way that *you* learn best, and to always proceed with your orientation clearly in mind. Quick example: If you are a visual learner and your assignment is to learn a list of vocabulary words, you'll want to devise a set of flash cards to help you with this task. If you are an auditory learner, you might want to make a tape of the words and their meanings so that you can listen while you commute back and forth to school. If you are a kinesthetic/tactile learner, you might learn best by being quizzed on the words by a friend while walking on a treadmill. The key here is to find what works for you—and do it!

LEARNING STYLES

With a nod to our visual learners, we'd like to recap some of the information we've covered in the form of this chart.

TASK	VISUAL	AUDITORY	KINESTHETIC/ TACTILE
Learning new words	See the word; flashcards	Sound out the word; phonetics	Write it out; connect it to an object
Concentrating	Distracted by mess (other people's)	Distracted by conversation (other people's)	Distracted by activity (other people's)
Remembering people	By their faces	By their names	By experiences or activities you've shared with them
Reading	Likes descriptive passages	Likes dialogue	Likes action scenes
Trying something new	Needs demonstrations, diagrams, etc.	Needs to talk it out with the teacher	Likes to just jump in
Assembling something	Looks at the diagrams	Tears hair out over badly written directions	Ignore the directions and figure it out as you go along
Classroom discussion	Will draw a picture on the blackboard to make a point	Loves discussion, even debating	Will tend to act something out with gestures and experssive movements

Think about It

No matter what type of learner you are, a large part of your job as a student will be to develop your thinking skills. People who wish to assume a role in society—to hold jobs or otherwise perform valuable work; to participate in community activities; to vote—are people who must hone their capacity for *critical thinking*. Critical thinking has, in fact, become something of a hot button issue in today's culture. Parents and educators worry that young people are spending too much of their time watching television, surfing the Net, playing video games, and engaging in other such technology-oriented activities that fog the mind instead of reading books that might help foster critical thinking. Go to any educational conference today and you will hear quite a bit about the urgent need to turn students into critical thinkers.

The concept of critical thinking has been around for a long time. John Dewey, the pioneering American educator, is often credited as the "father" of critical thinking, which he called "reflective thinking." Dewey described reflective thinking as a kind of active, persistent, and careful

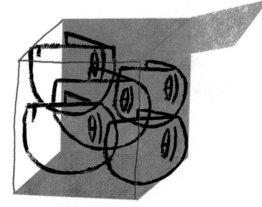

consideration of a belief or a supposed form of knowledge. What does this mean exactly? Well, consider a subject like modern art, for instance. There are some people who stand in front of a Jackson Pollack "drip" painting—widely regarded as a contemporary masterpiece—and say, "My 2-year-old could do that." Are such people thinking critically? Are they basing their opinions on any kind of knowledge base? Dewey's reflective thinking—what we are now calling "critical thinking"—allows you to look at modern art, or anything else, in a way where your evaluation will be thought-out and worthwhile. Critical thinking gives you the tools for making valuable considerations of wide-ranging issues.

The operative word around critical thinking is that it's *active*. People who possess the **faculty** of critical thinking are initiators, not simply recipients. They think things through for themselves. They raise questions. They locate information that will help them reach decisions and form judgments. They place a central importance on *reasoning*. Consider this definition by researchers Robert Ennis and Stephen P. Norris: "Critical thinking is reasonable, reflective thinking that is focused on deciding what to believe or do." [Norris, S. & Ennis, R. (1989). *Evaluating critical thinking*. Pacific Grove, CA: Midwest Publications, p. 1.]

Critical thinking will serve you well in many different areas of your life. Let's say that you're voting in your first presidential election: how will you decide which candidate to support? After all, you're being bombarded by television and radio ads, with both sides accusing the other of various forms of wrongdoing. Who are you going to believe?

Or maybe it's time to buy a car—a used car, as that's all you're able to afford. Your salesman, who is way too tan for someone living in

faculty any special skill or unusual ability

Nebraska in February, is promising you the moon with this 1992 Ford Escort with "just 143,000 miles." What can you believe? What should you be asking? How will you reach a decision?

These are just two real-life situations where critical thinking can make all the difference. In both instances—deciding who to vote for or whether to buy the car—the critical thinker will do the appropriate research in order to make the informed decision. Throughout your college years, you will be asked to use this kind of critical thinking. When you read an essay by George Orwell or when you are studying the Russian Revolution or when you are exploring Islam in your comparative religions course, your critical thinking will help you bring miscellaneous facts into the realm of solid understanding.

Critical thinking allows you to hold up a subject and examine all its facets. It teaches you not to take things at face value or to blindly accept other people's opinions as your own. In our society today, where the media is so subject to conglomerization (a word of recent coinage that means the taking over of industry by **conglomerates**), it is more important than ever that we question the validity of the news we hear. Critical thinking also encourages us to be sensitive to stereotypical thinking with regard to race, gender, religion, and so forth. When you look at a catalogue that comes to you in the mail, for instance, look at it *critically*. What is it trying to tell you and sell you? That the only way to be happy in this society is to be rich and own things and be white and thin? Critical thinking allows you to see things in new ways that can change the way you think altogether.

Testing for Logic

Hopefully, in the discussion you've had about ads, a healthy **infusion** of logic took place. What is logic? There are many definitions, but a good, all-purpose one is "reasoned and reasonable judgment." Logic doesn't mean *just because I said so* or *I picked it out of a hat* or anything like that. When you turn to logic, you are looking for answers that make the most sense.

Answers tend to make sense when they are based on a foundation of *reasoning*. One form of logical thinking is called *deductive reasoning*.

conglomerates a group of diverse corporations that is run as a single organization
subliminal below or beyond the threshold of consciousness
unsubstantiated lacking solidity or strength
infusion pouring in

**OPEN FOR DISCUSSION:
DO YOU BUY IT?**

Bring in some ads that you know will solicit a wide range of reactions and opinions. Pick out one ad to discuss as a group and try to dissect what's going on in the ad. Who is the ad trying to appeal to? Who is the ad excluding as a market? What are its **subliminal** messages? Does the ad make any claims that are **unsubstantiated**? Give it a long, hard, and *critical* look and see what you come up with.

With deductive reasoning, your conclusion is based on the validity of the steps that got you there. In other words, the conclusion is true if the information that led you there, also called the *premises*, is true. Here's an example of deductive reasoning:

Premise: Doctors must be licensed.

Premise: An orthopedist is a doctor.

Conclusion: Orthopedists must be licensed.

Deductive reasoning is a kind of common sense, and we use it all the time. "Red octagonal signs in the street mean STOP. I see a red octagonal sign. I stop." Or how about: "The bank is closed on national holidays. Memorial Day is a national holiday. The bank is closed on Memorial Day." The main point to remember with deductive reasoning is that the conclusion is true if the premises are true. (You can explore the truth of a premise by conducting your own research. Are banks closed on national holidays? *Do* doctors have to be licensed?)

Another form of logical thinking is called *inductive reasoning*. With inductive reasoning you are asked to make a *conjecture*, or an educated guess, based on the information you have been given. This information doesn't allow you to go from A to B quite as decisively as you did with cases where deductive reasoning applied, so you have to make a judgment as to the ultimate validity of the statement. Let's look at an example of where inductive reasoning comes into play:

Premise: English is the official language of Ghana.

Premise: As an American, I speak English.

Premise: When I go to Ghana and speak English, I will be understood.

With inductive reasoning, the conclusion you reach is very likely to be true … but not always. So you have to proceed with caution. Looking at the previous example, for instance, we can understand why you, as an English-speaking American tourist in Ghana, where the official language is English, would expect people to understand what you're saying. But, then again, you might encounter some areas in the country where only African languages like Akan, Ewe, Ga, and Moshi-Dagomba are spoken. And even if you are speaking with a Ghanaian who speaks English, the issues of accents and idioms might still make it difficult for English speakers to make themselves understood to each other. So, in this case, there's no such thing as a sure thing.

Got a Problem?

Critical thinking, with its tools of logic and reasoning, is a vital ingredient in *problem solving*. So is creativity, which we will be examining in depth in the next chapter. Like critical thinking, problem solving has become a popular buzzword in our contemporary culture. Maybe because our society is struggling with so many problems—unemployment, environmental hazards, racial disharmony, global terrorism—we have an ever-increasing need for problem solvers. Then again, our world has always needed problem solvers—men and women like Leonardo da Vinci, Galileo, Martin Luther King, Madame Curie, Gandhi, Thomas Edison, Susan B. Anthony—people who could think "outside the box."

As a student, you started your problem-solving career way back in grade school with mathematical problems that involved apples and oranges or pieces of pie. The skills you used to solve those problems will still work to solve the problems you encounter as you move through the world today. If you're a talented problem solver, you will always be welcome in the world of work, where too many people suffer from limited imagination and can only follow, never lead.

Problem solving is a process that you can rely on to take you from one step of a task to the next. To figure out where you are in the process, *always ask questions*. Consider the following questions and use them when you need to do some fast figuring:

1) *What's the problem anyway?* There's no better place to start than with this question. Let's say you have a flat tire in the middle of the road—that's a problem. You've identified it—it's a dangerous situation to be in—and now you have to solve it. Or let's say you've made plans with two different friends at the same—that's a problem. You may have to cancel one of them, which can cause hurt feelings. Whenever there's a problem to be solved, your first step is to be absolutely clear about what the problem is exactly.

2) *What's the response?* You're not sure yet, but you know that you need to get the car off the road, change the tire, and resume your trip. If you've made two sets of plans for the same time, you know that you have to fix your social calendar somehow. That's your objective.

3) *What are my options?* There could be any number of them. You could call a road service or put up a flare and wait for some

Good Samaritan to come along or you could get the instruction booklet out of the glove compartment and try to remember what you learned in driver's ed. If you've made plans with two friends for the same time, you might consider going out of town or, failing that, doing something that would include both parties, if you think that would work.

4) *Where will each option lead me?* Time for quick figuring: waiting for the road service could take a while, your Good Samaritan might turn out to be a homicidal maniac, and your efforts to change the tire yourself might be a total bust. As for the bungled social calendar, you might wind up alienating a sensitive friend or you might introduce two people and all have a lot of fun together.

5) *What are the pros and cons?* Most solutions have their good points and their bad points. It's up to you to weigh them and to come away with something that makes you feel confident.

Problem solving is a skill that can develop throughout your lifetime. The more you do it, the better you become at it.

Remember … What Was That Again?

As you know, when you come to the end of a chapter in this book, you will find review material. This material is there to reinforce *retention*—the effective storing of learning in the brain. Retention is a function of memory, and memory is one of the most important functions of the brain. The brain reminds us when to eat, when to sleep, how to locate our car in a crowded parking lot, where the Magna Carta was signed (that field in England called Runnymede—do you remember from Chapter 1?), and how to move our fingers to pick up a doughnut.

For students, the issue of memory is a particularly pressing one. On this big learning curve called the college years, you'll be asked to remember so many things. Mitochondria, Mugwumps, Matisse, Meriwether Lewis … yikes! Now wait a minute. Don't panic. You can do it—you really can. Your brain is wonderfully receptive. You just need to master a few techniques that will help you with memory function.

IN OTHER WORDS

"You cannot get out of a problem by using the same type of thinking that got you into it."
—Albert Einstein

IN OTHER WORDS

"Memory is the mother of all wisdom."—Aeschylus, Greek dramatist (525–456 BCE)

MEMORY: HOW IT WORKS

Before we suggest specific ways to boost your memory, it helps to understand the general workings of your memory. Essentially, memory comes in three forms: *sensory memory*, *short-term memory*, and *long-term memory*.

With sensory memory, we perceive a sensation—we hear, smell, taste, or feel something—and that sensation becomes something we store in our minds. Obviously, we could not hope to store all the sensory memories we process. We are not going to remember that piece of toast we ate last April or the time we stubbed a toe taking out the garbage. We do store many *significant* sensory memories, however. The taste of Grandma's apple pie; the time we stepped on a rusty nail; the sound of rain on the tin roof of the tree house we loved as a child.

Some portion of our sensory memories makes its way into the *short-term memory*. In the short-term memory, we store information that we associate with our sensory memories. For instance, if we smell mustard, we may be reminded of the hot dog that is sitting in our short-term memory from last week's visit to the ballpark … and suddenly a hot dog is what we crave for lunch. The short-term memory is a kind of holding tank, and not a very large one at that. It can only accommodate a handful of memories at any one time. If we want to keep something in our short-term memory for a while longer, we may need to use repetition—"take a right at Forrest Street, take a right at Forrest Street"—or use some other kind of mind trick.

Some of our short-term memories make their way into the "Memory Hall of Fame"—otherwise known as *long-term memory*. The long-term memory is almost limitless in its storage capacity. People hang on to so much in their long-term memories, from the state capital of Idaho (Boise) to the numerical equivalency of pi (3.14) to the lyrics of "America the Beautiful." Elderly people suffering from *dementia* ("impairment or deterioration of mental capacity") may be unable to remember the name of a visiting relative or what they said 5 minutes ago, but they might totally remember entire songs from their childhoods or the catechisms they recited when they were in Sunday school.

MEMORY BOOSTERS

Even if you feel that you have a poor memory, don't despair. There are many clever and easy ways to improve your memory—in fact, there are far too many tricks of the trade for us to comprehensively cover here. (For more information on memory improvement, consult the Links

section at the end of this chapter.) Right now, we'd like to focus on some particularly effective memory boosters that you can master without difficulty:

1) *Repetition*. We've already mentioned this earlier in this chapter, but, since we're talking about repetition, we'll mention it again. Of course, you've been using this memory booster all your life, haven't you? If you've ever taken French, for instance, you've spent a good deal of time repeating over and over and over again the conjugation of the verb *to have*. You went through it hundreds of times—*j'ai, tu as, vous avez, il a, elle a, nous avons*—until you got it down and it became second nature. You learned the same way when you were in grade school and were taught your multiplication tables. Repetition works but, then again, not everything lends itself to repetition. Some material is too complex for such an approach.

2) *Organization*. Miscellaneous information is more likely to stick in the mind if we organize it clearly and consistently through some system of categorization. Let's imagine, for instance, that you have an enormous extended family and you're trying to remember the names of your 50 first cousins. You'll have a better chance of accomplishing this task if you think in terms of "Uncle Sid and Aunt Joyce's kids" and "Uncle Phil and Aunt Lil's kids" and "Uncle Bernie and Aunt Ann's kids." Or perhaps you'll want to go from oldest to youngest or geographically or some other system you've devised. The other way that you can use organization to remember things is to make lists, even it they're just on the back of envelopes. (We'll be talking more about this in Chapter 7: Managing Your Time … Organizing Your Life.)

3) *Mnemonics*. Mnemonics are mind enhancers that help people to remember things. For instance, if you're trying to remember the names of the Great Lakes, you might rely on *HOMES*, that trusty old mnemonic device wherein *H* stands for Huron, *O* for Ontario, *M* for Michigan, *E* for Erie, and *S* for Superior. There are quite a few famous mnemonics like that one, but feel free to make up your own. For instance, if you're running into the supermarket for five items—bread, milk, apples, eggs, and rice—you'll have an easier time if you keep the word *AMBER* in your head (*A* for apples, *M* for milk, *B* for bread, *E* for eggs, *R* for rice). It may

**STUDENT TALK:
ANOTHER GOOD IDEA**

"My husband says my mind is like a sieve. I do forget a lot, but it's just that I have a lot going on right now, with school and kids and my job and everything. So what I'll do if I have something really important to remember—like picking up birthday candles for my daughter's cake, for instance—is I'll leave a message for myself on my cell phone. This has saved my life more times than I want to admit!"

—Maria Z., 29, Houston, TX.

What Did We Learn?

Let's see how much we managed to remember from this chapter on memory and other matters of the mind.

1. Define "cognition" and give examples of some cognitive functions that human beings perform.

2. IQ tests were once considered definitive predictors of achievement. What are some of the flaws that are now seen with regard to traditional IQ testing?

3. Who developed the theory of multiple intelligences and what are the various forms of intelligences according to this theory?

4. How does emotional intelligence manifest itself?

5. What are the three predominant learning styles? Which style would you say you prefer?

6. What are some characteristics of critical thinking?

7. Discuss the differences between deductive and inductive reasoning.

8. Identify some key questions you would ask to initiate productive problem solving.

9. Name three phases of memory.

10. What are some useful ways to enhance memory? Identify specific, practical tools.

take an extra helping of linguistic intelligence to think up such mnemonics but, once you get the hang of it, they come fairly easily. Making up a song or a rhyme can help too. (Columbus sailed the ocean blue in 1492.) Another mnemonic device that some people appreciate is called *the journey method*. With this, you create a little narrative in your mind that moves you down memory lane. For instance, your mother has asked you to pick up apples, milk, bread, eggs, and rice on your way home. So, in the interest of remembering these items, you make up a tale that situates you on some imaginary farm. You pluck an *apple* from the tree in the front yard, you pass the cow who gives you *milk*, you feed *bread* to the horse, you get *eggs* from the chicken and ... rice? Well, we'll have to work on that one.

4) *Customizing for learning styles.* Do you remember that we talked about learning styles? (We hope so—it was just a few pages ago!) You will be more likely to remember important material, as in the case of textbook review, when you key your review to the learning style that you have identified as closest to your own. For instance, if you are a kinesthetic learner, when you are reviewing an important point in your text, you might want to tap and untap your pen or pencil to reinforce the absorption. As we discussed, visual learners can reinforce their learning with flash cards and auditory learners stand a better chance of absorbing material if they can reinforce their learning with tapes or other auditory enhancements. Again, whatever works best for you.

Probably the simplest mnemonic device is tying a string around your finger. That tells you that you have to remember *something* ... but what is it again? Developing your memory requires practice and creativity. Which leads us to our next chapter: The Act of Creation.

Bibliography

Browne, M. N., & Keeley, S. M. (2003). *Asking the right questions: A guide to critical thinking* (7th ed.). Upper Saddle River, NJ: Prentice Hall.

Fisher, A. (2001). *Critical thinking*. West Nyack, NY: Cambridge University Press.

Forbes, R. (1993). *The creative problem solver's toolbox: A complete course in the art of creating solutions to problems of any kind.* Tucson, AZ: Solutions Through Innovations.

Gardner, H. (1993). *Frames of mind: The theory of multiple intelligences*. New York: Basic Books.

Gardner, H. (1993). *Multiple intelligences: The theory in practice*. New York: Basic Books.

Howard, P. J. (1999). *The owner's manual for the brain* (2nd ed.). Austin, TX: Bard Press.

Kotulak, R. (1997). *Inside the brain: Revolutionary discoveries of how the mind works*. Kansas City, MO: Andrews McMeel.

Lapp, D. C. (1995). *Don't forget! Easy exercises for a better memory*. Boston: Addison-Wesley.

Lorayne, H., & Lucas, J. (1996). *The memory book: The classic guide to improving your memory at work, at school, at play*. New York: Ballantine.

Priest, G. (2000). *Logic: A very short introduction*. New York: Oxford University Press.

Links

EverythingBio: An all-encompassing biology resource. Retrieved November 18, 2005, from http://www.everythingbio.com/

Howard Gardner, Multiple Intelligences and Education. Retrieved November 18, 2005, from http://www.infed.org/thinkers/gardner.htm

The human brain. Retrieved November 18, 2005, from http://www.meaningoflife.i12.com/brain.htm

The human brain: Some interesting facts. Retrieved November 18, 2005, from http://www.uwf.edu/jgould/BrainFacts.pdf

Singleton, J. K. Memory enhancement. Retrieved November 18, 2005, from http://www.ec-online.net/Knowledge/Articles/memoryenhancement.html

Tim Van Gelder's Critical Thinking on the Web. Retrieved November 18, 2005, from http://www.austhink.org/critical/

Word Smart

Don't forget these:

- adept
- arbiter
- arbitrary
- conglomerate
- faculty
- infusion
- intuitive
- nuance
- rote
- rudimentary
- subliminal
- synergy
- unsubstantiated

THE ACT OF CREATION

Sadly, there are too many people who go through life convinced that they're "no good" at things like music or dancing. They have been told—perhaps by parents or siblings or teachers—that they "can't carry a tune" or that they are "uncoordinated" or "clumsy." Such appellations **can damage a person's self-esteem and rob that person of the right to enjoy the pleasures in life that should be available to everyone. At some point in *your* life, you may have received the same kind of confusing and wounding message about creativity. Think back: when you were a child and went to the beach, did everyone *ooh!* and *ah!* over your brother's sand castle while ignoring your efforts? In first grade, did your clay turtle sit on the back of the shelf while somebody else's elephant was given a place of honor? When you took Art in high school, did you get less than a good grade? Did you grow up feeling that creativity was something for "other people?"**

If that was the case, we're sorry for the disappointment you must have felt then, but we urge you not to stay in that place. The fact is that creativity is a force and a resource that is available to everyone. The task lies in learning how to tap into it. In this chapter, we'll show you how.

appellations names or titles

Creativity Is ...

Often when people think of creativity, they immediately associate it with extraordinary artists like Michelangelo, Leonardo da Vinci, or Mozart, whose genius and vision transforms the way other human beings see the world. Genius can be thought of as creativity taken to its ultimate heights, but creativity is also present in the lives of ordinary people. When you come up with a solution for how to sell more footballs at the sporting goods store where you work, you've used creative thinking to solve your problem. When company is coming for dinner and you forgot to pick up dessert, maybe you'll think creatively and freeze a can of pears. You throw the frozen fruit into a blender and *voilà*! Pear sorbet! Once again, creative thinking has come to the rescue.

A good, all-purpose definition of creativity is that it's a new way of looking at something. Creativity involves coming up with original ideas and solutions. But, as we've suggested, you don't have to be a genius to be creative. You just have to know how to break out of the box. So, what stops us from doing that?

In fact, the thing that holds us back is called *functional fixedness*. This term, used in cognitive psychology, refers to the kind of narrow and limited thinking that often inhibits the problem-solving process. When a person thinks only in terms of functionality, then that person is said to be functionally fixated.

One of the first people to identify this problem was German psychologist Karl Duncker, who devised the following experiment. He divided his subjects into two groups. Members of the first group were shown into a room where they saw the following items placed on a table: a half-open box containing a few pins, a few matches, and a candle. They were told to attach the candle to the wall and light it, using the items available to them. In fact, the way to solve this problem was to use one of the pins from the box to attach the pin box to the wall so that it could support the candle, and then melt some candle wax to affix the candle to the box. This was not a problem that required genius to solve, yet very few people in this group were able to come up with a solution.

With the second group, there was a slight adjustment to the playing field: Duncker showed the pin box to this group with the pins already scattered on the table. As a result, the majority of the people in the second group were able to solve the problem. How did that slight change enable the members of the second group to "break out of the box?" The problem with the first group was that they could not get beyond the

notion that the primary use for the pin box was to contain pins. They were functionally fixated in terms of how they saw that box. The second group, however, realized that the pins were distinct from the box, and this freed them up to do some real creative thinking.

Access Your Creativity

The people in Duncker's second group were not geniuses. They were not even unusually intelligent or talented. They were simply ordinary people who were provided with the kind of circumstances that allowed them to access their creativity. Some people believe that creativity can only occur under certain very exacting conditions. "Maybe if someone bought me a box of beautiful pastels I'd start painting. Maybe if I had a whole week to myself I could start writing." While it's true that certain circumstances can facilitate creativity—the author Virginia Woolf wrote about the pleasures of writing "in a room of one's own"—creativity is more consistently brought to the surface through one's own **autonomous** actions. In this chapter, we will explore these autonomous actions—those that you can always have with you as general ways of thinking and being as well as those specific actions that can free you up when you're stuck. We don't really like the idea of "rules" to govern creativity, so we're not going to use that term to structure the list we're about to give you. Creativity is all about *ideas*, so here are some good ideas to help you get into a creative mode.

Eight Good Ideas to Help You Access Your Creativity

Whenever you're striving to think creatively, follow these pointers:

1) *Forget about failure*. When a writer sits down to a blank sheet of paper or a painter confronts a blank canvas, it is perfectly normal to feel anxious, even to the point of nausea. After all, every creative act has the potential for disappointment, and the tension between striving and achieving can be quite intense. But when fear of failure becomes too intense, then creativity can be short-circuited. That shouldn't be allowed to happen. And what's so bad about failure anyway? Herman Melville, the author of *Moby Dick*, one of the two or three greatest American novels, put it this way: "It is better to fail originally than to succeed in imitation."

autonomous functioning or existing independently

OPEN FOR DISCUSSION: *BOXED IN*

At some point or another, we've all experienced functional fixedness. Fixated thinking doesn't just have to concern objects, like the pins in the box of Duncker's experiment. It could pertain to abstract concepts, people, or ideas. When have you felt "boxed in?" What did you do to break out of the box? Is there anything that's going on in your life right now that is making you feel "fixed?" Try having this discussion in small groups, and then report back to the larger group with any thoughts you'd like to share.

IN OTHER WORDS

"The best way to get a good idea is to get a lot of good ideas."
—Dr. Linus Pauling, Nobel Prize-winning scientist

2) *Pay close attention.* Despite what many media critics have to say, there are quite a few excellent things to watch on television. There's a big difference, however, between selecting and watching a quality television show and being plugged in mindlessly and endlessly to the boob tube. The same thing goes for music. Are you actually listening to music or are you using it to screen out the world? Again, there are times when the world may need a little screening out—when you're sitting on a crowded bus or train, looking for some peace of mind—but the more we screen things out, the more we run the risk of not seeing. Learning to see—to stop and open your eyes and really look around you—is an important part of the process of developing your creativity.

3) *Let accidents happen.* Creative people realize that they aren't in complete control of the world. Rather, they see themselves as conduits or receptors for information and input. Sometimes the most incredible discoveries are made simply "by accident." Consider the discovery of penicillin, for instance. Sir Alexander Fleming was growing bacteria in a Petri dish when a spore of a certain mold, later identified as *Penicillium notatum*, blew into the culture and ultimately killed the bacteria. Fleming isolated the active ingredient, and—by **felicitous** accident—the world had a miracle substance that would go on to save millions of lives.

4) *Hang on to your ideas.* Is there such a thing as a bad idea? It's hard to say—even dill pickle ice cream might have its fans. If an idea digs its hooks into you, chances are it's because it has some merit. Try to store away your ideas and then reexamine them periodically. Perhaps you'll want to keep an "Ideas File" on your computer or jot them down in a notebook. A set of index cards is an excellent way to organize a file of ideas, particularly if you label each one with an identifying word in the upper right-hand corner. "Time Savers." "Ways to Save Money." "Entertaining." "Potential Businesses"—the labels are up to you.

5) *Put in the sweat equity.* Creative ideas are great, but there can be such a thing as pipe dreams too. Just spinning out ideas can border on fantasy—"I'm thinking of a machine that would brew your coffee, toast your English muffin, and wake you up all at the

FOOD FOR THOUGHT: PAYING CLOSE ATTENTION

In 1948, when Swiss engineer George DeMaestral went walking in the woods, he noticed some burrs sticking to his socks and trousers. He took the burrs back to his lab and, as he examined them under a microscope, he saw that they had tiny hooks that engaged with the tiny loops on the fabric of his clothing. DeMaestral was inspired to create a new fastening device that was called ... Velcro. Now *there* was a man who was paying close attention!

Source: The Online Learning Center. Retrieved November 28, 2005, from **http://www.tki.org.nz/r/ science/scienceschool/resources/1999/sticky2.htm**

felicitous happy

same time!"—so let the less valuable ones fall by the wayside (or, if you're not sure, stick them in your Idea File) and devote some extra thought to the ones that seem to merit it. The extra thought might involve research, brainstorming with others (we'll discuss brainstorming later in the chapter), actual experimentation, and more. You may also find that doing the work can stimulate other ideas. As the great Russian composer Igor Stravinsky once said, "As appetite comes from eating, so work brings inspiration."

6) *Listen to others … but let the decision be yours*. In general, creative people should be open to input and feedback, which can, of course, be immensely valuable. As a creative person, however, you may also be getting some really inferior input and you will have to learn how to tune that out. Extraordinary creative minds are so visionary that lesser mortals may be unable to understand them. In the words of the song "They All Laughed" by George and Ira Gershwin, "They all laughed at Christopher Columbus when he said the world was round/They all laughed when Edison recorded sound."

7) *Have fun*. Creativity often involves an enormous amount of hard work, but it should also be a source of pleasure, fun, and even joy. If you ever spend time around young children, you will see that their play is chock full of creativity. A stone becomes a mountain; a leaf in a puddle magically turns into a boat. Madeline L'Engle, the author of the classic young adult novel, *A Wrinkle in Time*, once wrote, "All children are artists, and it is an indictment of our culture that so many of them lose their creativity, their unfettered imaginations, as they grow older" [Maggio, R., ed. (1997). *Quotations on education*. Prentice Hall: Upper Saddle River, NJ, p. 149].Truly creative people know better than to let the culture rob them that way.

8) *Focus on process before product*. Creative people love the creative act. In fact, they often enjoy the act more than the product itself. Alfred Hitchcock, the brilliant director of such suspense classics as *Psycho*, *Vertigo*, and *Rear Window*, so thoroughly enjoyed the creative process involved in figuring out his films with an intricate system of storyboarding that by the time he actually got around to shooting the film, it was more or less a formality for him. Creative people relish the figuring out, the correcting, the polishing, the tearing apart and the putting back together again. An incredible

example of a creative person whose work is so much about process is the Scottish artist Andy Goldsworthy, whose creations have won him international acclaim. Goldsworthy creates sculptures out of twigs, leaves, stone, snow, ice, reeds, thorns, berries, feathers, and whatever else nature has to offer. He regards all his creations as temporary, and his goal is to understand nature by directly interacting with it as intimately as he can. "Movement, change, light, growth, and decay are the lifeblood of nature, the energies that I try to tap through my work," Goldsworthy says. "Each work grows, stays, decays. Process and decay are **implicit**. **Transience** in my work reflects what I find in nature." Goldsworthy has discovered joy in the creative process, even more than in the satisfaction of his finished work.

CREATIVITY AT-A-GLANCE

There is a lot to absorb in the information above. Repeating it as a simple list will help you remember:

- *Forget about failure*
- *Pay close attention*
- *Let accidents happen*
- *Hang on to your ideas*
- *Put in the sweat equity*
- *Listen to others … but let the decision be yours*
- *Have fun*
- *Focus on process before product*

Tools for Creativity

We've been speaking in general terms about how to instill, promote, and experience creativity in your life. Now we'd like to focus on some of the specific tools and techniques that can help you free up your creative spirit. Let's begin with mind-mapping.

MIND-MAPPING

In Chapter 3, if you recall, we discussed the different types of learning styles. Visual learners will be particularly drawn to the technique of mind-mapping, but your orientation really needn't be that visual for you

implicit implied; not specifically stated
transience temporariness

to benefit from this technique. Mind-mapping is a quick, easy, and effective way to free up the creative thinking that gets locked up inside us all.

With mind-mapping, you begin by writing down a central idea and then you let all kinds of new ideas radiate out from that hub. If nothing else, mind-mapping gives you the feeling that you are actually *doing* something. After all, it offers **tangible** evidence that some thinking has occurred. Let's imagine, just for now, that your central idea is *starting a video club*. After all, you're a total film freak and there must be other people like you on campus, right? The campus policy states that if you can find a certain number of like-minded individuals, the school will support you in your effort to start a club. So, from this central idea—the hub of your mind map—you start to look for relationships.

What's the best way to denote these relationships? That's up to you. You may decide to use arrows or dotted lines or colors to show how you get from one place to another. Accordingly, if the central idea is *starting a video club*, then perhaps some of your relationships might be things like, *screenings on the first Mondays of every month* or *creating a lending library of videos*. Now, don't worry if your pencil doesn't have an eraser. You're not going to **expend** any effort with erasing things or crossing out ideas or in any other way censoring yourself. The cardinal rule of mind-mapping is that all thoughts are equal, at least in the beginning. Later on, there will be time for evaluation and then you can discard those thoughts that do not make the grade. As you may come to see, the most fascinating thing about mind-mapping is that this visual record of your thoughts will sometimes surprise you in the end. That idea that sat quietly in the left-hand top corner of the page may prove to be the one that you finally come back to in the end.

Another good mind-mapping tip is to give yourself lots of space. A mere scrap of paper is not going to accommodate an expansive mind-mapping session. Roll out a big sheet of brown wrapping paper and let the ideas flow. There is a famous **dictum** in architectural circles: "Less is more." This saying does not apply to mind-mapping, where more is more!

Mind-mapping is a tool you can take anywhere. Although we've recommended that you do your mind-mapping on a nice big sheet of paper, you can get started on the back of an index card if you're stuck on a subway or a bus and want to make the most of your time.

tangible concrete
expend use up
dictum pronouncement

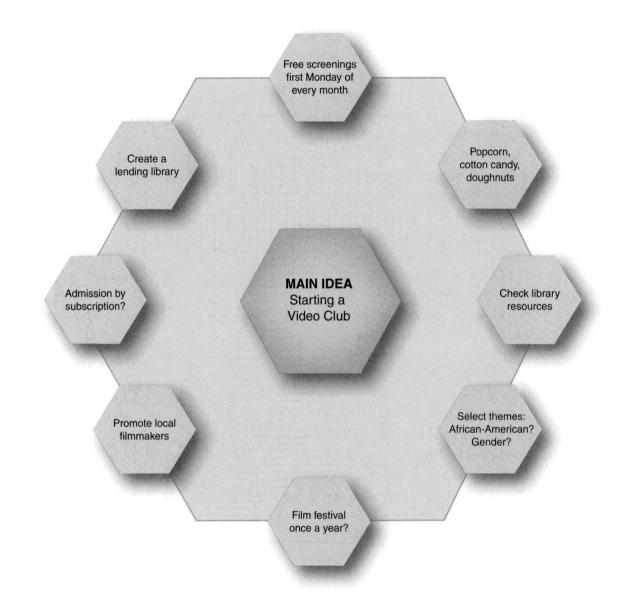

Free screenings
first Monday of
every month

Create a
lending library

Popcorn,
cotton candy,
doughnuts

Admission by
subscription?

MAIN IDEA
Starting a
Video Club

Check library
resources

Promote local
filmmakers

Select themes:
African-American?
Gender?

Film festival
once a year?

BRAINSTORMING

Our lives are full of problems, big and small, which require creative
thinking, and so getting into the habit of thinking creatively will serve
you well. One of the best methods for uncorking creative thoughts and
solutions that may be bottled up inside is brainstorming.

Like mind-mapping, brainstorming is an excellent way to generate
ideas. Again, the goal here is *more*. You want lots of ideas, and whenever
there are a lot of ideas in a room, some of them are bound to be wild
and crazy and perhaps ultimately useless. But, then again, some of the
greatest ideas in human history have seemed to be wild and crazy at first.

Brainstorming can work as a solo activity, but it's really designed to be done by groups, who are looking both for answers to shared problems and to develop their solidarity through shared problem solving. Here are some tips for making the most of your brainstorming sessions:

- *First, determine if your subject lends itself to brainstorming*. You'll want to reserve your brainstorming sessions for those subjects and topics that genuinely have the potential to generate a lot of ideas. Brainstorming on a subject like "Preparing a Budget" might not lead anywhere. After all, preparing a budget is a fairly **circumscribed** activity. There aren't all that many directions you can go with it. On the other hand, choosing a topic like "How to Save $20 a Month" could prove to be a very fruitful subject for brainstorming, with lots of ideas coming from each participant.

- *Build your group brainstorming on individual brainstorming*. If you're planning a brainstorming session, alert your participants and give them a couple of days' notice to start working up some ideas. This kind of preparation will provide a great head start for your group session.

- *Appoint a facilitator*. Too many ideas flying around a room can easily get out of control, so make it one person's job to maintain order in the group and designate another to record the ideas.

- *No criticism allowed*. This should be one of your absolute ground rules. Allowing people to criticize others in the room—"Are you crazy? That would never work in a million years. Bad idea!"—will not only inhibit the creative process but will use up valuable time to boot.

- *Push yourself beyond your limit*. Whether you're brainstorming solo or as part of a group, force yourself to go even further than you think you can go. If you're brainstorming by yourself, just when you think you've exhausted all your reservoirs of genius, tell yourself to put in another five minutes. You'll be amazed by what can come out of running that extra lap. Similarly, in a group situation, when you collectively feel like you've come to the saturation point, push the group to come up with three more ideas—"Just three more, guys. Really. We can do it."

- *Go crazy*. When it comes to brainstorming, no idea is too wild or crazy. People might say (if they were allowed to criticize you, which

FOOD FOR THOUGHT: THEY SAID WHAT?

You've heard the expression "famous last words"? Consider these infamous "first words" that greeted some of history's greatest ideas:

- "I think there is a world market for maybe five computers."—*Thomas Watson, chairman of IBM, 1943.*

- "Who the hell wants to hear actors talk?"—*H. M. Warner, of Warner Brothers, on the coming of talking pictures in 1927.*

- "This 'telephone' has too many shortcomings to be seriously considered as a means of communication. The device is inherently of no value to us."—*Western Union internal memo, 1876.*

- "With over 50 foreign cars already on sale here, the Japanese auto industry isn't likely to carve out a big slice of the U.S. market."—*Business Week, August 2, 1968.*

- "Radio has no future. Heavier-than-air flying machines are impossible. X-rays will prove to be a hoax." —*William Thomson, Lord Kelvin, British scientist, 1899.*

Source: Things people said: Bad predictions. Retrieved November 28, 2005, from http://rinkworks.com/said/predictions.shtml

circumscribed confined within bounds; restricted

REFLECTIONS: *YOUR HISTORY*

People who teach composition often ask their students to try a technique called *freewriting*. With freewriting, there are no rules, no rights or wrongs, no inhibitions. Students are simply instructed to write for 5 or 10 minutes with the only "rule" being that anything goes. Use punctuation or don't. Capitalize or don't capitalize. Sentence fragments? Why not?

Try some freewriting now—just write for 10 minutes and *do not stop*—and then, when you've finished, see if there are any valuable ideas that are waiting to be culled from your writing. Even if you've written, "This is stupid this is stupid this is stupid" for 10 minutes straight, it might be interesting for you to ask yourself why you chose that particular path.

In a way, freewriting is a kind of brainstorming. It also makes a fine limbering exercise for any writing assignment that you are asked to do. If, after you try this, you find that freewriting has worked for you on some level, keep it in mind as something you can go back to whenever you choose to help loosen you up and stretch your writing and thinking muscles.

they aren't), "Are you out of your mind? Do you have any idea how much that would cost?" But that's not the point. Budgets, practicality, political correctness—these are not issues that should bog you down when you're brainstorming. Sure, your idea might be outrageous in terms of its budgetary demands, but even a crazy idea can contain the kernel of something truly valuable.

• *Provide some follow-up recourse.* Brainstorming sessions can sometimes create a ripple effect. When people leave a session and then talk to friends, they may come up with other kinds of insights or information and are soon ready to share again. It can be difficult to schedule actual face time, so at least make sure that everyone has each other's contact information. That way, the sharing can continue.

We will be revisiting the subject of mind-mapping and brainstorming in Chapter 12: Word Perfect, when we explore those techniques further and show how they can be used specifically with regard to writing assignments. For now, however, we'd like to continue with our discussion of creativity, looking specifically at journaling.

JOURNALING

Maybe you were one of those kids who loved to curl up at night with a little notebook of your own. *Dear Diary*, you wrote, *this has been a very special day*. If you were such a child, there's no reason to be shy or self-conscious about it. There's nothing corny or hokey about keeping a diary. In fact, it's a wonderful impulse, and you, more than anyone, probably realize how much it helped you at that time and how it got you into the habit of examining your life as you live it. Socrates, the great Greek philosopher whose teachings were **expounded** by his student Plato, said, "The unexamined life is not worth living for a man." Socrates said this over 2,400 years ago, but it couldn't be truer today. If you've never kept a diary or a journal—we are using the terms interchangeably here—maybe it's time you tried. There isn't much to learn—keeping a journal is not like changing the spark plugs on a BMW—but there is so much to benefit from, particularly in how it can help you access your creativity.

Journaling is an express train to your inner thoughts—those that are so internal that oftentimes you're not even aware of them. Why are

expounded set forth in detail

you keeping them inside of you? It could be for any number of reasons. Maybe they're scary or threatening. Maybe they seem "silly" or unattainable. Maybe you feel that you simply can't find the time in your life for interior exploration. And who needs to look at these feelings and thoughts anyway?

You do. Remember what Socrates said? Examining your life gives you the advantage of understanding what really drives you, what your motivation is, what your hopes are, how you anticipate dealing with disappointment, what you're looking for in other people, what you value, what you shrink away from … we could go on and on. But the point is for *you* to go on and on … in your journal. And we don't mean "on and on" in the sense of having a marathon session. Journal writing is perhaps best done in short stints. We mean "on and on" in the sense that this kind of exploration should become an ongoing part of your life.

So, what do you need in order to get started? First of all, you need something to write in. Beautiful leather-bound journals make lovely presents, but they're hardly essential. A spiral notebook from your local stationary store will do just fine. So will a legal pad. Just make sure that your notebook and your pen or pencil feel comfortable. Some people like to write their journal entries on their laptops, and if that works for you, fine. Others like the **spare**, pared-down feeling of a pen and paper.

Where should you do your journaling? Again, wherever it feels good to you. Some people like to do it in bed or on the bus or train or in the student lounge or library or at a café. More important than the materials you select or the place where you choose to write is *when* you write. The idea is to really engage in this activity so that it becomes a kind of habit. That's why it's probably a good idea in the beginning to try to do your journal writing at the same time each day. And let's not hear about how you don't have enough time for this. All you really need is an extra 5 or 10 minutes a day. You may well find it worthwhile to get up 5 minutes earlier in the morning so that you can have this kind of restorative time alone with yourself.

As for the process, we want to borrow an important point from our earlier discussion about brainstorming: *no criticism allowed*. Now we don't mean that there shouldn't be any self-critiques in your diary. You may want to write about things you see in yourself that you'd like to

spare not elaborate or fussy

> ### STUDENT TALK:
> ### A SPECIAL PLACE
>
> **"**I've kept a journal since I was 12. In the beginning, it was a 'Dear Diary, do you think Bobby Wagner likes me?' kind of thing. I'm glad to report, however, that I've moved beyond Bobby Wagner. What my journal has become for me is a place where I can really go to *think*. It's not just about my personal feelings, thoughts, problems, and so on—although there's plenty of that in it. It's also a place where I'll jot down all kinds of interesting stuff I read about in the papers or hear on the news—stuff I don't want to forget. Frankly, I don't think I could live without my journal. Well, I guess I could, but it wouldn't be the same. I think it would feel kind of shallow, if you know what I mean."
>
> —Lauren P., 18, Wilmington, DE.

change or improve. When we say "no criticism," we mean that we don't want you to criticize your writing. Don't say, "Oh, that's a really stupid sentence." Just let it go. Don't cross things out. Don't dwell on what's not perfect because nothing is. Let your thoughts go to the paper and just let them be. After all, your thoughts have a right to express themselves, and expression can lead to creativity.

"But what am I supposed to write?" you ask. The answer is, "Whatever you wish." There is a lot going on in your life right now. You have undertaken a huge responsibility, enrolling in college. You may have doubts and insecurities about yourself. You may be pulling away from familiar situations and people. You're meeting new people who **pique** your interest and your journal is a good place to explore your thoughts about them. You're learning a lot of interesting things in your classes as well. Maybe you've been discussing issues that have come up in your history or science or psychology class. Your journal is an excellent place to explore these issues in more depth. If you're interrupted in

pique arouse

CASE IN POINT: SIMON RODIA

Creativity can turn up anywhere and can transform ordinary lives into extraordinary ones. In south Los Angeles, in the community known as Watts that became notorious as the site of one of the worst race riots in our nation's history, there stands a monument to one man's spirit, ingenuity, determination, and creativity. Simon Rodia, also known as Sabato "Sam" Rodia and "Don Simon" by his neighbors, single-handedly built a group of sculptural forms on a lot at 1765 107th Street that has become famous all over the world.

Rodia was born in 1879 in southern Italy and came to America when he was 12. He labored in coal mines in Pennsylvania and then, when he moved to California, he worked in rock quarries, as a logger, and in railroad camps. In 1921, he bought a humble house on a wedge-shaped plot of land in Watts. There Rodia dedicated himself to his life's work, building a masterpiece that he called "Nuestro Pueblo" (meaning "our town"). Nuestro Pueblo consists of nine sculptural forms made of steel that are covered with shards of ceramic, pottery, sea shells, and broken glass. The tallest of these edifices is nearly 100 feet high and contains the longest slender column of reinforced concrete in the world.

How did Rodia achieve this engineering marvel? Without the benefit of any special equipment, scaffolding, or drawing board designs. For 33 years he worked solo on his towers, using only the simple tools of a tile-setter and a window washer's belt and buckle. The Towers of Simon Rodia have been named a National Historic Landmark and are listed on the National Registry of Historic Places. Beyond that, they are an internationally recognized symbol of how the creative spirit can thoroughly captivate a human being and benefit not only him, but the rest of the world as well.

Source: Los Angeles: Watts Towers. Retrieved November 28, 2005, from http://www.kcet.org/lifeandtimes/arts/watts/php

the middle of an important thought, just jot down a word that will act as a prompt for your memory when you're able to return to it later.

As you become more accustomed to writing in a journal, you may find yourself becoming more responsive to the world around you and more aware of all kinds of stimuli. You may see things in nature—a leaf, a stone, an insect—that you would not have noticed before you developed this habit of examination. Maybe you'll start remembering your dreams and perhaps you'll want to explore their meaning in your journal. Maybe you'll become more attuned to language and you'll go on and try your hand at poetry. As you start to think more creatively, you'll notice that the world feels more vibrant and alive. It's an incredible discovery.

Having now had a look at how the brain works, how goal setting works, and how to foster critical thinking, problem solving, and creativity, it's time to start looking at how you can develop some of the hands-on study skills that will serve you well as a student. These will be explored in Chapter 5.

© BananaStock Ltd.

What Did We Learn?

Look at the following questions and activities to remind yourself of the most important points in our discussion of creativity.

1. Define creativity.
2. What is meant by "functional fixedness"?
3. What are some of the most effective ways to access your creativity?
4. Describe the process of mind-mapping.
5. What are some guidelines for assuring productive brainstorming sessions?
6. Define "freewriting."
7. What is the value of keeping a journal?

Bibliography

Csikzentmihalyi, M. (1997). *Creativity: Flow and the psychology of discovery and invention*. New York: Perennial HarperCollins.

Ayan, J. (1996). *Aha! 10 ways to free your creative spirit and find your great ideas*. Three Rivers, MI: Three Rivers Press.

Foster, J. (1996). *How to get ideas*. San Francisco, CA: Berrett-Koehler Publishers.

Hall, D. (1996). *Jump start your brain*. New York: Warner.

Nadler, G., & Hibino, S. (1998). *Breakthrough thinking: The seven principles of creative problem solving*. New York: Prima Lifestyles.

Thompson, C. (1992). *What a great idea! The key steps creative people take*. New York: Perennial HarperCollins.

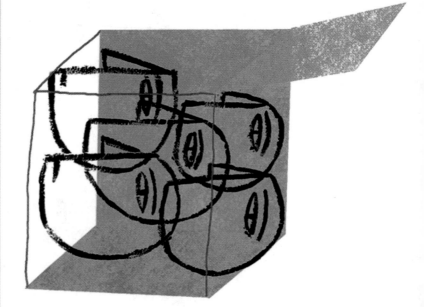

Links

Bouton, E. Journaling tips. Retrieved November 28, 2005, from http://www.whole-heart .com/tips.html

Eight basic heuristics of directed creativity. Retrieved November 28, 2005, from http:// www.directedcreativity.com/pages/Heuristics .html#DCHeuristics

Horowitz, R. Functional fixation. Retrieved November 28, 2005, from http://www .start2think.com/fixedness.html

McKenzie, J. Building good new ideas. Retrieved November 28, 2005, from http:// fno.org/jun01/building.html

Walonick, D. S. Promoting human creativity. Retrieved November 28, 2005, from http://www.survey-software-solutions.com/ walonick/creativity.htm

Word Smart

Below are some words from this chapter that you should learn. They're bound to come up again at other points in your life—you'll see!

appellation
autonomous
circumscribe
dictum
expend
expound
felicitous
implicit
pique
spare
tangible
transience

PART TWO

GETTING
SERIOUS

THE HOW-TO OF STUDYING

One of the keys to becoming a successful student is to develop a set of study skills that you know will work for you. This chapter will be looking at those specific skills, as well as the environmental factors that can influence how you study.

Finding Your Inner Student

Earlier in this book, we looked at the various learning styles—auditory, visual, and kinesthetic. Now, before we go any further, we want to reinforce the idea that, just as we all learn in different ways, we also choose to study in different ways. For instance, some people study best with a certain amount of noise buzzing in the background. They like to take their notes to the neighborhood coffeehouse, and in the liveliness of that atmosphere, they're best able to settle down to work, which would have been impossible for them if they were stuck in the absolute quiet of the library. Other people thrive on that kind of absolute quiet and can be distracted in an atmosphere that has even a hint of liveliness.

As a college student, you may be experiencing the kind of independence that you've always looked forward to or, if you're an older student, you've probably become accustomed to being independent for a while now. Independence is great—it means getting to do things your own way, at least to some extent. Part of doing things your own way, however, is doing them in a way

that nets the best results. You don't need us to tell you that the stakes are now high and the learning is serious, but we'll tell you anyway: *The stakes are high and the learning is serious*. That's why you'll need to figure out what works best for you and how you can ensure that you get what you need in order to succeed.

Owning Your Learning

If we were to name one **attribute** that distinguishes students who are successful, it's that they have a real sense of ownership around their learning. They are active learners, not passive ones. A passive learner sits there in class, waiting to be told what to do. An active learner is fully engaged in the learning process and understands that the relationship with the teacher is a collaborative one.

How does a sense of ownership **manifest** itself with regard to studying? It does so in two principal ways: through quantity (how much you study) and quality (how well you study). With regard to quantity, we recognize that there is no "right" amount of study time. It will vary from student to student. Some people are lucky—they are "quick studies." They can glance at a page of facts and digest it easily and speedily. Unfortunately, most of us cannot do this. Studying for us involves setting aside sufficient time for the material to sink in. How long is "sufficient" time? Again, this is a highly personal matter. All we can say is that if you shortchange yourself you'll know it. You'll wind up cramming, and when you show up at the test, you'll have that queasy feeling that signifies how inadequate your preparation has been.

attribute quality or characteristic
manifest show

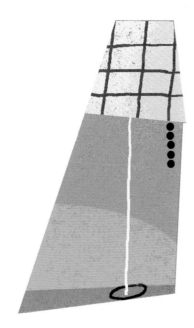

In terms of "quality," we're talking about the nature of the studying itself. A person can put in lots of study hours, but if those hours are peppered with phone conversations or romps with your dog or trips into the kitchen every 5 minutes, then the kind of *uninterrupted* study time that spells real quality will never be attained.

The quality and quantity that characterize good studying and that speak to a real sense of ownership around your studying stem from the right kind of motivation. Motivation is very much at the heart of being a successful student, and it really comes into play around studying. The fact is that very few people look forward to sitting down and studying because they love it so much. On the **hierarchy** of life's activities—swing dancing, windsurfing, Texas hold' em poker—the idea of sitting down with a hefty textbook to review complex material may not rank high. Studying requires discipline. And where does that discipline come from? You guessed it—from motivation.

Some people call motivation "willpower." Others refer to it as "self-discipline." Whatever you want to call it, we're sure you know what it is. When you're studying for a big Biology test, and something comes along to tempt you—a call from friends to go to the beach; your kid's final game of the soccer season; going to a movie with your partner—motivation is that part of you that says "No." Now it's hard to say no—we all recognize that. The idea of your family and friends having fun while you're stuck in the house with cytoplasms, membranes, and mitosis can be almost unendurable. But there are those who are able to endure such deprivation and then there are those who throw over their work and head for the boardwalk, the soccer game, or the movies. And therein lies the difference....

How can you develop the kind of motivation that will help you make the right choice in such situations? A good place to begin is by understanding where motivation comes from. Essentially, there are two types of motivation: *extrinsic* and *intrinsic*. Extrinsic motivation comes from outside of you. Let's say you're taking Biology, and your rich Uncle Leo, the cardiologist, has offered you $150 as a reward if you get a B or better in the course. That $150 could go toward paying for the teeth whitening you've been dreaming about, and so you hit the books. The motivation is all external—you're more fixated on your teeth than on your learning—but sometimes that's all the motivation you need to get you over the hump.

hierarchy a group of things, people, ideas, etc. ranked in order of importance

The other kind of motivation—intrinsic motivation—comes from inside of you. You're taking Biology because you've always wanted to become a doctor. Your cousin Tommy almost died in a car accident, but when you saw what his doctors were able to do for him, you decided that this was what you wanted to do with your life. Your dream is to help people, and you'll do whatever is necessary to accomplish your goal. The motivation is inside of you, where it's far less susceptible to the **vicissitudes** of all that's going on around you.

Is intrinsic motivation better than extrinsic? We'd have to say yes, in the long run. Extrinsic motivation often involves rewards, and for rewards to be sufficiently sweet and enticing, it may be necessary to up the ante. Uncle Leo's $150 might make you yawn after a while, and if he's not willing to contribute more to your motivation fund, then where will the motivation come from? Intrinsic motivation, on the other hand, is ultimately more solid, and when the goal you've set for yourself is a very ambitious one that can take a long time to accomplish, a really solid reservoir of motivation will get you through the rough patches.

Most people, at various times in life, will rely on a combination of intrinsic and extrinsic motivation to move them toward their goals. For example, you may have to take certain required courses that simply do not interest you, and you'll have to find some way to make the best of it. Here are some good tips about motivation for those times when you feel like you need a boost:

- *Praise*. Praise is usually thought of as a strictly extrinsic kind of motivation, but it does a fine job of inspiring most people to do better. After all, who among us is above being told that we're great? When we get an A on a paper, we're motivated to write our next paper. When a teacher says, "Good question," we're motivated to contribute more to the classroom discussion. Even when we don't have others showering us with praise, we can always play a little trick on ourselves by turning the extrinsic praise inwards, making it into a kind of intrinsic motivation. Otherwise put, we can praise ourselves. If you think this sounds terribly **contrived**, just step back and give it a chance. Return to our discussion of Positive Self-Talk in Chapter 1, and think about how that positive self-talk can be used to bolster your motivation. For instance, when you're feeling low, initiate a dialogue with yourself. "You're doing great. Okay—you've had a rough

STUDENT TALK: BREAKING THE HABIT

" I think the clearest example of how motivation has worked in my life has been around the issue of my smoking. I took up smoking when I was 14, even though I knew it was bad for me, and I got totally hooked. It wasn't long before I came to realize that there were a lot of reasons why I needed to give it up—my girlfriend thought it was disgusting; I was on the basketball team and it's not exactly great for your wind; and it cost me money I didn't have. But all those reasons were external. What finally got me to give up smoking was that I started asking myself *why* I was doing this. Why was I taking something into my body that was toxic? When I realized that what I really wanted was to have a long and healthy life, I didn't need a lot of other reasons. That one was plenty good enough."

—Mitch B., 24, Bakersfield, CA.

vicissitudes irregular changes or variations
contrived overly planned; artificial

patch—but you've worked hard and, given your natural abilities, there's no reason why you shouldn't realize your goal." It's called being your own best friend, and it does the job for a great many people.

- *Use your friends and family*. Praise is particularly nice when it comes from objective sources, but if you need a boost and you're tired of praising yourself, enlist the support of your friends and family. Be proactive and upfront about it. "Tell me something nice about myself," you might say. "I need a mental hug." Be careful not to overdo this—after all, even friends and family have their limits—but there's absolutely nothing wrong or weird about asking for some stroking when you feel the need.

- *Don't discount pledges, oaths, vows, and promises*. Making a commitment is a good way to keep the motivation alive. Some of us are more prone to guilt than others, and the potential guilt we would feel at not meeting our commitments motivates us to get the job done. Telling yourself that you must do something by a certain time—or, better yet, writing your deadline down—can be very effective.

- *Remember your anti-procrastination tips*. Procrastination is that wet blanket that can stifle your motivation. Look back to Chapter 2 where we first discussed procrastination, and review some of the tips we offered there. For instance, breaking a large task into smaller ones is a good way to head off procrastination and thereby preserve motivation.

- *Find a role model*. Inspiration and motivation go hand-in-hand. If you feel that you can't possibly succeed because there are simply too many cards in the deck stacked against you, consider someone like Oprah Winfrey, for instance, who overcame poverty, child abuse, and racism to become one of the nation's most successful and wealthy people. Better yet, find a role model in your immediate world who you can look up to and use as a resource. This could be a family member, a teacher, an employer, an older friend—someone you admire who can answer important questions and give you some of the support you'll need to get ahead.

- *Don't neglect the creature comforts*. Human beings exist on at least two planes. One is the cerebral plane, where we deal with ideas. The other is the physical plane, where we look to satisfy our bodily needs. Bringing these two planes into harmony will serve you well,

REFLECTIONS: *YOUR HISTORY*

Have you experienced a situation in which you set a goal for yourself and then saw your motivation start to sag? What caused this to happen? Were you able to reinvigorate your motivation? How did you manage to do that? Write a short piece in which you recall the situation and reflect on how you dealt with it.

and will help to preserve your motivation, rather than sapping the energy and will from you that are necessary to succeed. This means that you should always pay attention to your physical needs and reward yourself in ways that make you feel good and comfortable. Studying under a warm afghan on a cozy chair might be a lot more effective for you than sitting on a hard-backed chair in a drafty library (unless all that comfort lulls you to sleep). Whipping up a batch of fudge or ordering in a pepperoni pizza could do the trick when it comes to studying for your statistics exam. A nap, a walk, a bath—you decide what it takes to make you feel good and provide some relief from the **onus** of studying.

© BananaStock Ltd.

Setting Up a Study Space

What is your dream study space? Does it have one of those little refrigerators, stocked with chocolate milk, apples, peanuts, and cheddar cheese? Is there a window seat to stretch out on, where the sun beats down on you and you feel all warm and cozy? Is a tabby cat curled up on your chest? Do you have Bach on in the background or Miles Davis or Norah Jones? Do you have a friend in the room who is studying the same thing, so that you can share thoughts and ideas?

Like fingerprints, no two dream study spaces are exactly the same. Some like it hot, some like it cold. Some like absolute silence, some like a little noise. Some like to lie down, some like to sit up. The bottom line is whatever works. And, of course, budgetary constraints and other practical factors will have a significant bearing on the kind of study space you can create. A massage chair would be lovely, but keep in mind that some of the highest achievers in history did perfectly well studying at the kitchen table, while the rest of the family went about their chores.

Here are some general tips to keep in mind when it comes to setting up your study space:

1) *Keep it light.* Has anyone ever come into your room and said, "What's the matter with you? It's so dark in here. You're going to go blind!" Did you sigh and ignore these comments? If so, you may not yet have discovered that insufficient lighting can lead to

onus burden or obligation

OPEN FOR DISCUSSION:
IF I COULD STUDY ANYWHERE ...

Try a brainstorming session in which the class collectively shares its ideas of what constitutes an ideal study space. Note the differences between what people like and what they don't like. Are there any absolutes?

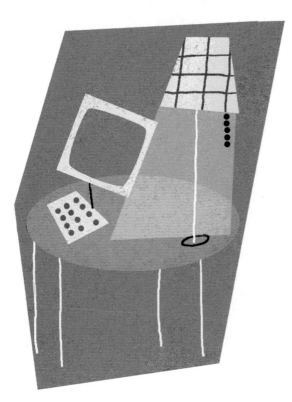

eyestrain, which can significantly reduce the quality and quantity of your study time. It is a good idea to have at least two sources of light in your study space.

2) *Check for drafts and adjust the thermostat.* Warm-blooded animals like we humans are quite sensitive to sudden changes in temperature. And most of us are particularly sensitive to drafts and changes in temperatures when we're holed up in a room by ourselves, trying to study for an exam with nothing else to distract us. Being comfortable is very important. Dress warmly or coolly, as the temperature dictates, and try to ensure that your study space has the benefits of an efficient heating or cooling system.

3) *Choose the right chair.* If you're planning to be sitting for a while, then try to find a chair that has good back and seat support. You know what it feels like to go for a long drive in a car with a bad seat? You don't want to duplicate that discomfort in your study sessions. But don't get overly comfortable, either. Studying in a recliner, for instance, can result in an ill-timed nap.

4) *Come supplied and make sure you have enough space.* Take an inventory of your needs before you sit down to study. You don't want to waste time running out for paper, pens, pencils, scissors, dictionaries, or anything like that. And if you're going to be laying out a lot of materials, make sure you have a large enough table at your disposal.

5) *Clear away obvious distractions.* If you're working at a desk that has a lot of mail on it, stick the mail in a box and place the box in a closet while you're studying. The less distractions, the better.

6) *Enlist the cooperation of others.* As we already mentioned, kitchen tables have traditionally served as study spaces for people who don't have other options. But don't expect the kitchen to become the reading room at the public library. After all, people will be coming and going. You can, however, ask them to come and go *quietly.* Suggest that they keep their kitchen visits to a minimum. Maybe you can convince them that the best time to start making lasagna is not while you're in a high-gear study mode. Chances are, if the people who share your life genuinely care about you (which, chances are, they do), they'll understand and cooperate—even your kids or little brothers and sisters.

Studying often means sitting still for long periods of time, often at a computer, poring over information. This can lead to eyestrain and back strain, both of which can take a serious toll on your studying. Here's how to sidestep those pitfalls:

Avoiding eyestrain:

- Keep your reading materials at a comfortable distance.
- Stay on top of the glare. This may require adjusting lights and blinds, shifting your position, and so on.
- Regularly clean your monitor, per the manufacturer's instructions. A dirty computer screen can contribute to eyestrain, as will jittery or flickering images.
- Take breaks at regular intervals to rest your eyes. Also rest your eyes by closing them and rolling them around.

- Use humidifiers to combat dry air, which can aggravate eyestrain.

Avoiding back strain:

- Adjust your chair seat so that you are sitting upright with your feet firmly planted on the floor and your lower back well supported.
- When using a computer, set the chair height so that your hands and wrists are at approximately the same level as the keyboard.
- Arrange your work area so that you're directly facing the monitor and keyboard and don't have to twist your body. Keep frequently used items within easy reach.
- Break up your desk time. Ten minutes of every hour should be devoted to something other than desk time—walking around, stretching, and so on.
- There are other stretches that can be done while you're seated at your desk. These include:
  - Shoulder rolls: Gently roll the shoulders forward, then up, and then drop them back. Do this slowly and rhythmically, five or ten times.
  - Finger stretch: Gently open and close your hands, stretching your fingers wide when they are open.
  - Trap stretch: Sit on your hands to help stabilize yourself and then tip your head down, as if looking into your shirt pocket. Hold this position for a moment.

- Side bending: Lower your head toward your shoulder and then repeat on the other side.
- Shoulder blade pinch: Rotate your arms to your back, pinching your shoulder blades together.
- Hug stretch: Grasp your arm at the elbow. Pull your arm forward and across your body as if you're hugging somebody. Repeat with the other arm.
- Chin tuck: Keeping your head level, slide your chin back to make a double chin. Hold for two seconds and then release.
- Hand stretch: Make a gentle fist. Open your hands at the first joint, keeping your fingers bent. Then open your hands, straightening out your fingers all the way.

Avoiding Distractions

You're finally ready to sit down and study and then something happens: *distractions*. Now, there are genuine, unavoidable distractions, like a power outage in the middle of a storm or your cat suddenly choking on a fur ball but, the truth is, most distractions are actually ways that you've thought up to sabotage yourself. Let's look at some of these distractions:

- *Procrastination*. The daddy of them all, and the one that is most likely to undermine your efforts. We talked about avoiding procrastination in Chapter 2: The Goal Zone. If you don't remember them, go back and review the tips in Chapter 2 that we offered to help you avoid procrastination.
- *"Stuff" happens*. Of course it does, but you'll need to find ways to anticipate and then deal with any and all distractions and crises that come your way. If your study schedule is so tight that you absolutely cannot be bothered for the next 12 hours, then it's your responsibility to enlist a back-up team that can field the "stuff" that happens during this period. That's what mothers, fathers, spouses, partners, grandparents, siblings, aunts, uncles, cousins, friends, and children (of a certain age) are for.
- *Concentration deficits*. You find that you can't focus and you blame it on the subject? That sounds to us like the easy way out. Examine your recent behavior—have you been sleeping enough? did you party too much last weekend?—before you blame your problems on Gestalt psychology, the Hundred Years War, or whatever it is that you're supposed to be studying. Then correct the behavior—get more sleep; cut down on the partying—before you sit down to study again.
- *Technology overload*. Technology surrounds us—televisions, telephones, and the like. Put them all on hold. Tape the show you wanted to watch for *after* your exam. Do not answer the phone. That's what answering machines and voice mail are for.
- *Weak resistance*. If you're not taking sufficient care of yourself, you can come down with colds, headaches, and all kinds of other bodily distress. Some people use sickness as an excuse to get out of studying; others get sick because they feel so guilty about *not* studying. Either way, you lose. Check out Chapter 13: The Whole You in this book for our discussion of wellness.

Reading Your Textbook

So far in this chapter we have spent quite a bit of time discussing the physical surroundings that can have an impact on your studying as well as the motivational, psychological, and emotional factors that come into play. We'd now like to look at the nuts-and-bolts of reading textbooks and taking notes—two academic issues that play an important part in how you study.

As textbooks go, *The Complete Student* is not going to be the most demanding one in your backpack. You will surely encounter others in your college career that are more dense, more complex, and more intimidating. But the same principles that you'll find at work in *The Complete Student* will most likely apply to all your textbooks, for the fact is, that any textbook worth its salt has been designed to lead you carefully and surely to rich veins of knowledge and information.

Generally speaking, reading—and learning—should never be passive. The more engaged you are as a reader and as a learner the more easily and naturally the learning will occur. So, the most important thing to keep in mind when you're reading a textbook is that you have to allow yourself to participate in the dialogue that the authors have set up. They have devised ways to enlist your interest and attention, and you need to meet them halfway by relaxing your resistance to material that may, at first, seem too difficult and foreign for your mind to absorb.

Now there is no way to make a textbook on economics or sociology read like *Lord of the Rings*, so you're just going to have to adjust your expectations. Reading a textbook is a different kind of reading experience but, on its own terms, it too can be quite satisfying. A good textbook is a marvelously structured creation that has been designed to lead you at a calm and orderly pace through a **thicket** of facts and other data. The process by which you will most easily get what you need out of your textbook has three tiers that we are going to label as:

- *The Overview*
- *In the Trenches*
- *Looking Back*

Let's think of this process as *OIL*—it's like hitting a gusher that can fill you with knowledge.

1) *The Overview*. This is the step that orients you to the chapter you've been assigned. Sometimes chapters in a textbook can be very long

thicket a thick growth, as of underbrush

and weighty. In the overview stage, you quickly look through the pages to see how the chapter is structured, and you become aware of the various indicators (colored heads, bullets, bold type, etc.) that point out the most important material. Set aside 10 minutes or so to preview the key elements of the chapter, like the title, the introduction, the various subheadings that run throughout the chapter, any special charts or diagrams, and so on. (In *The Complete Student*, as you may have noticed, you'll find such recurring features from chapter to chapter as Reflections, Open for Discussion, Food for Thought, What Did We Learn?, Word Smart, and more.) Then, assuming the role of the engaged learner, start asking questions. What does the main thrust of this chapter appear to be? Is the organization clear? How difficult does this material seem to be and how long do I think it's going to take me to read this? The point is that you may have a small mountain to climb here, and you may not want to take it on all at once. You may want to **apportion** your time in a way that feels manageable to you.

2) *In the Trenches.* Now that you've had your overview, it's time to roll up your sleeves and get to work. But, boy, oh boy—what a lot of work this is going to be! Forty pages on covalent bonds in your Chemistry textbook? It feels totally overwhelming. It doesn't have to be, however. The way to overcome that overwhelmed feeling is by breaking the chapter down into much smaller, more digestible units. Of course, the authors of the textbook have already done that to a considerable degree. No doubt they have provided a good many sections and subheadings. But you may need to divide those even more. It's up to you. What can you handle? A half page at a time? A column? A paragraph? Go at your own rate—just don't sit there! Remember, the best way to approach this kind of reading is to be engaged and active. One way you can accomplish this is by asking yourself a question as you begin each new section. For example, the section you're reading in this textbook right now is called Reading Your Textbook. This subhead should spark some questions for you. "Are there tips and strategies to reading a textbook?" (Yes, there are—and we're clueing you into them right now.) "Is this going to help me understand things better?" (We certainly hope so.) When forming your questions, remember these five basic prompts: *who, what, where, when,* and *how* to help you out. One more

apportion to divide and assign proportionately

thing: it *is* hard work to read 40 pages on covalent bonds (at least it is for us). So, in addition to dividing up the chapter into manageable bites, also factor in break time. Read for half an hour or even 20 minutes, and then go do 100 sit-ups or pop some corn or make a phone call to a friend (putting a limit on the time) before you hit the books again.

3) *Looking Back.* This may be the most important step in the process. Research shows that between 40 and 50 percent of the material we read is forgotten very shortly, often within 15 minutes from the time we read it. To prevent all this valuable knowledge from going down the drain, we suggest that you try the following: (a) underline or highlight key points and/or make notes in the margin; (b) read key points and passages aloud (particularly effective for auditory learners); (c) outline the chapter on a separate piece of paper to reinforce your overall understanding of the relationships of key points in the text; and (d) go over the chapter with a study buddy, quizzing each other on what you've read. And, once again, keep your learning style in mind when you're in this review mode. If you're a kinesthetic learner, you might want to walk around or pace while you're reviewing. If you're a visual learner, you might want to make up flash cards for yourself.

We mentioned the idea of making notes in the margins of your textbook. Now we'd like to expand on the subject of note-taking.

The Fine Art of Note-Taking

One place where it is obviously very important to take notes is in the classroom, when the instructor is lecturing. It can be challenging to get down the important points, particularly if the instructor talks fast, talks low, mumbles, or has a heavy accent. Fortunately, there are some very solid techniques to help you with your note-taking.

THE TWO-COLUMN FORMAT

When you use this technique, you will be taking notes on a lined pad or in a lined notebook as you read. Your page will have two columns—one that is narrow; the other wider. In the narrow column, you will write down your *key idea words*. These are the words that help you recall the "bones" of the lecture you're listening to or the chapter you're reading. In the wider column, you can jot down significant facts and ideas that you think may show up on a test. During a lecture, the instructor will

often clue you in to potential test questions by saying things like, "This could appear on your test." Listen carefully for such clues.

What would the two-column format look like for a section you've recently read in this book? Go back a few pages to look at the section on Avoiding Distractions. The following chart shows how you could use the two-column format for your notes on that section.

Chapter 5: Study Skills	
Avoiding distractions	Distractions include: • Procrastination • Crises • Lapses of concentration • Too much technology • Sickness
Dealing with distractions	Take these measures: • Procrastination (see Chapter 2 for tips on how to avoid) • Crises (established back-up support teams) • Lapses of concentration (correct behaviors that lead to it, like too little sleep and too much partying) • Too much technology (unplug the TV and use your answering machine) • Sickness (pursue wellness, as discussed in Chapter 15)

PICTURE THIS

Visual learners will love this note-taking technique, but even if you're not that visual in your orientation, you may find it useful. The idea is to put a visual spin on material that is presented in straight text. Often, your textbook will already provide some of these kinds of diagrams, but there's no reason why you shouldn't make your own timelines, pie charts, mind maps, and other such tricks of the trade. The following chart shows what the section on Avoiding Distractions from this book might look using a mind-map approach.

One other important point about note-taking: try to put the thoughts in your own words, rather than just taking words down **verbatim** from

verbatim word for word

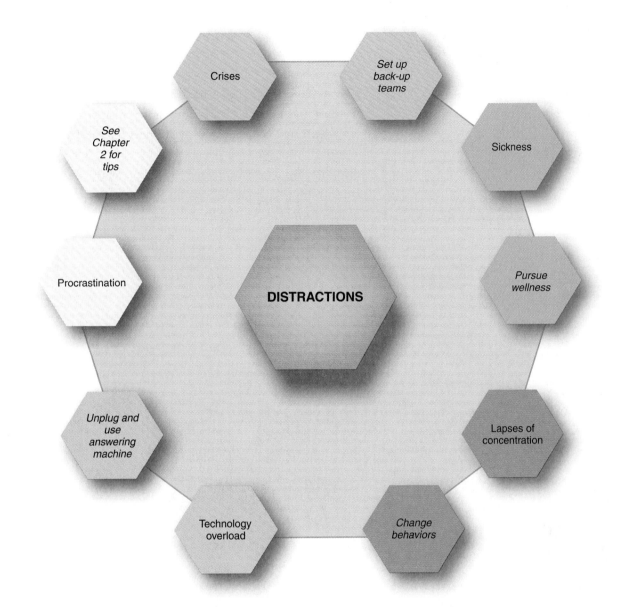

the book. Putting things in your own words is a good way to make them take hold in your memory—which is what studying is all about. Of course, in a lecture, you probably wouldn't have time to take the instructor's words down verbatim anyway, unless you're a trained stenographer.

A WORD ON CRAMMING

Cramming is not a very good way to study. Learning happens best when you allow time for new information to settle into your brain. Cramming involves filling your short-term memory with a lot of facts and figures right before an exam instead of allowing those facts and figures

IN OTHER WORDS

"I was thinking about how people seem to read the Bible a whole lot more as they get older; then it dawned on me … they're cramming for the final exam."— George Carlin, comedian

What Did We Learn?

**Remember the *Looking Back* part of *OIL*?
That's what we're doing here.**

1. What are the two types of motivation? Explain their differences.
2. Name some tips that will help you to boost your motivation.
3. What are some key factors to keep in mind when you're setting up a study space?
4. Cite five kinds of distractions that typically divert students from their studies.
5. What are the three components that make up the acronym *OIL*?
6. Describe the two-column format of note-taking.
7. What is an alternative approach to note-taking beyond the two-column format?

Bibliography

Allen, D. (2003). *Getting things done: The art of stress-free productivity*. New York: Penguin.

Bryant, T. (1999). *Self-discipline in 10 days: How to go from thinking to doing*. Seattle, WA: HUB Publishing.

Kesselman-Turkel, J., & Peterson, F. (2003). *Note-taking made easy*. Madison: University of Wisconsin Press.

Kornhauser, A. W. (1993). *How to study: Suggestions for high-school and college students*. Chicago: University of Chicago Press.

to move nicely into your long-term memory. Studies, in fact, have shown that information learned while cramming is almost entirely forgotten within 72 hours of its acquisition. Nevertheless, there are certainly going to be times in life when things come up and you just can't stay on schedule. Suddenly you'll find yourself facing a quiz or an exam that you haven't studied for and this situation does call, in all fairness, for some cramming. When we get to Chapter 9: Testing, Testing …, we will be offering tips on productive cramming versus totally panic-stricken cramming. Right now, we will proceed to our next chapter, where we will be taking a tour of one of the most important places on campus: the library.

Links

Kishwaukee College Learning Skills Center: How to read a textbook. Retrieved November 29, 2005, from http://kish.cc.il.us/lsc/ssh/textbook.shtml

Tips on avoiding eyestrain. Retrieved November 29, 2005, from http://www.bytesoflearning.com/UltraKey/Posture/Eyestrain.html

Tips to avoid RSI (repetitive strain injury). Retrieved November 29, 2005, from http://homepages.inf.ed.ac.uk/dch/Safety/tips.html

Word Smart

Why bother with vocabulary? Because some of the new words that you're learning will help you say what you want to say better. Good vocabulary adds liveliness and color to your writing and your speech.

apportion

attribute

contrived

hierarchy

manifest

onus

thicket

verbatim

vicissitude

THE LIBRARY

In most segments of our popular culture, libraries do not enjoy the best public relations image. The joke is that they are places of funereal **quiet, presided over by elderly women with their hair tied tight in buns who severely shush anyone making any noise. We are pleased to report that this stereotype no longer has any relevance to what's going on in the real world. Today, libraries are seen as vital centers in the life of the community and the college campus. In fact, in the words of the renowned Civil War historian Shelby Foote, "A university is just a group of buildings gathered around a library." In this chapter, we will be taking a tour of the library to review its systems and to find out how you can best take advantage of its extraordinary resources. By extension, this chapter will also serve as a** primer **on basic research.**

Where to Start?

Even at a small college, a visit to the library can feel overwhelming. To start with, there are an awful lot of books in there! Consider, too, the thousands of periodicals, either bound on shelves or stored electronically. A new student, who hasn't had an orientation to the system, may have little idea of where to turn.

funereal solemn, mournful
primer an introduction to a topic

One of the very first steps you should take as an incoming college student is to visit the library and become part of an orientation session—either group or individual—with a reference librarian. The librarian will tell you where things are and will show you how to get the most out of the library's many and varied resources. Let us point out that this chapter is not intended to serve as a substitute for that kind of orientation session. Each library is unique in its own way, and you will need to understand the specific one in which you'll be spending so much time. On the other hand, all libraries have certain features in common, and hopefully this chapter will prove useful in orienting you to any research facility you happen to find yourself in.

Where shall we start? The answer is with the logic behind library research. Once you get the hang of that logic, you'll feel far more empowered to use the vast holdings and resources that are available to you. Let's choose a subject that we can carry through this chapter as an example of something we might want to research. How about the potential impact of stem cell research on juvenile diabetes? Sound timely?

WHAT DO I LOOK IT UP UNDER?

Your passport into the world of library research will be your understanding of *subject headings*. Subject headings are also referred to as *controlled vocabulary*, which corresponds to precise terms designated by the Library of Congress. (In case you're not exactly sure what the

REFLECTIONS: *YOUR HISTORY*

Spend a few moments writing about your experience with libraries. For some of you, the library may have been a stuffy, stale, and intimidating place. For others, it was a wonderful refuge from the difficulties of the world. Now is the time to explore your feelings, because your preconceptions can negatively influence your present experience, and you want to be able to start thinking about the library as an important and positive place in your life.

© BananaStock Ltd.

Library of Congress is, it is the national library of the United States. The Library of Congress oversees copyright protection and has developed a classification system that is used by most research and university libraries.)

As we've already mentioned, the essential nature of subject headings is that they are precise. For instance, if you were to attempt a subject search in a library catalog under the heading "Teen Pregnancy," you would discover that this is not a recognized subject heading. The term recognized by the Library of Congress—and, hence, by your own college library, which uses the Library of Congress Classification system—is "Teenage Pregnancy." The subject heading is a uniform, agreed-upon word or group of words used to gather in one place all items about a single topic, including all the different synonyms and similar words closely related in meaning.

Now if you were to use the Basic Search section of the online catalog of the Library of Congress (which can be accessed at http://catalog.loc .gov), and you typed in Stem Cell Research, 25 subject headings would come up. These would include such headings as:

> STEM CELLS
> STEM CELLS CYTOLOGY
> STEM CELL TRANSPLANTATION
> STEM CELL TRANSPLANTATION ETHICS

… and 21 more. Let's imagine that your paper on stem cell research and juvenile diabetes was for a Sociology course, and you were going to focus on some of the ethical issues that surround this research. You would then follow the path to Stem Cell Transplantation Ethics for your leads.

Using subject headings in a thoughtful way provides a good start to your research. You can also start by using a *keyword* search. When you are searching online for something, your keyword is the word or phrase that alerts your software—that is, whatever search engine you're using—to the topic that you're looking for. Then, at mind-boggling speeds, the database software will rifle through unimaginable volumes of information until it makes a match.

BOOLEAN SEARCHING

Your keyword searching—so vital to your research—will be vastly improved by your understanding of a technique called *Boolean searching*. Boolean searching involves the combination of terms through the use of the words *and*, *or*, and *not* (and sometimes *near*). These words—referred to as *Boolean operators*—allow you to expand or restrict your search by specifying the relationship of the terms being searched.

The Boolean operator *and* is a command that requires all terms to appear in a record. If, for instance, you were to log onto the Google search engine (which can be accessed at http://www.google.com)—arguably, the leading search engine today—and search for Stem Cell Research and Juvenile Diabetes, Google would call up over 70,000 results (also known as "hits"). On Google and other sophisticated search engines, the *and* is taken for granted when you type in two words or phrases in the Search spot. That is to say, if you typed in Stem Cell Research Juvenile Diabetes, you would get the same results as if you typed in Stem Cell Research *and* Juvenile Diabetes. The *and* is there by default (this is not true of all search engines, however). For all of you visual learners, that principle looks like this:

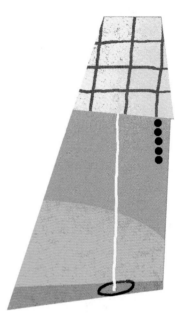

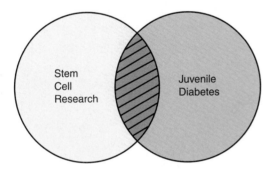

AND: All terms are present

Other examples of what we're talking about here might be:
- Diamonds *and* Mining (retrieving material relevant to both diamonds and mining—over one million results).
- Red Sox *and* Curse (retrieving material relevant to both Red Sox and curse—over one million).
- Pinky *and* Exercises (We thought we'd be a little silly here and come up with something that would give us a really low hit result. In fact, the combination of "pinky" and "exercises" yielded over 200,000! It turns out that not only are there a great many exercises designed to help with such hand problems as carpal tunnel syndrome, but there are pinky exercises for guitar players.)

The Boolean operator *or* retrieves records that has either term in them.

FOOD FOR THOUGHT:
GEORGE BOOLE

Where does the word "Boolean" come from? It's taken from Boolean logic, a mathematical breakthrough formulated by George Boole, a man so interesting that it is worth spending a moment to look at his life. Boole was born in the English industrial town of Lincoln in 1815 to a poor working-class family. Given his circumstances and the rigidity of the class structure in England at that time, Boole shouldn't have had a prayer of breaking out as a mathematical genius ... but he did. Boole was translating Latin poetry by the age of 12, and, as a young teenager, was fluent in German, Italian, and French. At 16, he became an assistant teacher, and by the time he turned 20, he had opened his own school. At the age of 24, he published his first paper—"Researches on the Theory of Analytical Transformations"—in the *Cambridge Mathematical Journal*. Boole's most lasting contribution to mathematics was his development of a notational system that represented logical statements by algebraic equations. Applied to set theory, Boolean algebra described the relationship between groups, reducing them to simple equations. His system, linking logic with mathematics, was instrumental in the development of digital computer systems. Boole's work not only facilitated the incredible possibilities of the computer age, but his life also gave glorious **credence** to the idea that genius can occur anywhere, anytime, and can thrive even in the most difficult circumstances.

Sources: George Boole. Retrieved December 1, 2005, from http://www.kerryr.net/pioneers/boole.htm and George Boole: Mathematician. Retrieved December 1, 2005, from http://www.who2.com/georgeboole.html

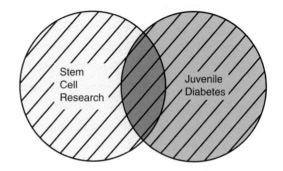

OR: Either of the terms are present

The Boolean operator *not* excludes terms, retrieving material when the first term is desired but not the second term. Stem Cell Research *not* Juvenile Diabetes excludes Juvenile Diabetes from the discussion. You might use this function, for instance, if you are looking for a more generalized discussion of Stem Cell Research.

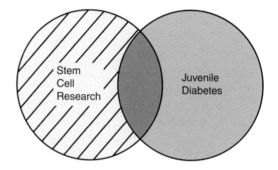

NOT: First term is present but not the second

ALL ABOUT THE WEB

The odds of a high school or college student in the United States or Canada picking up this book without ever having been on the Internet are remote. The latest figures on global Internet usage show that out of an estimated 2004 worldwide population of 6,390,147,487, some 360,993,512 people are Internet users. That's 12.7 percent of the population, which represent a 125.2 percent rise since 2000. In North America, however, out of a total population of 325,246,100, some 222,165,659 people use the Internet. That's 68.3 percent of the total population, with a rise of 105.5 percent since 2000. In 1996, President Clinton said, "When I took office, only high energy physicists had ever heard of what is called the World Wide Web. Now even my cat has its own page."

credence confidence based on external evidence

If we consider the overall increase of global Internet use, and then consider the fact that this book is aimed at college students, it is relatively safe to assume that you're plugged in. But like all things that are more or less free in this world—air, water, and such—we tend to take the Internet for granted, hardly even remembering that relatively recent time when it didn't exist. So let's take a moment to review some popular terms here. What is the Internet? What is the World Wide Web? And how do they relate to each other?

The Internet is the physical infrastructure of computers, networks, and services that are connected across the globe. The World Wide Web— now generally referred to simply as the Web—is the global environment in which all information accessible on the Internet, whether it be in the form of text, pictures, audio, or video, can be reached in a consistent, simple way by using a standard set of naming and access conventions.

The Web is easy to navigate, endlessly adaptable to text, graphics, and other kinds of data, and makes the gathering and **dissemination** of information truly global. And, through libraries and other publicly subsidized sources, this information is free for everyone.

When the Web was conceived, its main **tenet** was that there would be no central control. Rather, the Web would work because anyone who operated within its boundaries would subscribe to agreed-upon guidelines. The Web ethic dictated that anyone could publish on it, and anyone authorized to do so could read the published information (excluding minors from certain material). All Web browsers were designed to use the same language—HyperText Markup Language, otherwise known as HTML—and a great sense of democracy would rule.

The Web has remained faithful to these core beliefs and has been an extraordinary social and political force in the 21st century. It is used throughout the world to convey government information, library information, to provide online news and financial information, for reference information, for companies to communicate externally and internally, for shopping, games, dating, chat rooms, music, and countless other purposes. It is estimated that the World Wide Web contains more than *three billion* documents and this figure increases **exponentially** from year to year.

Documents on the Web are not arranged according to subject headings, as with the holdings of the Library of Congress, but, rather, by

dissemination distribution; spreading
tenet any of a set of established and fundamental beliefs
exponentially rapidly becoming greater in size

keywords. You have to guess what keywords will lead you to your sources, and you also have to guess what keywords your sources are offering as clues to get you to reach them. Fortunately, there are amazing search engines—computer programs that create indexes of Web sites based on the titles of files, keywords, or the full text of files—that can lead you almost instantaneously to where you want to go. The most popular search engine in the world today is probably Google, but others worth checking out include Gigablast, Yahoo!, WiseNut, Excite, Teoma, HotBot, AltaVista, Ask, and many more.

A BRIEF LEXICON OF INTERNET TERMS

If you're going to be surfing the Web, it's a good idea to get your terminology straight. Here are some important terms to understand.

Bookmarks: Also called "hotlist" or "favorites," these are a list of the Web addresses that you most frequently use.

Browser: A program used to view information on the Web. Netscape, Mosaic, Safari, and Internet Explorer are examples of browsers.

Chat: Real-time interaction among users on the Internet.

Cookie: A piece of information sent by a Web server to a user's browser.

Cyberspace: The entire range of resources available on computer networks.

Domain name: The unique name that identifies an Internet site.

FAQ: Frequently asked questions—a popular informational format.

Hit: A way of counting the number of visitors to a Web page, or the number of sites returned by a search engine in response to a search.

Home page: A starting point for accessing information on a Web site.

Hyperlink: Usually known simply as "link," this is the part of a document that will direct you to another document or another location within the same document.

JPEG: A file tag and method of compressing image files.

Login: The nonsecret account name used to gain access to a computer system.

Maillist: A system that allows people to send E-mail to one address, whereupon their message is copied and sent to all of the other subscribers to the maillist for the purpose of forming a discussion group. A *listserv* is the most common type of maillist.

Newsgroup: The name for discussion groups on USENET (see below).

Password: A secret code used to gain access to a locked system.

Spam: Unsolicited "junk mail" sent out on mailing lists or USENET.

URL: Uniform Resource Locator. A unique address of a specific site on the Web.

USENET: A worldwide system of discussion groups.

Webmaster/Web Goddess: The person who creates and maintains a site on the Web.

Source: Understanding Internet terminology. Retrieved December 1, 2005, from http://ollie.dcccd.edu/library/Module2/Internet/webspeak .html

By the Book

No doubt, you will be doing a great deal of your research, no matter what area you're working in, on the Internet. It is just as likely, however, that when you are asked to do a research paper, you will be required to use actual books and periodicals as well. Finding these sources in your library is not difficult, once you develop a good overview of the way things work.

Every book in your college library has a *call number* based on the Library of Congress classification system, and this call number enables you to locate a book on the shelves. Call numbers begin with one, two, or three capital letters followed by numbers. The letters are arranged alphabetically. If the first letter is a G and the next letter is an A, then the following call numbers in the sequence would be GB, GC, GD, and so on. The second line of the call number is always numerical—1, 2, 3, and so on. The third and fourth lines of the call number are alphabetical and decimal.

We went to the Library of Congress Web site and in the Basic Search mode, using the Keyword choice, we typed in "Stem Cell Research and Juvenile Diabetes." Among the books that came up was one entitled *Bioethics in the Clinic: Hippocratic Reflections* by Grant R. Gillett (Johns Hopkins University Press, 2004), which interested us as a possible source. The call number for this item was R724.G549 2004. The components of the call number break down as follows:

R Alphabetical
724 Numerical
.G549 2004 Decimal

Libraries have two kinds of shelves: open shelves and closed shelves. Open shelves are open to all users; closed shelves are accessible only to librarians and designated users. With regard to open shelves, you will probably find that your library posts guide signs at either end of each

© BananaStock Ltd.

row of shelves. When looking for *Bioethics in the Clinic: Hippocratic Reflections*, the "R" indicates that it is in the Medical section. If the first letter in the call number was an "S," let's say, you would then follow the alphabet, moving along the shelves until you came to S. You would then proceed down the S shelves until you come to the section that corresponds to 724. Then you'd follow that section until you come to G. Then you'd explore the G section until you reach 549. Then you'd hope that nobody had taken out the book!

You should also be aware that most college libraries offer inter-library loan, which allows you to request a book from a library other than the one on campus. Most probably, you'll be able to make inter-library loan requests online or by visiting the library and speaking with the librarian. You should also become familiar with the reserve desk. This is the area in the library where instructors arrange for certain books and materials to be placed. These books and materials will not circulate, but you can make a time to use them in the library.

BOOKS ON THE INTERNET

Each year, each month, and each day, more and more books are being made available in their entirety on the Internet. The majority of these books are novels—usually classics—that have become part of the *public domain*—the condition of being freely available for unrestricted use and not subject to copyright or patent protection. (After a certain number of years, all copyrighted materials become public domain.) You may wish to visit the following sites to see which books exist there in their entirety.

- *netLibrary*—includes thousands of public domain eBooks, free to registered netLibrary users.
- *The Internet Public Library Online Texts Collection*—contains over 10,000 titles.
- *The On-Line Books Page*—over 17,000 listings.
- *Project Gutenberg*—an ambitious attempt to bring the most significant world literature together online.

Periodicals

Periodicals—the label given to publications such as magazines, professional journals, trade journals, and so forth, that are published at fixed intervals of more than one day (hence, not *newspapers*)—will prove to be an invaluable resource for your research. Again, however, the issue is how to find what you need. Once you know your way around a library, the opportunities are virtually limitless.

We'd like to begin by familiarizing you, if you're not already familiar, with some key terms relating to periodicals. These include:

- *Abstract:* A brief summary of a book or article. Some indexes (see below) only give an abstract, not a full text.
- *Citation:* A complete reference to a particular quote or to a source that has been used as an authority. (We will have a brief discussion of citations at the end of this chapter.)
- *Database:* A large collection of data, arranged into individual records, and organized for rapid search and retrieval by a computer.
- *Index:* A reference tool used to identify citations to library materials. There are indexes for periodical articles, newspaper articles, plays, poems, short stories, and much more.
- *Journals:* Often referred to as professional journals or scholarly journals, these specialized periodicals contain reports of current research, articles, reviews of related books, etc. Journals are indexed in subject indexes like ERIC (Education Resources Information Center) or the Humanities Index, to name but two of many.
- *Microfiche:* A 4 × 6 sheet of films that holds several hundred miniaturized document pages.
- *Microfilm:* A roll of continuous film that can hold several thousand miniaturized document pages.

In this discussion of periodicals, we'd like to move from the general to the specific. Let's start with *print indexes*.

PRINT INDEXES

There are a great many print indexes—far too many for us to list here—but it is useful to offer a brief overview of at least a few. Most of these are self-explanatory. Those that aren't are accompanied by brief descriptions.

- *Readers' Guide to Periodical Literature*. An index of articles from over 200 popular periodicals, this easy-to-use source is arranged by subject and author and goes back over a hundred years.
- *SIRS-Social Issues Resources Series*. Large notebooks, each devoted to a broad topic like Economics, Youth, Pollution, etc.
- *Applied Science & Technology Index*.
- *Art Index*.
- *Bibliographic Index*. This indexes bibliographies from more than 2,800 periodicals and 5,000 books each year.
- *Biography Index*.
- *Biological & Agricultural Index*.

- *Business Periodicals Index*.
- *Current Index to Journals in Education*.
- *Education Index*.
- *Engineering Index*.
- *Humanities Index*.
- *Library Literature*. Indexes key library and information science periodicals.
- *Psychological Abstracts*. The premier reference guide to the international literature in psychology and related disciplines.
- *Public Affairs Information Service*. This source publishes indexes and abstracts that help people identify and locate documents about important, political, economic, and social issues.
- *Social Sciences Index*.

Used properly, these indexes will direct you to a wealth of material, but you will also need to consult with the reference librarian to see which periodicals are actually archived by *your* library. The library will maintain a list that details all of its periodical holdings.

INDEXES FOR NEWSPAPERS

You will also want to become familiar with those indexes that cover newspaper articles. Some of the better known include:

- *New York Times Current Events Edition Index*. Indexing articles on microfiche from the daily and Sunday *New York Times*.
- *Wall Street Journal Index*. Articles from the nation's premier business newspaper.
- *NewsBank Index*. An index to newspaper articles published in over 450 U.S. newspapers.
- *Editorials on File*. An index of editorials reprinted from U.S. and Canadian newspapers.

CURRENT EVENTS SOURCES

Another area that most college students will need to explore at some point or another is current events. Some important resources that can help with your research in this area include:

- *Annual Editions*. Contains reprints of significant recent articles on topics like drugs, marriage and family, economics, the environment, and more.
- *Congressional Quarterly Report*. A weekly summary of U.S. congressional and government activities, with special reports on key issues.

- *Facts on File*. A weekly digest of world news and events.
- *Information Plus: Information Series on Current Topics*. Each volume offers a summary of facts and statistics on the topics covered, from abortion to capital punishment, gun control, the homeless, and much more.
- *A Matter of Fact*. Full text abstracts of material from the *Congressional Record*, as well as over 200 newspapers and periodicals on public policy issues.
- *Taking Sides*. Well-selected, sharply differing viewpoints on issues of the day.
- *Vital Speeches of the Day*. Each semimonthly issue contains the full texts of speeches given by notable persons on subjects of current issues and controversy.
- *Weekly Compilation of Presidential Documents*. What did the President say this week? Find out with this source that offers the text of his speeches, news conferences, and so on.

ONLINE SOURCES FOR CURRENT EVENTS RESEARCH

Some excellent online sources exist for current events research. You might want to check out the following sites for ideas and information.

- *The Best Information on the Net* (http://library.sau.edu/bestinfo/Hot/hotindex.htm). Maintained by the O'Keefe Library at St. Ambrose University, this has an excellent index of Hot Paper topics.
- *LookSmart* (http://www.findarticles.com). This site allows you to search from some 5.5 million articles from over 900 publications.
- *International Affairs.com* (http://internationalaffairs.com/). Here you will find highly useful links to a wide variety of resources addressing matters of international interest.
- *Public Agenda Online* (http://www.publicagenda.org/). This site, created and maintained by a nonpartisan, nonprofit public research and citizen education organization, offers valuable information on major policy issues.
- *SpeakOut.com* (http://speakout.com/activism/issues). Nonpartisan and free to users, this site provides information into major issues of the day with no slanting and far more depth than you would find from traditional news sources.

This is just a brief glimpse into the world of periodicals. Check with your reference librarian to find out about the many other resources available to you.

FACTS AND STATISTICS

Where do you turn when what you're looking for is primarily facts and statistics? If you're in the library, head straight for the reference librarian. If you're on your computer, check out these sites:

- *Statistical Resources on the Web* (http://www.lib.umich.edu). An excellent site maintained by the University of Michigan that will link you to a wide range of statistical sources covering many different topics.

- *Fast Facts* (http://www.freepint.com/gary/handbook.htm). Compiled by Gary Price of George Washington University, this is a list of sites that point you to information from almanacs, fact books, statistical reports, and other reference tools.

- *Data on the Net* (http://odwin.ucsd.edu/idata/). From the University of California, San Diego, comes this gateway to 361 Internet sites offering Social Science statistical data, data catalogs, data libraries, and more.

- *The World Factbook* (http://www.odci.gov/cia/publications/factbook/index.html). Maintained by the Central Intelligence Agency, this is a highly useful site that has country profiles, maps, and facts about governments around the globe.

- *The Data Web* (http://www.thedataweb.org/). A network of online libraries covering topics that include data on the census, health, economics, unemployment, income, population, labor, cancer and crime rates, transportation, vital statistics, and much more.

- *Stat-USA/Internet* (http://www.stat-usa.gov). Maintained by the Department of Commerce, this site offers valuable information on trade, business, and economics.

Citations

At the end of your research paper, you will include a "Works Cited" section, where you will be listing citations for the books, periodicals, and other sources you used in your work. Take note that it is critical for you to cite your sources in order to protect yourself against any charges of plagiarism. Keep in mind, however, that your citations are governed by a very complex and sometimes confusing set of rules that have been known to cause students a great deal of anxiety. Professors will often take points off the final grade for mistakes in citations, and the fact is that there is much opportunity for error in this area. Indeed, the issue of citations is more complicated than ever in our online era. Now we have to figure out how to cite abstracts on a CD-ROM, subject encyclopedia

articles from Web-based full-text databases, conference proceedings,
E-mail correspondence, and newsgroup postings, not to mention books,
periodicals, videos, radio interviews, television interviews … yikes! But
don't panic. In the short space allotted to us here, we may not be able
to give you all the formatting information you'll need for your citations,
but we *can* direct you to authoritative sources on the subject. Here
are some of the various citation styles and where you find out about
them:

- *MLA*. For literature, arts, and humanities papers. See *MLA Handbook for Writers of Research Papers, 6th Edition* (Modern Language Association, 2003).
- *APA*. For psychology, education, and other social sciences. See *Publication Manual of the American Psychological Association, 5th Edition* (American Psychological Association, 2001).
- *AMA*. For medicine, health, and biological sciences. See *American Medical Association Manual of Style, 9th Edition* (Lippincott Williams & Wilkins, 1997).
- *Turabian*. Designed to be a "universal" citation style for use by college students with all subjects. See Kate L. Turabian's *A Manual for Writers of Term Papers, Theses, and Dissertations, 6th Edition* (University of Chicago Press, 1996).
- *Chicago*. Used with all subjects in the "real world" (i.e., non-academic), including books, magazines, newspapers, and non-scholarly publications. See *The Chicago Manual of Style, 15th Edition* (University of Chicago Press, 2003).

Consult with your reference librarian, who can answer your specific
questions on citations and who can show you where in the library you
can find these manuals.

Head for the Library

This chapter has been a whirlwind tour through an institution that is
going to figure large in your life—in your college years, at the very least,
but hopefully beyond as well. We have offered some useful tips in these
pages regarding research, but, before we leave this subject, we want
to stress that you should also try out the library as a place to study. In
Chapter 5, we stated that all learners have different study styles, but,
nonetheless, the seriousness of the library—that sense of purposeful
quiet and of being surrounded by great books—is not something that
can be duplicated elsewhere. You may find that the library really *is* the
perfect place to study. Most college libraries have very pleasant reading

rooms that provide good light, comfortable chairs, and the chance to be in the presence of other serious learners, and these factors can make a big difference in helping you establish good study habits. You may find that the library is not only filled with interesting materials, but with interesting people as well.

CASE IN POINT:
JERILYNN ADAMS WILLIAMS

We started this chapter by saying that stereotypes of librarians still influence the way people think. As a matter of fact, American toy manufacturer Archie McPhee & Co. recently reinforced these stereotypes by introducing the "Librarian Action Doll"—a female figure in dowdy clothes and sensible shoes with glasses, hair tied in a bun, and a "shushing" button that, when activated, moves the figure to raise a finger to her lips. Stereotypes aside, there are librarians today who are playing an historic role in a society where First Amendment rights are too often coming under attack. Jerilynn Adams Williams, director of the Montgomery County (Texas) Library, was the 2003 recipient of a First Amendment Award sponsored by PEN, the international literary organization, in conjunction with Newman's Own (the food company founded by actor Paul Newman). In August 2002, when a dozen angry community member stormed a meeting of the

Commissioner's Court in Montgomery County to demand that a book called It's Perfectly Normal: Changing Bodies, Growing Up, Sex & Sexual Health be removed from the county's library shelves, Ms. Williams stood fast. Countering charges that the book was "obscene" and "promoted homosexuality," she spent three solid months tirelessly educating public officials and the community at large about the proper way to challenge library materials. Fighting to defend the library's right to offer this critically acclaimed book that tactfully and sensitively explains human sexuality to young readers, Ms. Williams received personal threats and calls for her termination. In the end, however, she prevailed and the Commissioner's Court returned the book to the library shelves.

The American Library Association publishes a list of the 100 Most Challenged Books—those that are most frequently censored in schools and libraries. On the list are such classics as The Adventures of Huckleberry Finn, The Catcher in the Rye, The Color Purple, Of Mice and Men, I Know Why the Caged Bird Sings, To Kill a Mockingbird, Lord of the Flies, as well as the Harry Potter series and even Where's Waldo? The efforts of librarians like Jerilynn Adams Williams to preserve First Amendment rights in the face of personal danger and sacrifice truly are heroic. The Librarian Action Doll? Think again, Archie McPhee!

Sources: American Library Association press release. Jerilynn Adams Williams receives 2003 PEN/Newman's Own First Amendment Award. Retrieved December 1, 2005, from http://www.ala.org/PrinterTemplate .cfm?Section=archive&template=/ contentmanagement/contentdisplay .cfm&ContentID=27921 and American Library Association. The 100 most frequently challenged books of 1990–2000. Retrieved December 1, 2005, from http:// www.ala.org/ala/oif/bannedbooksweek/ bbwlinks/100mostfrequently.html

What Did We Learn?

Indeed, there was a lot to learn in this chapter. Look at the following questions and activities to see how well you retained the information.

1. Explain *subject heading*. What is an alternative term for subject heading?
2. What is the Library of Congress and what are two of its chief responsibilities?
3. Explain *keyword*.
4. What is Boolean searching?
5. Explain the difference between the Internet and the World Wide Web.
6. How are documents on the World Wide Web arranged?
7. Define *call number*.
8. Define *public domain*.
9. What is a periodical?
10. What is a citation? Name five distinct citation styles.

Bibliography and Links

This is not a chapter where it makes great sense to provide a bibliography and links. The best link you have is walking into your library and getting to know it. Although every library resembles other libraries in key ways, each one is also distinct. And the staff is ready to help you—just ask them. We have located a few links, however, that might be of use to you.

Things to know before you begin searching.
Finding information on the Internet: A
tutorial. Retrieved December 1, 2005, from
http://www.lib.berkeley.edu/TeachingLib/
Guides/Internet/ThingsToKnow.html#
WhatSearching

What Is the "World Wide Web"? Retrieved
December 1, 2005, from http://www.cio
.com/WebMaster/sem2_web.html

World Internet usage. Retrieved December 1,
2005, from http://www.internetworldstats
.com/stats.htm

Word Smart

Not too long a list this time around:

credence

dissemination

exponentially

funereal

primer

tenet

MANAGING YOUR TIME ...
ORGANIZING YOUR LIFE

It's time to interrupt our discussion of study skills to issue this caveat. **You can have the best study space imaginable and you can be a whiz at locating what you need in the library and you can be totally up to speed on the technology front, but if you haven't developed basic organizational skills, then your chances of becoming a first-rate student are slim. Along with procrastination, poor organization is probably the fastest route to self-sabotage. Losing things, forgetting things, and missing deadlines are all symptomatic of poor organization, and can all lead to serious academic problems.**

One reason why your organizational skills may not yet have developed by the time you enter college is because somebody else—your mother, your father, your significant other—have been doing your organizing for you. This chapter is designed to help you understand that you don't need that kind of support anymore. In fact, such support may be **antithetical** to your personal growth. You've reached that point in your life when you ought to be able to organize yourself *by* yourself. You need to know when your assignments are due, where you put your car keys and wallet and glasses, and when to send the rent check so it arrives on time. These essentials are up to you—not your mother,

caveat something said as a warning, caution, or qualification
antithetical contrary

not your father, not your partner, not your spouse, and not your room-mates. But not to fear—we have every confidence in your abilities.

It's about Time

In order to brush up your organizational skills, you have to have a real sense of time. The essence of time is that it's highly relative—60 seconds or 60 minutes can feel a certain way on one occasion and altogether different on another. Think about those times when you've taken a 4-hour road trip somewhere. On the way out, the trip felt really long, didn't it? And yet on the way back it sped by. In fact, those same 4 hours are the same 240 minutes and the same 14,400 seconds. But they don't feel the same. Why? Because time is relative.

Ten minutes in a Swedish-language film in which people are talking about the nature of marital relationships doesn't feel like 10 minutes in an Indiana Jones movie when Harrison Ford is running away from people with spears. Sitting in your classes will probably furnish you with more examples of what we're talking about. Fifty minutes might fly by in Psychology but crawl by in Statistics (or vice versa).

Your key to becoming an organized person is to start getting a handle on time, because once it's gone, it's *gone*. So how can we keep the sands of time from funneling down the hourglass too quickly? We can start by becoming increasingly aware of how we're spending our time.

Logging On

To begin this exploration of how you spend your time, you'll want to take a fairly scientific approach to the subject. Many people, when asked to account for their time over the course of any given day, will actually have little idea of what was spent where, when, and how. As a student, you might not have that problem, as your life is tightly sched-uled, but you may also be feeling "time-poor." Between your course work, your extracurricular activities, the demands being made on you by friends and family, not to mention the pressures of holding down a job, you could definitely use an extra 3 or 4 hours a day. But you simply don't have them. So you have to make the most of what you've been given to work with—24 hours exactly. No more, no less.

We propose that for one solid week, you keep a log of how you spend your time. That means that whenever you have a change in activity, you take out your little pad or notebook and you record what you're doing. Okay, so maybe people will look at you like you're weird, but you can handle being weird for a week, can't you? Just explain that it's an "experiment"—enough said.

Many people have a highly ambivalent rela-tionship with time. Some worry that they are constantly behind the eight ball, never quite able to catch up. Others are always "bored," feel-ing as though time just creeps by. Some people get a nice brisk buzz from working at things they enjoy, while others only feel relaxed and easy when they're doing "nothing." Take a moment to write down some of your thoughts about time. Does time feel like a tyrant to you? Are you get-ting better or worse at managing it? What is your history around the issue of time? Are you often late for appointments? Do you find yourself in a panic trying to get to places on time? Do you have a reputation for being punctual or tardy? Think about the role that time has played in your life, and what you'd like to change.

Your log should look like a grid. On top, you will have a column that will denote each day of the week. On the left hand margin, you'll have slots for every hour of the day. (Yes, even 4 o'clock in the morning. You may not be busy then, but hey—you never know.) Now you're ready. On your mark, get set, go. Write down each activity as you come to it.

	Monday	Tuesday	Wednesday	Thursday	Friday	Saturday	Sunday
12:00 AM							
1:00 AM							
2:00 AM							
3:00 AM							
4:00 AM							
5:00 AM							
6:00 AM							
7:00 AM							
8:00 AM							
9:00 AM							
10:00 AM							
11:00 AM							
12:00 PM							
1:00 PM							
2:00 PM							
3:00 PM							
4:00 PM							
5:00 PM							
6:00 PM							
7:00 PM							
8:00 PM							
9:00 PM							
10:00 PM							
11:00 PM							

How specific should you get? Well, you don't have to put down 2 minutes for brushing your hair, 2 minutes for brushing your teeth, and 20 seconds for rinsing, but you should add up all those tasks and then record the time block—"morning bathroom routine"—which might amount to 20 minutes altogether. Everything goes down on your log. Doing the laundry, commuting, sitting in class, walking the dog, shopping, studying, going to the bank, chatting online, talking on the phone. (If you talk on the phone while you're commuting, your log entry can say something like, "Bus/Phone to Sandy.") Specify on your log the person you've been talking to, because, at some later point, you may want to review how much of your day is devoted to personal calls as compared to school-related or work-related calls. Be very aware of each activity, and write down when you're "doing nothing." You may ultimately discover that "doing nothing" represents a great deal of what you're doing after all.

After a week of keeping your log, sit down to **scrutinize** what you've recorded. Try to assign a number value to each of your activities—let's say, 1 is very valuable, 2 is valuable, 3 is somewhat valuable, 4 is not very valuable, and 5 is not at all valuable. Consider each of the activities carefully. Studying for a Biology test—well, it may not have been fun, but it certainly was valuable, wasn't it? On the other hand, spending an hour on the phone with your cousin arguing about which was better—*The Matrix* or *The Matrix Reloaded*—was not particularly valuable, was it?

In analyzing your activities, consider which you would have liked to devote more time to, and which you feel you devoted too much time to. Were there any activities in the course of your week that you never got around to? Cleaning the fish tank? Getting your hair cut? Exercising? Cleaning out your book bag? Make a note of those, too.

ANALYZING YOUR LOG

So there it is—in black and white—the complete record of what you did with yourself over the course of a week. A week is a long time. Seven days. One hundred and sixty-eight hours. Ten thousand and eighty minutes. (We'll spare you the seconds.) While it's true that none of us wants to live and die by the stopwatch, it's sobering to think that with all that time on our hands, we didn't accomplish nearly as much as we had hoped to. Why not? What went wrong? Ask yourself: Did you waste

scrutinize examine closely and carefully

time? And what constitutes "wasted time" anyway? T. S. Eliot, the great 20th century poet, once wrote, "Time you enjoyed wasting is not wasted time." We all enjoy a little downtime now and then, vegging out with a bowl of popcorn while we catch a favorite flick, trying out a new video game, of playing Frisbee with friends. But if these kinds of activities take up too much of your time, you'll have to wonder if they're worth it.

Examine your routines, as reflected in the log, and be sensitive to where you may be wasting valuable time. Do you really need to talk to your friend on the phone four times a day? Might not once or twice suffice? Does lunch have to last a full hour? Are you spending more time on your appearance than necessary? After all, do you really have to dress up to go to the laundromat?

You may also be having difficulty prioritizing. Giving equal time to shampooing your dog and studying for a History final does not signal wise thinking. Allowing your day to be submerged in trivia can be a form of procrastination—that dreaded mind-fogger that can derail goals so **insidiously**. After all, it's easier to shampoo your dog than it is to study for your final, and yet there's something vaguely virtuous about shampooing your dog, so you trick your mind into believing that you're not *really* procrastinating ... are you?

insidiously slowly and subtly harmful or destructive

FOOD FOR THOUGHT: THE LEISURE TIME PARADOX

Are you feeling overburdened in this hurried world? Most Americans, when asked that question, would probably reply affirmatively. But, in fact, studies show that the leisure time of Americans is actually on the rise. In their controversial book *Time for Life*, John D. Robinson, professor of sociology and director of the Americans' Use of Time Project at the University of Maryland, and Geoffrey Godbey, professor of leisure studies at Penn State University, spent 10 years, starting in 1965, studying the time-diaries that they asked a cross-section of Americans to keep of their days. They discovered that sleep hours increased over the years to nearly 8 hours a day among the 9,000 participants in the study, and time spent working decreased while leisure time expanded.

Americans, on average, now watch television more than 15 hours a week. This compares to less than 3 hours a week that is, respectively, spent on reading, hobbies, sports, education, and religion—all activities that used to take up more of our time. Robinson and Godbey believe that television is a "quick fix" that leads us to believe that our problems can be solved in 30 minutes or an hour. As we watch TV, we are bombarded with advertisements that suggest how a certain skin cream, shampoo, food product, car, or some other material item can cure our ills. This "quick fix" mentality puts us on an ever rising-and-falling pattern that may explain why people today feel more pressured while actually having more time on their hands.

Source: Time for life: The surprising ways Americans use their time. Retrieved December 1, 2005, from http://www.sleephomepages.org/books/timeforlife.html

Once you've analyzed your log, if you feel that you're misusing your time or even wasting it, then the question becomes, What *can* you do to manage time? The good news is that there's a lot you can do, and learning new habits to help you deal with time is something that can be mastered fairly quickly.

How to Get Organized ... Fast!

A person's organizational skills are, to some degree, manifestations of personality and, on the other hand, are markers of one's place along a particular developmental timeline. It's true that some people can be wildly successful and at the same time be wildly disorganized. Such people may have very carefree personalities that **abjure** organization, but they may also have sparks of genius that carry them to professional heights nonetheless. These very talented people may find mentors or managers or associates who can do their organizing for them—lucky people! Most of us, however, are not so lucky. We have to organize ourselves, and this is a task that some of us manage to master sooner than others. Often, college is the place where people genuinely *learn* how to become organized. In order to learn, it helps not to have your mother, father, or the usual crew doing the things for you that you ought to be doing for yourself.

THE FUNDAMENTALS OF ORGANIZATION

To accomplish what you set out to do, you have to *remember* what you set out to do. Keeping your eye on the prize is key—remember Helen Hooven Santmyer, the writer who waited decades between books and whose novel ... *And Ladies of the Club* hit the best-seller lists when she was in her late eighties? Her goal was clear and unshakeable, surviving the many, many years when she was forced to put her dreams on the back burner.

To keep *your* goals clearly in your mind, write them down. Stick them on your bulletin board, in your notebook, or wherever you will see them on a regular basis. Writing down goals is probably the best way to achieve them. Think of the practice of writing down your goals as a contract with yourself.

PRIORITIZING

"Prioritizing" is one of those words you hear often in the business world, but it has just as much applicability to the world of academics. Very few of us enjoy the luxury of pursuing one goal at a time. If we did, life would be

abjure reject or avoid

FOOD FOR THOUGHT:
ORGANIZATIONAL DISABILITIES

In some individuals, lack of organization is actually a form of learning disability that can go undiagnosed all the way through grade school, high school, and even college. Some individuals who are unable to organize themselves suffer from temporal-sequential disorganization. They find it extremely difficult to allocate and estimate their time, to follow schedules, meet deadlines, and solve problems in stages. Other "disorganized" people grapple with material-spatial organization. They can't seem to keep track of possessions like pencils, books, and calculators, and their notebooks and desks are in perpetual disarray. Having problems with transitions and being unable to settle down and function effectively when expectations or settings change are further signs of organizational disability. If you feel that you suffer from such a disability, talk to your teachers, your guidance counselor, or whoever you feel comfortable confiding in. Whatever you do, don't just give up!

Source: Levine, M. D. Childhood neurodevelopmental dysfunction and learning disorders. Retrieved December 1, 2005, from http://www.nldontheweb.org/levine.html

so much easier. "Ah, today is the day I get my oil changed … *and nothing else!*" Sorry, but today is the day you get your oil changed and your Biology report is due and you need to meet with your English professor to zero in on a topic for your paper and you have an appointment to get your nails done and you have an interview for a job at the shoe store and you have to buy a present for your cousin's birthday party and … shall we go on?

The way to deal with busy lives is to prioritize. To prioritize means to set priorities—to determine those most important tasks that go to the top of the list, and those that can be put off until another day. Let's take a closer look at the list we started compiling above:

- *You have to get an oil change.* Ask yourself: is it absolutely necessary? While it's true that it's good to change your oil every 3,000 miles, and you've already gone 3,220, you won't put on that many more miles by the end of the week and the shop will probably be able to accommodate you whenever you happen to drive in. If we're prioritizing along the lines of A (must do); B (would be good to do); or C (I could put this off), let's give this a *B*.

- *Your Biology report is due.* There's no arguing with this one. Your instructor is very strict about deadlines (as you should assume all your instructors are). To hand this in late would be a clear case of self-sabotage. Give this one an *A*.

- *You need to meet with your English professor so you can zero in on your paper topic.* This is important, and it's true you've been putting it off, but you're still pretty much in the safe zone as to when this paper is due. You could probably put it off another day or two, if need be. Let's give it a *B*.

- *You have an appointment to get your nails done.* Okay—you *want* to get your nails done, and if you cancel your appointment, they're going to be annoyed with you because you've canceled before. On the other hand, they'll continue to take your business, and you can still go for your job interview without your nails being perfect. We could really give this a *C*, couldn't we?

- *You have an interview for a job at the shoe store.* There's no give here. You want that job. The pay's good, it's conveniently located, and you need the money. This is an *A*.

- *You have to buy a present for your cousin's birthday party.* The party is tonight. But your cousin's been known to miss or be late with birthday gifts herself. You could always say you left the present at home. Or you could order her something over the Internet and tell her what it is. This one's a *B* … maybe even a *C*.

Do you see the kind of thought processes that go into prioritizing what needs to be done on a typical day? At the top of the list are school and work responsibilities, which is exactly where they should be. Other matters are important, and, if they are delayed, they mustn't be allowed to get lost in the shuffle. At least one matter is fairly unimportant and can go to the bottom of the heap. In short, when it comes to your to-do list, all things are *not* created equal.

TO-DO LISTS

Essentially, prioritizing allows you to arrange your to-do list in order of importance. What is your to-do list? You guessed it—a list of things you need to do. Some people believe that they can go through life without keeping such a list, and, if that's true, then all the more power to them. The fact is that very few people in this day and age live such **unencumbered** lives that they can afford to go list-less.

unencumbered not burdened with cares or responsibilities

A to-do list doesn't have any real logic to it until you apply the process of prioritization. As you prioritize your list, ask yourself these key questions:

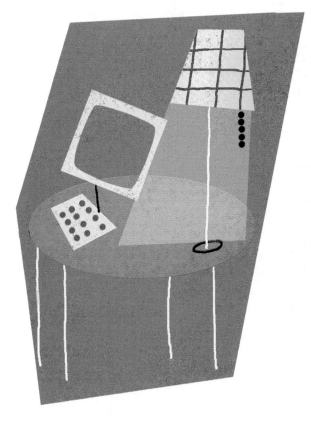

- *How long will each task take?* Sometimes you can reasonably estimate—20 minutes for the conference with your English professor; half an hour for the job interview—while, in other cases, your estimates may be less reliable. When you go in for an oil change, for instance, there could be a longer wait than usual. The same goes for the nail salon. Too many of these "iffy" activities in a packed day can spell trouble.

- *Are any of your "to-do" items dependent on each other?* Let's look at one of your items—meeting with your English professor to discuss the topic of your paper. In order for you to do that, you have to go to the library first to look up a few more background facts. So you'd better add that to your "to-do" list, hadn't you?

- *Can you play around with your to-do list?* That is to say, can you combine things? Usually, you have your oil changed at the service station over on Main Street, but you could just as well go to the station on Second Street and that way you'd be next door to that trendy new shop where you could buy your cousin her birthday present while you're waiting. Killing two birds with one stone is always welcome (to everyone but the birds, that is).

- *Are you clear as to what's flexible and what isn't?* Certain aspects of your day are non-negotiable. You know that you'll have to get some sleep in the course of 24 hours. You know you'll have to eat something. You know you'll have to walk your dog. When you are going over your schedule, you must factor in these non-negotiable activities so that you have a clear sense of your available time.

Once you have a firm grasp on the art and science of prioritizing, you can then move ahead to the next step in your time management campaign: scheduling.

Scheduling

Scheduling occurs once you've made up your to-do list, and you're ready to figure out how to get done all there is to do. Keep in mind those factors beyond your control that can affect your output—like the weather, for starters. If it's snowing, you can assume that your schedule is going to take a beating. Similarly, if you have a terrible head cold, you're not going to be circling the track as speedily as usual. On a

Another buzzword in today's frenzied global economy is *multitasking*, which means the ability to work effectively at more than one thing at a time. For some people, multitasking evokes Dilbert-style nightmares of worker exploitation in the 21st century, but successful executives recognize that the need to multitask—and thereby stay competitive—is not going to go away. Some of these executive notions can be applied to your own student experience, where multitasking can come in handy. Here are some good tips collected by Fast Company, a Web site that offers prescriptions for success.

- *One size does not fit all.* Different strokes work for different folks. Be clear on which work habits best enable you to achieve your goals. For instance, some people only feel productive if they check their E-mail 20 times a day. Others limit this activity to twice a day. Whatever works....

- *People are a nonrenewable resource—don't waste them.* When you have the opportunity to be with someone who can help you—a friend, let's say, who can provide you with a little informal tutoring on some difficult math problems—don't use up his or her valuable time talking to another friend on your cell phone. Turn the phone off and give that person your undivided attention.

- *Delegate: it's the ultimate time-saver.* Executives know the truth of this. Get help where you can and don't micromanage. If your younger brother offers to put on your snow tires for you, don't follow him to the garage to make sure he's doing it right.

Source: The art of multitasking. Retrieved December 1, 2005, from http://www.fastcompany.com/online/63/multitasking.html

normal day—if there is such a thing—you should be able to adhere to your schedule. Keep the following scheduling tips in mind for peak effectiveness:

1) *First and foremost, be realistic.* Sure, you want to get everything done, but if your to-do list is as long as your arm, it's simply not going to happen. There are only so many hours in the day; there is only so much energy we can expend. Winnowing down your to-do list will make it much more likely that you will actually accomplish what you set out to do.

2) *Know when you're at your peak and when you're heading into your valley.* We often hear individuals speak of themselves as "morning people" or "night people." The point is that different people experience differing rates of energy at different times of the day. Pay attention to your cycles, if you feel that you have them, and schedule your most demanding activities for when you are most energized.

3) *Schedule in some "free time" just in case.* Things have a way of happening when you least expect them. Your mother/sister/partner might get a flat tire, and you'll be asked to come to the rescue. Your babysitter doesn't show up. You lose your wallet and have to retrace your steps. Make sure, when you're scheduling, that you give yourself some wiggle room so you can deal with these eventualities.

4) *Work with big building blocks.* We don't have to tell you what occupies most of your day—your school responsibilities, your work responsibilities, and your domestic responsibilities. Schedule those duties first and then fit the other stuff—oil changes, pet shampoos—around them.

5) *Don't lose the forest for the trees.* Sometimes people can only see what is directly in front of them, at the expense of the bigger picture. You should really be factoring some activities into your day that work toward your longer-range goals. For instance, if you're graduating this year, you know that you'll need to pull your resumé together and you know that you have to make time for networking, job research, and so forth. You can't afford to neglect these longer-range activities. Review your schedule to make sure you're allowing room for them.

THE RIGHT STUFF

If you truly believe that you can keep all of your responsibilities, duties, and tasks in your head, that's great. We know we're unable to, however, and we wouldn't be surprised if, down the line, you decide that you can't either. It's an enormously difficult and risky thing to do. Writing your schedule down—preferably in the same place every day—is a simple, easy habit to acquire and it will take you a long way toward realizing your goals.

PLAN ON A PLANNER

What is a planner? It's essentially a calendar that is set up in such a way as to facilitate your planning. Walk into any stationary store and you'll find dozens of options to choose from. You can select from pocket planners, weekly planners, monthly planners, and more, all the way down the line from fancy leather-bound versions to plain, simple, and highly affordable choices.

When you choose a planner, you'll have the option of picking one that displays a day-at-a-time (actually, two days at a time, as the daily pages will face each other), a week-at-a-time, or a month-at-a-time. Personal preference will dictate your choice. Although it is good to keep the long-range view going, most people don't think quite so long-range that they're comfortable with the month-at-a-time option. You'll also be cramped for actual writing space if you go with a monthly planner. On the other hand, the week-at-a-time gives you a nice overview, but, again, if you have a very packed schedule—as so many students do—you may opt for the two-day-at-a-time choice.

A pocket planner will probably be your best bet for now. To get into the habit of using a planner, it helps to have it with you at all times. Once you get used to pulling it out, jotting down your notes, and referring to it often in the course of the day, using a planner becomes second nature. Some people prefer to use a desk calendar, often in conjunction with a pocket planner. This is not a bad idea, as pocket planners can get mislaid rather easily, and the desk calendar offers you substantial insurance against the potential catastrophe of floating rudderless in your crammed schedule. Your desk calendar and/or your pocket planner can be complemented with a wall calendar that shows the entire month (thereby giving you some of that long-range view you could benefit from). Depending on how techno-savvy you are, you may choose to use a computer-based calendar or a personal digital assistant (PDA) for your scheduling needs.

The People Problem

We love to tell jokes and trade stories, to sit around and **schmooze**. Who doesn't? But there comes a time when duty calls and people become a temptation you have to resist. How do you deal with the demands that other people make upon your time? Here are some good ideas:

- If you're in a public place, like a reading room or a lounge, turn your chair to the wall. The less you see, and the less you *are* seen, the less chance you have of being distracted from your work.
- When it comes to phone calls, don't spread them out through the day, but, rather, designate a phone call "hour." That way, you can limit the time you're turning over to that activity. Lunch hour might work well, as other people tend to be busy then and so your calls are more likely to be brief.

schmooze talk idly or casually, in a friendly way, derived from Yiddish

FOOD FOR THOUGHT: QUICK FACTS ABOUT PDAS

No, PDAs are not the pollutants that foul our rivers or some kind of baseball statistic you've never heard of. PDAs stand for Personal Digital Assistants—one of the fastest-selling consumer devices in history. Since their inception, more than 9 million of these cunning little gadgets have been sold, the vast majority from one company—Palm, Inc. PDAs centralize everything—your calendar, your address book, your memo pads, your to-do list, and your expenses—in one very small hand-held item. Not only can it maintain your day-today schedule, notes, lists, and contacts, but a PDA can also download information from the Internet and can be used for crunching numbers and playing games or music. PDAs can be synchronized with your desktop or laptop computer. There are many excellent PDAs on the market. When selecting one, ask yourself the following questions:

- *Do you prefer a PDA that you can carry in your briefcase or your pocket?* They come in both hand-held or palm-size models—you choose.
- *What type of data entry do you prefer?* Most hand-held PDAs use a miniature keyboard for data entry, which can be difficult for some people to manage. Palm-sized PDAs use a stylus/touch-screen technology that involves learning some shorthand alphabet. This, too, can be difficult for some people.
- *What operating system are you most comfortable with?* This is like choosing between a Mac and an IBM clone. PDAs use one of two types of operating systems: Palm OS or PocketPC. Palm OS takes up less memory, runs faster, and is easier to use. Pocket PC is great on graphics and standard Window packages like Excel or Word, but it takes up more memory, is slower, and is more complicated to use.

Shop around to determine what you like and where you can get the best price, and then, if you're ready, join the latest in 21st century technology.

Source: How PDAs work. Retrieved December 1, 2005, from http://www.howstuffworks.com/pda.html

- A "Do Not Disturb" sign on your door works wonders. People get the message fast.
- If you're really pressed for time, and someone wants to meet with you—let's say your friend has a problem he wants to discuss—do it on his turf. When *you* go to *him*, it's a lot more likely that you'll be able to quickly wrap up the visit than if he comes to you.
- If it looks like you can't avoid being interrupted, insert a marker or a prompt in what you're reading or writing so that you can resume the activity quickly when you return to it.
- "Give" people time. If your mother's been pressing you to have a heart-to-heart, say something like, "Okay. I have 15 minutes." You're *presenting* her with something, rather than *resisting*, and she may very well be satisfied with that "gift."

… AND THEN THERE'S CHILDREN

As any parent will tell you, nobody or nothing eats up time the way children can. Fortunately, most of the ways they eat up time are thoroughly delightful. Even parents who are harried students will have to make time for eating ice cream cones with the kids on a summer day—that's what life is all about and you don't get enough turns on the carousel to ignore such opportunities. But, of course, if you are going to be a student and you do have kids, then you will have to allocate the day-to-day responsibilities of child care to others—at least to some degree. If you have a partner who can take up the slack, so be it. If you have an extended family—grandmas, grandpas, aunts, uncles— who can help out, all the better. Even if such support is available to you, you will probably also be relying, to some extent, on some kind of child care for hire, whether it's a sitter, family day care, or through a child care center.

If you are a matriculated student who has a child or children, check with your college or university to see what kind of child care options they offer, if any. Many schools now have child care centers on site, which are immeasurably helpful to adult students who are attempting to combine studies and parenting. Also check to see if you are eligible for a child care subsidy. The federal Child Care Access Means Parents in School Program was established to help institutions of higher education provide campus-based child care services to low-income students. You may qualify. For information on this program, visit the U.S. Department of Education's Web site at http://www.ed.gov/programs/campisp/index.html.

© Digital Vision

Adopting a Time-Saver Mentality

We've talked about to-do lists, scheduling, organizers and planners, and other fundamentals of organization. Now we'd like to discuss the kind of mindset that develops as you feel yourself becoming a more organized person. In writing widely over the years on student and career success, we've collected hundreds of time-saving tips that cover many areas of everyday life. We'd like to share some of our favorites, to give you an idea of how you can save valuable minutes all over the place.

- Check out automatic services that might save you a trip to the bank.
- Try shopping on the Internet. Use a search engine like Google or Yahoo! and type in your keyword. For instance, if you're looking for a wedding present for your cousin and you want to get her an item from a certain line of cookware, you would type in your request and, chances are, many reputable dealers with great prices would come up. That way, you won't have to spend half a day in a crowded mall.
- Carpool! Not only does it save money on gas, but it saves you the time of having to look for parking everyday.
- Get off junk mail lists. Call up the 800 numbers of all those catalogs and whatnot that are pursuing you and ask to be removed. Similarly, register with the National Do Not Call Registry at https://www .donotcall.gov. This keeps those pesky telemarketers from bothering you when you're trying to get things done.
- Stop losing things! Always keep your vital items—keys, wallet, glasses, mail—in the same place everyday. It's incredible how much time you can waste looking for stuff.
- Work at clutter control in an easy, ongoing way that will keep you from having to spend lots of frustrating time cleaning up when things get out of hand. When you leave a room, pick up something that doesn't belong there and put it back in its rightful place. Carrying one thing at a time on a regular basis is a lot easier than moving loads of things every few weeks.
- Cook double portions of food and then freeze away a portion. That will save you a lot of time on food preparation.
- With regard to food shopping, keep a running list on your refrigerator door and then, before you go to the supermarket, group the items on your list by category—Dairy; Meats and Poultry; Dry Goods. That way, when you get to the store, you won't have to waste time repeatedly going up and down the aisles.

We could go on and on with such tips, but space limitations prevent us from doing so. Anyway, more important that the actual tips themselves is the idea that saving time is something you can become good at, if you practice. Becoming conscious of where your time goes, and using prioritizing and scheduling to control your time, is your avenue to higher achievement. Now let's explore in our next chapter what happens when your organization breaks down and nothing is going right. In other words, stress!

What Did We Learn?

Review the following questions and activities to make sure that the things you need to remember from this chapter have sunk in.

1. Do Americans have more or less leisure time now than they used to?
2. Why should you write down your goals?
3. Explain the process of prioritizing.
4. What are the key questions to ask yourself when you're prioritizing your to-do list?
5. What are the five most important tips with regard to scheduling your time?
6. Cite several actions you can take to prevent people from distracting you from your work.

Bibliography

Davidson, J. (2001). *The complete idiot's guide to managing your time, 3rd ed.* Indianapolis, IN: Alpha.

Kolberg, J. (1999). *Conquering chronic disorganization*. Decatur, GA: Squall Press.

Nakone, L. (2005). *Organizing for your brain type: Finding your own solution to managing time, paper, and stuff.* New York: St. Martin's Press.

Schlenger, S., & Roesch, R. (1999). *How to be organized in spite of yourself: Time and space management that works with your personal style.* New York: Signet.

Links

How PDAs work. Retrieved December 1, 2005,
from http://www.howstuffworks.com/pda.htm

How to make a to-do list. Retrieved December
1, 2005, from http://www.ehow.com/how_
3812_make-list.html

Setting priorities. Retrieved December 1,
2005, from http://www.jou.ufl.edu/sji/1999/
features_02.htm

The art of multitasking. Retrieved December 1,
2005, from http://www.fastcompany.com/
online/63/multitasking.html

Word Smart

Here is this chapter's crop:

abjure

antithetical

caveat

insidious

schmooze

scrutinize

unencumbered

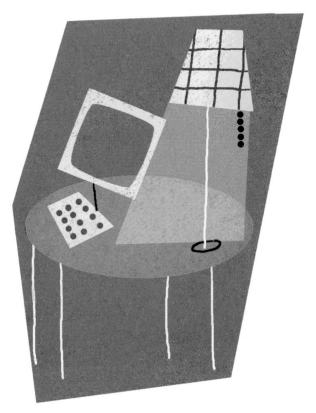

STRESSED OUT

Stress is no joke. We don't have to tell you that. You know what stress does to you. You feel it when you have a paper due and you haven't even started the research yet. You suffer from it after you've taken an exam that was a lot harder than you expected and you're waiting for your grade. Stress gnaws at you when you look at your dwindling bank account or your burgeoning credit card bills. You're overwhelmed by stress when you've had a big fight with someone you care about, and you surrender to stress when the alternator on your car conks out as you're trying to get to an important appointment on time.

Many people think of stress as a modern-day problem, but, in all fairness, it had to have been fairly stressful to run away from saber-toothed tigers or to live through the Black Plague. Stress is simply—or not so simply—a part of the human condition. Everyone experiences it—even the high and mighty. Martha Stewart gets sent to prison … stress. Rush Limbaugh is accused of abusing prescription drugs … stress. Britney Spears breaks a nail … stress. Think about it: What causes you stress and how do you generally respond to stressful situations?

burgeoning growing or expanding rapidly

"Into each life some rain must fall." Those are the lyrics of a well-known old song. For some people this "rain" is money woes. For others, it's relationship problems or health issues. No one goes through life unscathed or unstressed. Take a few moments to explore the areas that are causing you stress in your life right now. This is just for you—share it only if you want to. Ask yourself how you handle stress. Do you curl up into a fetal ball? Hit the vodka? Kick the dog? Or do you practice yoga, breathe deeply, go for a run, watch a Mel Brooks movie, or talk it out with a friend? Everyone has stress. How you handle your stress is a subject worth exploring.

Stress: A Modern Societal Epidemic

Stress, as we've noted, has always been around, but efforts to quantify the amount of stress in our lives and its impact are relatively recent, historically speaking. Now that we have begun to amass significant data, we can see how serious the problem of stress really is. Seventy-five percent of the general population experiences at least "some stress" every 2 weeks, and half of the population experiences levels of stress that are "moderate or high." In fact, the World Health Organization recognizes job stress as a worldwide epidemic.

With the uncertain climate of post–9/11 life, as we face the specter of terrorism and a difficult economy, millions of Americans are feeling more stressed than they can ever recall having felt before. Globally, stress can affect others even more critically. Consider the lives of people in war-torn countries or those living in dire poverty, in disease-ridden areas, or in parts of the world that are prone to earthquakes, typhoons, droughts, or other natural disasters. According to the American Psychological Association, two-thirds of all office visits in the United States to family physicians are due to stress-related symptoms [*Source:* APA Help Center Web site. Retrieved August 11, 2005, from http://www.apahelpcenter.org/articles/article.php?id=103]. The medical costs alone for the treatment of stress-related illnesses in the United States have been estimated at well over a billion dollars a year. Stress costs industry approximately $150 billion a year in increased health insurance costs, burnout, absenteeism, reduced productivity, and accidents.

In terms of your own experience as a student, consider all the **stressors** affecting your life at the moment. Perhaps you're thinking about going to graduate school and, knowing how competitive it is to get in, you're worried about your ability to keep up your grades. Maybe college is a major financial burden for you and/or your family, and every time you get a bill in the mail, that band of anxiety around your head tightens. Are you holding down a job while you go to school? Does the job have its own set of pressures that are hard to cope with? Are you being pulled in one direction by friends or family and in another direction by school and work responsibilities? Do you feel that you never have enough time and that you can barely keep your head above water?

Before you get into bed and pull the covers over your head, we'd like you to consider the fact that, even when stress feels overwhelming, it is only *one* of life's experiences, not its totality. Indeed, stress can even be

stressors activities, experiences, or other situations that cause stress

When it comes to stress, it's really a case of different strokes for different folks. Some people have a very high threshold for stress. They are cool under pressure, and can think clearly even in highly charged situations. Others are easily excited, nervous, and prone to overreaction. Then you have your drama queens and kings, those who seem to thrive on stress and appear bored when things are not at a fever pitch. It is universally acknowledged, however, that certain life events almost invariably contribute to stress. Psychiatrist Thomas H. Holmes and his colleagues devised the Social Readjustment Rating Scale to assess these life events and give them a corresponding "stress point" value. Holmes discovered that people whose points exceeded 300 could be expected to develop an illness within a year or two. The following chart lists these events and their respective points. Test yourself, if you wish, and see if you have reason to be concerned.

Life Event	Value
Death of spouse	100
Divorce	73
Separation from spouse	65
Jail term	63
Death of close family member	63
Personal injury or illness	63
Marriage	50
Fired from work	47
Reconciliation with spouse	45
Retirement	45
Change in health of family member	44
Pregnancy	40
Sex difficulties	39
Addition to family	39
Change of financial status	38
Death of close friend	37
Change of career	36
Change in the number of marital arguments	33
Foreclosure of mortgage or loan	30
Change in work responsibilities	29
Son or daughter leaving home	29
Trouble with in-laws	29
Outstanding personal achievement	28
Spouse begins or stops work	26
Starting or finishing school	26
Change in living conditions	25
Trouble with boss	23
Change in work hours or conditions	20
Moving	20
Change in schools	20
Change in recreational habits	19
Change in social activities	18
Change in sleeping habits	16
Change in number of family gatherings	15
Change in eating habits	15
Vacation	13
Christmas or major holiday	12
Minor violation of the law	11

Source: Reprinted (TK) with permission from *Journal of Psychosomatic Research*, vol. 11, p. 213, Thomas H. Holmes and Richard H. Rahe, "The Social Readjustment Rating Scale," copyright 1967, Pergamon Press plc.

useful in certain situations. When you run a race or are about to give a solo piano performance, you may experience stress that will actually help lift you onto a higher plane of achievement. In any event, stress can be controlled and monitored, up to a point, so long as you learn to recognize it and know the necessary techniques that will keep it at bay. This chapter provides help on both of these counts.

The Physiology of Stress

Stress is a physiological phenomenon. Understanding how it works is a first step toward understanding how to control it. Walter Cannon, a physiology professor at Harvard University from the early 1900s to 1942, studied the physiological basis of stress and developed the concept of the emergency function of the sympathetic nervous system. Cannon identified a hard-wired human response—primitive, automatic, and in-born—that acts as a kind of genetic wisdom designed to protect us from perceived attack, harm, or threat to our survival. Cannon deemed this response "Fight or Flight," and found that it corresponds to the area of our brains called the *hypothalamus*. When the hypothalamus is stimu-lated—by something that causes anxiety, for instance—it triggers a series of nerve cell responses that release the chemicals and hormones that prepare our bodies for either running ("Flight") or combat ("Fight").

So then, if you will, imagine a caveman out looking for food who comes upon a saber-toothed tiger. The "Fight or Flight" response kicks in instantaneously, as he tries to figure out his next step. Bodily sub-stances like adrenaline, noradrenaline, and cortisol are released into his bloodstream. His respiratory rate increases. Blood flows away from his digestive tract into his muscles and limbs, providing him with the extra energy he'll need. His pupils dilate; his mouth goes dry. His awareness intensifies. And he … runs! (He's no fool, this caveman—he knows he can't fight a saber-toothed tiger.)

Now here you are, many, many thousands of years later, and you're walking to your car through a dark parking lot. Suddenly, you see a group of guys who don't seem like they belong here. You and that cave-man couldn't be more different from each other—after all, you use hair products and drink lattes and are entirely modern in your outlook—but your bodies respond in identical ways. Increased heartbeat and respira-tion. Dilated pupils. Dry mouth. Fight or flight? The group gets into their car. They drive off. You return to normal. No reason to panic after all.

At some point in your life, you've probably been in a situation where you felt that "Fight or Flight" response kick in. Maybe it was confronting a growling dog. Maybe someone with road rage was screaming horrible things at you. Did you ever get lost in the woods? Swim out too far at the beach and had a hard time swimming back in? If so, you know what "Fight or Flight" feels like … *and you know it doesn't feel good.*

Chronic Stress and Its Toll on Your Body

Unfortunately, it doesn't take saber-toothed tigers, growling dogs, or being lost in the dark woods to set off the "Fight or Flight" response. The fact is that complications and stressors besiege us all in the 21st century. Even matters that are routine can set off that same physiological reaction. Sitting in traffic, waiting on endless lines to get through airport security, dealing with outrageous prices at the gasoline pump, haggling with an insurance firm over medical reimbursement—these all have the ability to release the adrenaline, noradrenaline, and cortisol just as a growling dog would. Many of us believe that we become **inured** to the stressful things in modern life, and certainly some of us are better at dealing with these things than others. But, to some degree or another, these unpleasant aspects of life in the 21st century take their toll on all of us.

The real problem is that the wide-open spaces that were available to the caveman who was running away from a saber-toothed tiger are not so available to us today. Many times we find ourselves stuck in places that set off the "Fight or Flight" response—at the airport, on the freeway, in a tiny cubicle in an office building—and we can't just run. Nor can we take out our clubs—literally or metaphorically—and stand up to the tiger. If we scream or threaten people at the airline terminal or from our cars, we will be accused of airport rage or road rage and, depending upon how far we go, we could even get ourselves arrested if we don't watch out. What happens when all those chemicals and hormones stew in our bodies without the release of running up a tree or clubbing a wild animal to the ground? Nothing good. When stress hormones build up over a period of time without release, serious disorders can result. Among these disorders are tension headaches, irritable bowel syndrome, and high blood pressure. Cumulative stress can also bring on disorders of the hormonal and immune systems, which can lead to infection, chronic fatigue, depression, and such autoimmune diseases as rheumatoid arthritis, lupus, and allergies. In other words, too much stress, over too long a period of time, is extremely unhealthy.

inured used to something unpleasant over a long period of time

Stress not only takes its toll physically, but it also can have a major psychological impact that can show itself as irritability, anxiety, impaired concentration, confusion, frustration, anger, and poor judgment. When you are stressed, you are much less likely to be able to sit down and study or take a test. In fact, a test might spike your tendency toward stress, which is something we will be discussing specifically when we come to Chapter 9: Testing, Testing. So, how can you get a hold of this problem? How can you reduce the stress in your life or, failing that, improve your ability to cope with stress? The answer lies in changing your habits and altering the very way you think.

Making Changes

Stress comes not just from the external realities of our lives but from the internal responses we choose to listen to. It is reassuring to know that you can change them both.

When we speak of external realities, we are talking about the environment that surrounds us. To some extent, we may be limited as to how much we can alter this environment. Let's say, for instance, you are living in a crowded situation—four people in an apartment that would better serve two—and several of your roommates are sloppy or noisy. This type of living arrangement is highly stressful to you, but your budget doesn't allow you to pick up and move. Is there anything you can do? No, you say hopelessly. You're stuck.

Nonsense! There is always something you can do. You can start by openly discussing the situation with your roommates. "Are you kidding?" you reply. "That's confrontation, and confrontation stresses me out." It's true that making your wishes known can be difficult, and dealing openly with another person can be a challenge. But once you're able to get beyond your inhibitions, you may discover that the stress created by such an interaction is ultimately far less taxing than the stress of living with a chronic problem. In Chapter 10: Works and Plays Well with Others, we'll be offering some hands-on advice for dealing with difficult situations and people, but that is not the thrust of our discussion here. We are simply offering the above scenario as an example of how you may have to think creatively and positively in order to **allay** the stress in your life.

There may be many steps you can take right now to deal with issues that are causing you stress. If someone is making so much noise that you can't study or sleep, you could try using earplugs, for instance.

allay reduce the intensity of

(There are many extraordinarily effective earplugs on the market today, which you can investigate online by going to a consumer Web site like http://www.epinions.com.) If your feet hurt, which is causing you physical stress, you can try special shoes or orthotics, which are devices for orthopedic disorders. If your romantic relationship is starting to feel toxic, you can end it. You have the ability, in most cases, to at least begin the process of change. The question becomes: What's stopping you?

Just as we need to change our external environment in order to rid ourselves of stress, we may also need to change our internal responses. In fact, the very thing that may be stopping you from changing your external environment could be your particular set of internal responses. Your internal responses may be telling you that it's no use, it's hopeless, you're hopeless, so why even bother? You need to learn to not listen to these voices. You may need to develop more self-esteem, more confidence, and more resistance to the negativity that you've learned at the hands of others. The capacity to alter your internal responses does not develop overnight. It can take a long time to become aware of what your internal responses actually are, and then it can take more time to learn how to silence them and allow other, more compassionate voices to take their place. But before you do that hard work, you may first need to get a grip on your day-to-day stress and anxiety, and, to that end, we are offering an overview of methods and techniques that you can use to accomplish that task.

ON YOUR MARK, GET SET, BREATHE ...

The very best form of stress relief is universally available, completely free, and is absolutely **devoid** of any dangerous side effects. What is this miracle drug? It's called breathing.

Breathing is something that most of us take entirely for granted, but the way you breathe can enormously affect the way you feel. The fact is, however, that few of us really know how to breathe correctly, in a way that imparts a feeling of well-being and calm. Breathing improperly can create or worsen lung problems like asthma and bronchitis and cannot only be a symptom of stress, but can create stress.

When you are feeling stressed, try some conscious breathing. Sit in a straight, comfortable chair, take off your shoes, and focus all your attention on the process of your breathing. Do you see how your chest and

devoid not possessing

stomach rise and fall? Listen to the sound of the air as you inhale and exhale. It should be smooth and even—almost effortless.

Here are some excellent breathing techniques that can help you get an immediate grip on stress:

- *Square Breathing*. Sit with your feet flat on the floor and your hands relaxed in your lap. Close your eyes and slowly count to three as you take in a deep breath through your nose. Hold the breath for three slow counts, and then release the breath through your mouth for three slow counts. Hold still for three more slow counts, and then repeat the process two or three times, as needed. This is a valuable technique for acute situations.

- *In With the Good, Out with the Bad*. This is a simple and very effective stress reliever. As you inhale, tell yourself, "In with the good," and let yourself fill up with good feelings. On the exhalation, you say, "Out with the bad," and push out your negativity, which should make you feel lighter and less stressed almost immediately. Repeat as necessary until a sense of calm settles in.

- *Belly Breathing*. Find a comfortable place to sit or lie down and place one hand over your navel with your other hand on top. Through your nose, take in a deep breath, hold it for two to three seconds, and then feel the air come down into your belly so that your abdomen and hands rise. Hold the breath for several seconds, as you feel your body calm down, and then slowly exhale through your mouth. Repeat this four or five times to get the full effect.

MIND OVER MATTER

Another way to grab your anxiety by the tail is to let your mind work for you in positive ways. When you are feeling anxious, your mind is working in negative ways. You start spinning out worst-case scenarios and, before you know it, you've spun out of control. Of course, some people are more predisposed to anxiety than others. Some of that may be environmental. Perhaps you grew up in a family where losing your keys or losing your wallet was viewed as a calamity of epic proportions, on a scale with the sinking of the *Titanic*. If so, you will need to find new ways of thinking, but don't worry—you can. In fact, you can begin to counter your orientation toward anxiety and negativity, which may be leading you toward stress, by practicing some of the following techniques that are designed to give your mind the strength it needs to deal with most things that come up. Some of these techniques were discussed in Chapter 1, but are relevant to our current discussion as well.

- *Positive Self-Talk.* Here is one of the tools we've mentioned before— always available and free of charge. When people feel stressed, they may begin to dump on themselves. "What's the matter with you? Look at the mess you've made. Can't you do anything right?" This endless stream of disapproving, unconstructive, incomplete thoughts that invade our brains is sometimes called "mind chatter." Positive self-talk keeps those negative thoughts at bay and positions in their place a constructive feeling of hope and possibility. When using positive self-talk, avoid addressing yourself as *you*—"You don't do anything right"—and focus instead on *I*. Say things to yourself like, "I'm really learning this. I'm getting good at it. I know I can do it." Stay in the present tense—proactive and forward-looking.

- *Stop Thought.* Here's another one we've mentioned, but let's be re- minded of it now. If you feel yourself on the verge of overwhelming anxiety, hold up a stop sign in your mind and say to yourself, "STOP THOUGHT." Just stepping on the brakes that way can send you in a whole other direction.

- *Mindfulness.* Again, this method of calming oneself, which involves a very conscious focus on what is beautiful and relevant in the here and now, is an excellent way to alleviate stress. Turn back to Chapter 1 for a review of this method.

- *Visualization.* Here's a new one—a particularly good way to com- bat stress. Visualize yourself in a place or situation that feels good. Where would that be for you? A porch on a seaside house in Maine? Floating on a chaise lounge in a swimming pool, sipping nectar out of a pineapple? Sitting by a roaring fire on a snowy night in a ski lodge, after a long day on the slopes? You choose. This kind of visualization can be combined with the breathing practices we discussed earlier for some very fast and effective relief.

- *The Relaxation Response.* This antidote to the "Fight or Flight" response was first identified and named by Harvard cardiologist Herbert Benson. Benson **theorized** that the relaxation response cor- responded to a physical portion of the brain, located in the hypothal- amus that, when triggered, sends out neurochemicals that almost exactly counteract the "Fight or Flight" response. The relaxation re- sponse can be evoked by following a simple two-step method:

    1) Focus on a word or phrase that carries a positive charge for you. *Love. Happiness. Serenity. Family*—these are examples of

theorized to put forth as a theory; speculate

words that people often choose. Or you might use a phrase from a psalm, like "The Lord is my shepherd, I shall not want."

2) If you find your mind wandering from the word or phrase—if the mind chatter begins to buzz—turn it away and refocus yourself on the chosen word or phrase.

The relaxation response is hard-wired in the brain, just like the "Fight or Flight" response. Dr. Benson advocated practicing the relaxation response at least twice a day, for 10 to 15 minutes each time. Even if you do not feel immediate stress relief from practicing it, Dr. Benson argued that it is still good for you, like brushing your teeth or flossing, and the beneficial effects will become evident over time.

- *Relax your feet, relax your toes.* Another supremely calming technique is to lie down and, with your eyes closed, progressively relax each of your muscle groups as you move from your feet to the top of your head. Doing this in tandem with another person can be particularly useful and reinforcing.

There are many other such techniques that can help you relax in times of stress. Finding what works for you is a process of discovery. Just don't let the process become another source of anxiety. As you look for ways to relax, look in a way that is calm and relaxing.

Good Habits

We will be devoting an entire chapter later in the book to issues of wellness (Chapter 13: The Whole You), but we just want to mention here, while we're on the subject of stress relief, that embodying good habits is a very important factor in your quest for stress relief. Which habits are we talking about specifically? Consider the following:

- *A healthy, balanced diet.* Junk foods, high in sugar and fat, can **exacerbate** a stressful situation. Choose instead wholesome foods like fruits, vegetables, and grains.
- *Cut back or eliminate caffeine.* Yes, caffeine consumption *is* an addiction. Coffee, tea, colas, and chocolate—all high in caffeine—can overstimulate you and make a stressful day even more nerve-wracking.
- *Get plenty of sleep.* Different people need different amounts of sleep. Some do fine on 6 hours, while others crave 10. Studies have

exacerbate to make an already bad or problematic situation worse

shown, however, that sleep deprivation is a major stressor and can lead to a host of other physical and emotional maladies.

- *Exercise regularly*. The natural conclusion of the "Fight or Flight" response is vigorous physical activity. After all, you're either going to do battle or run, both of which will use up a lot of calories. When we feel stressed, and the "Fight or Flight" response is set off, one of the best things we can do for ourselves is to engage in some vigorous physical activity, to bring the cycle to a close and restore our body and mind to a calmer, more relaxed state. We are not talking about fitness here, although we **extol** fitness and will discuss it again in our chapter on wellness. Here we are talking about any form of activity that will work up a sweat for 4 or 5 minutes, thereby working off the stress hormones that have flooded your system. It might be jumping jacks, running up and down the stairs, jumping rope—whatever metabolizes those excess hormones.

Other Lifestyle Changes

In addition to the various techniques we've already discussed, there are other effective measures you can take to help you cope with stress. Consider the following:

- *Making time for family and friends*. Too much time spent alone can make a stressful period that much worse. Be with those who love you and like you, and accept their support. It will make you feel so much better.
- *Pursue interests and hobbies*. What? You say you have no time? Ten minutes looking over your coin collection or trimming your bonsai plant can go a long way toward clearing your head and calming your spirit. An hour volunteering with an organization like Big Brother/Big Sister or Meals on Wheels can take you away from your problems and reconnect you in a meaningful and constructive way with the world.
- *Be fiscally responsible*. Create a budget and live within its means. Being financially irresponsible and running up bills you can't afford will surely spike your stress levels.
- *Don't forget to laugh*. Laughter can work like a silver bullet to drive away your demons. If you're feeling stressed, play a Monty Python, Adam Sandler, or Three Stooges DVD and laugh yourself silly. You'll feel a whole lot better for it.

extol praise something or somebody with great enthusiasm and admiration

Annus horribilis is a Latin phrase meaning "horrible year." We all have them, now and then. The phrase was most famously used in recent years by Queen Elizabeth II, who described 1992 as her "annus horribilis." In March of that year, the Queen's second son, the Duke of York, separated from his wife, Sarah Ferguson ("Fergie"). Soon thereafter, a picture of a topless Fergie in clinch with a male friend was published in the tabloids, starting a scandal. In April, the Queen's daughter, Princess Anne, divorced her husband, Captain Peter Philips. In November, Windsor Castle, the Queen's primary residence, was badly damaged by a fire, and some priceless artifacts were destroyed. When the royal family asked the government to pay 40 million pounds to make repairs, a public outcry ensued and, to raise the necessary funds, the Queen was forced to open up several residences to tourists. On the 24th of November, in a speech, the Queen said, "1992 is not a year I shall look back on with undiluted pleasure. In the words of one of my more sympathetic correspondents, it has turned out to be an *annus horribilis*." The annus became even more horribilis a month later, when Prince Charles and Princess Diana separated.

How about you? Have you ever had an annus horribilis? Now is the time to share war stories with your classmates, and see who can come away with the medal for the worst luck and the most grit.

Source: WordiQ.com. Retrieved December 1, 2005, from http://www.wordiq.com/definition/Annus_Horribilis

When You Need Extra Help

There comes a time in most of our lives when our stress points add up to an unmanageable total and all the visualization and exercise and positive self-talk just doesn't seem to be managing the problem effectively enough. Every now and then you enter a period where it's all just too much. So what do you do then?

CONSIDERING COUNSELING

If you are starting to feel like your problems are overwhelming and you are unable to cope with them on your own, know that you are not alone. According to the National Institute of Mental Health, more than 30 million Americans sometimes seek counseling to help them with their problems. It is nothing to be ashamed of. Life is tough. There are marital rifts, illnesses, job losses, deaths of loved ones, family problems, financial problems, depression, burnout, substance abuse. When is it time to consider psychotherapy? According to the American Psychological Association, it may be when you:

- Feel overwhelmed and experience a prolonged sense of helplessness and sadness. Your problems are not getting better despite the intervention and support of family and friends. You don't know where to turn.
- You're finding it increasingly difficult to fulfill your everyday responsibilities. Concentrating on school and work is feeling harder and harder.
- You're always worrying, expecting the worst, and your pleasure in life is not what it once was.
- Your actions are harmful to yourself and to others, whether it's from drinking too much, using drugs, or an inability to control your anger.

If you're experiencing any of these "warning signals," now might be the time to seek professional help. So, then, the question becomes where to start?

Psychotherapists—whether they're psychiatrists, psychologists, licensed therapists, or clinical social workers—work with patients to change their feelings and attitudes and help them develop healthier ways of behaving. When you see a psychotherapist, whatever you tell him or her remains strictly confidential, except in certain very unusual circumstances that the psychotherapist can explain to you. A good way to find a psychotherapist is through the referral of another health professional, such as your physician. You may also call your local or state psychological

association for a referral or ask friends and family, if you're comfortable with them knowing of your interest, or you can speak with a clergy person or contact your area community mental health center. As a student, you should also have access to a psychotherapist who is on the staff of your college or university.

In order for you to feel as comfortable as possible with the therapist, and to yield the best results for yourself, it is important that you ask certain questions at the outset. These include the following:

- Are you a licensed psychotherapist?
- How many years of experience do you have?
- I've been having problems with (depression, controlling my drinking, sexual performance, or whatever your issue may be). What kind of experience do you have helping people with problems like mine?
- What are your fees?

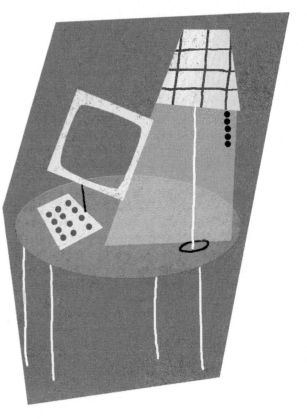

What Did We Learn?

If you know how to handle stress, you'll be way ahead of the game. Check out the following questions and activities to see what you've understood and remembered.

1. What is the Social Readjustment Rating Scale and, according to this scale, what are the five most stressful life events?

2. Explain the "Fight or Flight" response.

3. What are some of the physical disorders that can result from too much stress?

4. Describe three useful breathing techniques that can reduce stress.

5. What is positive self-talk?

6. Define visualization.

7. Explain the "relaxation response."

8. How does mindfulness work?

9. What are some circumstances that might lead you to seek psychotherapy?

10. What are some questions that you would ask when interviewing a potential psychotherapist?

Bibliography

Benson, H., & Klipper, M. Z. (1976). *The relaxation response*. New York: Harper Torch.

Davis, M., Robbins Eshelman, E., & McKay, M. (2000). *The relaxation & stress reduction workbook*. Oakland, CA: New Harbinger Publications.

Lazarus, J. (2000). *Stress relief & relaxation techniques*. New York: McGraw-Hill.

Posen, D. (2004). *The little book of stress relief*. Richmond Hill, Ontario: Firefly Books.

Wilson, P. (1999). *Instant calm: Over 100 easy-to-use techniques for relaxing mind and body*. New York: Plume Books.

- How much therapy do you think I might need?

- What types of insurance do you accept? Will you accept direct billing to or payment from my insurance company?

If you're able to find the right therapist, your chances of being helped are very good. One major study showed that 50 percent of people undergoing psychotherapy noticeably improved after 8 sessions, while 75 percent improved by the end of 6 months. In order to improve, it is important that you and your therapist establish clear goals. If you are suffering from depression, let's say, or a phobia, you will want a sense of what kind of treatment plan your therapist has in mind and what you can expect.

Keep in mind that the only mental health professionals who have the ability to prescribe drugs are psychiatrists and psychiatric nurse practitioners. There are many excellent and even revolutionary drugs available now to help people who are suffering from anxiety, stress, and depression. You've heard of many of them—Valium, Xanax, Prozac. Any psychotherapist you choose to see—psychologists or social workers—will be able to consult with a psychiatrist if medication seems necessary. Keep in mind, too, that while these "wonder drugs" may reduce anxiety and stress, they will not "cure" the underlying problems that cause them. These problems are best treated by counseling in conjunction with mind/body techniques and, if necessary, pharmaceuticals (which can have serious side effects like drowsiness, lack of coordination, and memory loss).

Speaking of Stress

Stress, as we've said, is a fact of life. It's not going to go away and, in fact, in our troubled world, it may become increasingly problematic. It's also very much a part of a student's life, as you juggle school, a job, and social responsibilities while you work toward your future goals, whatever those may be. (Not knowing what your future goals are can be a whole other source of stress.) In the next chapter, we're going to be looking at a particular situation that almost all of us will agree is an undeniable source of stress. We're talking about tests, exams, quizzes … those tension-filled performance situations that fill our stomachs with butterflies and our mouths with our hearts.

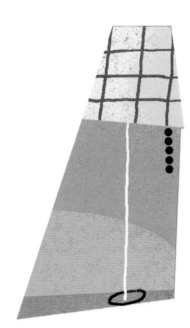

Links

About breathing. Retrieved December 1, 2005, from http://www.about-breathing.com

Anti-anxiety medications. Retrieved December 1, 2005, from http://www.healthyplace.com/Communities/Depression/nimh/medications_6.asp

Finding help: How to choose a psychotherapist. Retrieved December 1, 2005, from http://helping.apa.org/articles/article.php?id=51

Neimark, N. F. The fight or flight response. Retrieved December 1, 2005, from http://www.mindbodymed.com/EducationCenter/fight.html

Stress management. Retrieved December 1, 2005, from http://www.businessballs.com/stressmanagement.htm

Walter Bradford Cannon. The 6th APS President (1914–1916). Retrieved December 1, 2005, from http://www.the-aps.org/about/pres/introwbc.htm

Worldwide epidemic: Workplace stress. Retrieved December 1, 2005, from http://www.medicalcenter.osu.edu/patientcare/hospitalsandservices/publications/?ID=227&SIDS=15,8&o=0

Word Smart

Here are this chapter's words to remember:

allay

burgeoning

devoid

exacerbate

extol

inured

stressor

theorize

TESTING, TESTING ...

In reading this book, you've probably figured out by now that we're very interested in words—what they mean, how to use them, and where they come from. When we started to think about the whole issue of testing, we found ourselves wondering about the derivation of the word "test." (Word derivations—the study of how words in the English language evolve out of roots in Old English, German, French, Greek, Latin, or other languages—often appear in dictionary entries.) We discovered that the word "test" comes from the Old French, meaning a pot or, more specifically, a *cupel*—a small, flat, circular vessel that was used to determine the quality, and thereby the value, of gold or silver. When you take a test, do you sometimes feel like you're being placed in a vessel where your value is about to be judged?

Enter any location where a test is being given and you'll be sure to find three sets of people. There are those supremely confident individuals who seem to thrive in a testing situation and who remain as cool as the **proverbial** cucumber. At the other end of the spectrum, you'll find a segment that really doesn't care how they do. They too are quite cool and unbothered because nothing much is at stake as far as they're concerned. In the middle, representing the vast majority, are those who recognize that a lot is at stake, who care a great deal, and who are subject to much nervousness and anxiety going into the testing situation. If you find yourself in that middle

proverbial generally known or remarked

group, then this chapter is for you. It will address test-taking strategies and offer some constructive ideas on how to control test anxiety so that your efforts can be productive and successful.

Be Prepared

Obviously, the way that we prepare for tests and exams is very much related to the issue of study skills that we discussed at length in Chapter 5: The How-To of Studying. This is a good time, however, to review and expand on those skills that are particularly **germane** to test situations.

The first thing to understand when you're taking a test is that your ability to do well is directly linked to your ability to recall information. This, in turn, depends largely on how you've studied the material. Research shows that learning is at its most effective when you process small chunks of information over a period of time. In other words, it is best to review just a *few* ideas and to review them *many, many times*.

Another way to be sure that the relevant course material sinks in is to make your review of class notes another routine in your life, just like brushing your teeth or walking your dog. Spend a certain amount of time per day—how much is up to you—going over your notes and clarifying them, pruning out unimportant thoughts, and underscoring key ideas. This slow **accretion** of retained information will set you up well for your exams.

Essentially, as we see it, there are only so many ways to really study effectively for a test. Here are some of the ways that we think are best:

- *Silent review*. Read and review the information that you are being tested on, and then quiz yourself until you've reached a point where you can recall the information without referring back to your notes.
- *Recitation*. By adding an audio component to your silent review—particularly important for auditory learners—you will discover that the information lodges in your brain more effectively. Recite the information you are studying out loud—again, more than once—and let it take hold that way.
- *Diagrams and mind-mapping*. Just as an audio component can enhance your silent review, so can a visual component—especially important, obviously, for visual learners. Creating mind-maps and other diagrams reinforces retention.

germane relevant; pertinent
accretion an increase in the size or amount as a result of something accumulating or being added gradually

REFLECTIONS: *YOUR HISTORY*

We'd like you to start by writing down three or four words that you associate with testing. It could be #2 Pencil, Cramming, Nausea ... whatever comes to mind. Then look at your list, pick out one of the words, and write a paragraph that expands on that word. In doing so, explore why you feel such a powerful connection to that chosen word when you think about testing situations.

© Digital Vision

135

- *Cue yourself*. Introducing a motor activity—specifically, writing—may also help reinforce retention. Write out important points or jot down cues in the margins of your notes to signal what's most important.
- *Flash cards*. Ratchet up the writing component by creating your own flash cards and study cards. These reinforce visual learning as well.

There are also several techniques that are helpful when you're trying to absorb lists of information. The first technique is called *chunking*. You put information together in "chunks" that have some element in common, and this makes it easier to memorize what you've been assigned. For instance, if you're trying to learn all the contributing factors that brought about World War I, you would "chunk" these together by grouping them in terms of economic factors, social factors, political factors, and so on. This chunking fixes the information in your mind much more effectively than if the information was floating all over the place with no **discernible** logic.

Another proven way to remember items on a list is to use a *mnemonic device*. We talked about mnemonic devices in Chapter 3: It's All in the Mind, but, to reiterate, they are clever ways to trick your mind into remembering things. For instance, if you were trying to remember the Great Lakes, you might use the HOMES mnemonic we told you about in Chapter 3—H for Huron, O for Ontario, M for Michigan, E for Erie, S for Superior.

POPULAR MNEMONICS

You've heard of *Popular Mechanics*, so why not *Popular Mnemonics?* Here are some of our favorites:

- *Please Excuse My Dear Aunt Sally*. For remembering the order of calculations in algebra (Parentheses, Exponents, Multiplication, Division, Addition, Subtraction).
- *My Very Educated Mother Just Served Us Nine Pizzas*. The order of the planets (Mercury, Venus, Earth, Mars, Jupiter, Saturn, Uranus, Neptune, Pluto).
- *Kings Play Catch Over Farmer Gray's Shed*. For remembering the proper order of the biological grouping in taxonomy (Kingdom, Phylum, Class, Order, Family, Genus, Species).
- *Divorced, Beheaded, Died, Divorced, Beheaded, Survived*. For remembering the fate of Henry VIII's six wives.

discernible able to be seen, recognized, or understood

And If That's Not Enough ...

If you use some or all of the test-studying tips we've provided here, but feel you need even more help to set yourself up for your next test or exam, consider the following steps:

1) *Consult with your instructor*. Always operate under the assumption that your instructor is not your enemy, but, rather, is there to help you. Most likely, your instructor has been planting clues in his or her lectures about what will be covered on upcoming tests, but, if you're very concerned about a test, by all means schedule a conference with your instructor to find out what you will be tested on. Remember that few instructors wish to surprise their students by testing them on material that has not been emphasized in class. After all, when students do poorly on an exam, it can reflect poorly on the instructor as well.

© Digital Vision

2) *Join or form a study group*. You've heard the expression "safety in numbers"? There is much truth to that. When you study with other people—one, two, or maybe three others— you may find that somebody else's knowledge picks up where yours ends. Within a group, the likelihood of important information falling through the cracks usually lessens.

© 2003 Stockbyte

3) *If need be, cram*. Cramming is a court of last resort but, in all fairness, it's a court that most of us have had to visit at some point or another. If you've left yourself with no other options, and

you absolutely have to cram, you should know that there's a right way to do it and a wrong way. Cramming does not mean panicking. To get the most out of cramming—which, mind you, will not be giving you the kind of test preparation you could have gotten if you proceeded in a more orderly fashion—you should take the following steps. First of all, preview the material you want to cover. Second, skim the relevant chapters for the main points. (As we said in our chapter on study skills, the main points of chapters are usually quite clearly telegraphed.) Don't read information that you don't have time to review. You've painted yourself into a corner, so what you can manage to accomplish at such a late date may be limited, but, at least, given that, you can try to make the best of it.

Test-Taking Strategies

Obviously, the kinds of study skills that we've been describing in this chapter constitute your first line of defense when taking tests. That said, there are any number of specific, useful, test-taking strategies that we would like discuss here. In general:

- Always allot sufficient time to get to the testing place *ahead* of schedule. Showing up in a sweaty panic is almost sure to result in impaired concentration and lost points.
- Read all test directions carefully. The time you spend reading the directions should be regarded as part of your overall allotted time. In other words, if you have 50 minutes to take an exam, you should reserve several minutes of that time for carefully reading the test directions.
- Do a little quick, simple math to figure out the time you have available to you. For instance, if you are taking a 50-minute test that has 50 multiple choice questions, it's simple enough to figure out that you have about a minute per question available to you. That means you shouldn't spend 10 minutes trying to figure out one question, and then play catch-up with the rest.
- Read over each question carefully before answering. Rereading questions can be a good form of insurance against wrong answers.
- If you are confused about a question, you are well within your rights to ask the instructor or proctor to try to clear things up for you. If he or she feels that it compromises the integrity of the exam to do so, you'll be told. On the other hand, your question might be completely legitimate and thus deserving of a legitimate answer.

- Hopefully, you'll have some time left over at the end of the exam to review your work. Proofread your answers, make the necessary corrections, and use all of your available time to pull your test into the best possible shape.
- Need we point out that your eyes should be on your own paper only?
- You may come across a question that throws you for a loop. Don't panic. Memory lapses can happen to anyone. Put that question aside for the moment and go on to the next one.

There are also some *specific* test-taking strategies that will help you deal with the various test formats you will encounter.

ESSAY TESTS

Some students enjoy essay questions; others dread them. Regardless of your predisposition, make note of these rules and tips:

- Start with an overview of the exam. As you are reading through the various essay questions, jot down whatever ideas come to your mind for each of the questions. It's important, after all, to never lose a good idea.
- Start with the easiest question first. Getting at least one essay under your belt will fuel your confidence to go on to the others.
- Begin your essay with an opening that is crisp and **cogent**. Don't "tell the people what you're going to tell them." Get into the meat of your answer right at the top.
- It may make sense for you to create some kind of outline for each of your essay questions. Such an outline will hold you to a structure that will allow your essay to stand strongly on its own.
- Back up your points with details—specific examples, statistics, or whatever you feel will give your answer the necessary **ballast**. To do this requires that you study well, you are fully prepared, and that your knowledge is at your fingertips … or, more accurately, in your frontal lobe.
- Be particularly aware of the directive words in the essay question itself. Words like "define," "illustrate," "explain," or "defend" will indicate what the instructor is looking for in terms of an answer.
- Even with time constraints, it is important to write legibly and in complete sentences.
- If time permits, proofread and edit your answers.

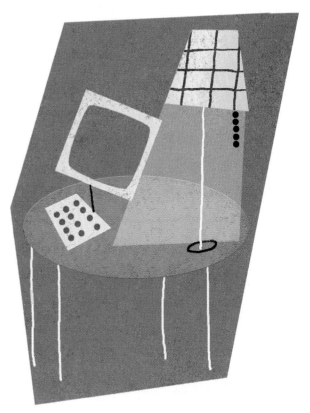

cogent forceful and convincing to the intellect and reason
ballast heavy material carried in the hold of a ship to give the craft increased stability

- Try not to leave any essays blank, even if you're running out of time. At the very least, if you run out of time, try to outline your points. A sympathetic instructor may give you some credit for showing that you have some kind of grasp on the answer.

OBJECTIVE TESTS

Is there a way to "out-think" those multiple choice and true-or-false tests? Maybe not entirely, but the following are some good approaches to keep in mind:

- Proceed in chronological order, starting with the first question. Don't jump around—you'll only confuse yourself and waste time later when you try to figure out what you've skipped. Mark any questions that stop you in your tracks, and return to those later.

- Read each question carefully. Grammatical inconsistencies between the question stem and the answer choice—like lack of subject-verb agreement, for instance—can often help you eliminate incorrect answers and leave you with a clearer choice for picking the right answer.

- The general rule of thumb is that your first answer is usually the correct one. Your brain is telling you to go in that direction and you should listen. Not that your brain is **infallible**, but the odds are definitely with you.

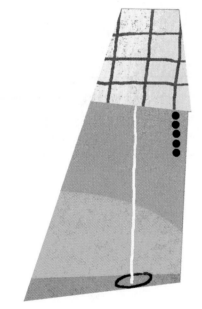

- If you're having trouble with a question, ask yourself if the answer you're leaning toward completely addresses the question. If the answer is only partially true, or true only part of the time, then it's probably not correct.

- Most instructors don't plant "trick questions" on tests. The "trick" in this case might be the one that your brain is playing on you. Maybe you're thinking *too* hard.

- Be suspicious of answers that contain negative or absolute words, like *always* or *never*. Try substituting a word like *seldom* or *sometimes* for *always* or *never*. If *seldom* or *sometimes* work, then you know that *always* or *never* cannot be correct.

- "All of the above" is often the right answer. If several of your answers work, it's very likely that "all of the above" deserves to be your pick.

- Always guess when there is no penalty to do so. If you will lose points for questions that are not answered, then why not make your best guess on any questions you are unsure of? Test takers often

infallible incapable of making a mistake

pick up more points than they lose with this method. (You can establish whether or not there is a penalty for unanswered questions by asking the instructor or proctor about this before the test begins.)

Conquering Test Anxiety

In our chapter on stress, we guessed that some of you might suffer from acute test anxiety. For those of you who qualify, we'd like to offer some suggestions on how to get beyond it.

A 10-STEP PROGRAM FOR OVERCOMING TEST ANXIETY

Here's how:

1) *Begin with preparation.* Even though we're sure you're aware of this on some level, we're going to say it again: if you're truly prepared for a test, your anxiety should be significantly diminished. On the other hand, if you haven't apportioned your time as you should have, and you've taken more than your share of study shortcuts, then it's perfectly understandable that you would be experiencing test anxiety.

2) *See if you can do a "dry run."* You know you have a problem—tests make you terribly anxious—so why not be forthright with your instructor about this? It's very likely that your instructor will allow you to take a practice test, which can go a long way toward boosting your confidence.

3) *Prepare yourself physically and mentally.* Think of taking a test as if it were a 5K race. If you were going to run a 5K race, surely you would do certain things to get yourself ready for it, wouldn't you? You'd try to sleep well for at least a few nights before the race. You'd eat healthy foods and keep your alcohol consumption to a minimum. Maybe you'd listen to some calming music, like Mozart or Celtic lullabies. Get into a serious mode for a major test the same way you would for a 5K race and it will definitely pay off.

4) *Give yourself time.* Again, don't rush. Running around right before a test will surely spike your stress level. Looking for a parking spot 5 minutes before you're supposed to be sitting in your seat at the testing place is a sure prescription for disaster. Get to campus 30 to 60 minutes ahead of test time, so that you can sit somewhere quietly, breathe, and get centered.

5) *Now is not the time to be social.* Yes, it's nice to see a friendly face when you're feeling nervous, but you may want to do your visiting in the hallway before the exam because once you enter the testing place, you'll probably be a lot better off sitting by yourself. That way, you'll be less susceptible to distractions and less likely to pick up on other people's test anxieties. Remember: anxiety is contagious. Avoid it like the plague.

6) *Face up to your worst fantasy.* Let's say you've done all of the above and anxiety still has you in a stranglehold. Spend a moment—just a moment—asking yourself what is the very worst thing that can happen if you fail. You'll have to retake the course? You'll be embarrassed? You'll have to defer other goals for a while? Is any of that so terrible that you should be putting yourself through this kind of misery?

7) *Use your anxiety.* Anxiety may not feel great, but it doesn't have to be a terrible thing. Actors routinely experience anxiety as they go on stage, but this does not generally impair their per-formances. Likewise, you can feel anxious before a test, but you can actually *use* your anxiety to boost you onto a higher level of awareness and alertness, so long as you understand the dynam-ics and don't let anxiety run away with the show.

8) *Remember your mind-over-matter techniques.* Some of the spe-cific techniques we discussed in our chapter on stress relief, like STOP THOUGHT, positive self-talk, and visualization, can be used in a test situation. Telling yourself, "I can do this, I can do this"—just like that Little Engine That Could—is a lot better than saying to yourself, "You're sunk. It's over. You're toast."

9) *Ignore the comings and goings of others.* Just because you see other people getting up and handing in their tests doesn't mean that you're falling behind. If you're working within the allotted test time, that's absolutely fine, and just because Joe Blow has whipped through his exam is no indication that he will do well and you won't. Don't worry about him. Just concentrate on your own work.

10) *Take a "time out" when you need it.* You may encounter mo-ments when you're feeling too overwhelmed by anxiety to func-tion. The words on the test sheet in front of you are swimming and your heart is beating at an unhealthy rate. This is when

you may need to take a "time out." Turn over your test, close your eyes, count to 10 or even 20 if you need to, practice some square breathing, and ride out the feeling. You should be in better shape to resume the test, with a clearer head, after you've tried this strategy.

Following this 10-step program should go a long way toward alleviating your test anxiety. As time goes on, you can build on your successes and become more resilient and stronger as you face each new test situation.

Contesting Your Grade

Tests and exams are developed by humans and hence, by their very nature, are imperfect. You may well encounter questions on a test that are poorly or vaguely phrased or that are, in fact, just dead wrong. If you think points have been unfairly taken off on a test or exam, by all means contest your case. There are very few instructors who would take **umbrage** over being questioned in a reasonable and rational way about some aspect of their test design. The problem is that too many students become overly emotional when arguing their points instead of bringing to bear the critical thinking skills they hopefully have been developing as part of their student experience.

In arguing your point, you need to proceed as if you were arguing a case in court. In other words, your **rationale** for whatever test answer you gave needs to be at least as strong as the basis for the instructor's asking the question in the first place. Where this situation differs from a court of law is that there is no jury. The decision is ultimately in the hands of the instructor, so the argument is weighted. You can only hope that the instructor will keep an open mind and wish to be fair, which is generally the case.

There are a few things you should definitely *not* say when you are contesting your grade. These include the following:

- "This is not what I really meant." Your instructor is not a psychic or a seer. If something was in your head but didn't make it onto your test paper, that's not a valuable argument.
- "A lot of people missed this question." Yes, a lot of people may have missed the question, and it's possible that they missed the question

umbrage resentment or annoyance, arising from some offense
rationale reasoning or principle that underlies or explains a particular course of action

Have you ever been in the position where you've contested a test grade with an instructor? Share your experiences with others in the class. How did you feel going into the situation? As you can recall it, what was your argument? How did the situation resolve itself? By sharing these memories, you can help others learn how to stand up for themselves in a constructive way, should such a situation arise.

© Digital Vision

because it was poorly designed, but just the fact alone that a lot of people missed it doesn't *prove* that it was a poorly designed question. It may simply have been a well-designed, very *hard* question.

- "I've never gotten this low a grade." Not a strong argument. There's always a first time for everything!

- "I'll never pass (get into medical school, law school, or substitute whatever frantic appeal applies)." That's your problem, and an instructor may feel sympathetic, but don't count on it.

If you use strong logic and critical thinking skills to make your argument, not only will your instructor be open to hearing you, but he or she may be very favorably impressed with the seriousness and intelligence that you bring to the situation.

When Failure Strikes

Most of us can look back to moments in our lives when tests were handed back and there was a great big D or—gulp!—F staring us in the eye. You remember what that felt like, don't you? Your stomach dropped, your heart leapt into your throat, your palms got sweaty, your extremities grew cold. Do you recall the "Fight or Flight" response we talked about in our chapter on stress? Getting a failing grade is a highly stressful situation, and your response may well be to flee to some secluded place where no one can witness your shame.

As perfectly normal as it is to react in this way to failure, it's also very important to understand that *everyone* fails at something at some time or another. People lose at elections and beauty pageants and at the Academy Awards. They get fired. Their romantic partners jilt them. They strike out and their team loses because of it. They don't live up to the expectations of others. Failure, as we said earlier in this book, is very much a normal part of life. The way a person reacts to failure, however, can be abnormal or unhealthy. The storm winds of shame that often swirl around failure do not have to be accepted as a natural and inevitable part of the process. You can fail at something without believing that you *are* a failure. Being able to make that distinction is a vital step in your personal growth.

When you've fallen short of the mark, and your palms start to sweat, we'd like you to try to keep the following thoughts in mind. They are comforting and constructive and remembering them in troubled times will do you a world of good.

- *Experience your shame and then shed it.* Shame—that feeling of being inadequate, unworthy, or somehow "bad"—is something that almost all people experience at some point or another. Shame, in and of itself, is not a crippling thing, but it can become so if you hold on to it. Shame can accumulate over time until it plays out as a major theme in your life. Experience your shame, look it straight in the eye, but be bigger than it.

- *Failure doesn't always require blame.* Sometimes it does. If a train engineer gets drunk and sends a train off the tracks, then he is to blame and he deserves to suffer guilt and shame. Failure often occurs, however, without blame playing any role whatsoever. A person may simply lack the aptitude to succeed in calculus, for instance. That is not the fault of that individual. That individual is not to blame. He may feel sorry or sad that he doesn't possess the innate skills to succeed in this subject, but he can redirect his efforts and energies to succeed in something else. Remember Howard Gardner's Theory of Multiple Intelligences (also in Chapter 3)? Someone who is not good at calculus might be brilliant at gymnastics or at party planning. There are so many different ways to be valuable and to succeed in this world.

- *Recognize that failure is just one stop on a local train.* When you're in a panic about failure, you tend to think of it as "the end of the line." It almost never is. Frank Sinatra and John Travolta are just two of the megastars who were said to be "washed-up" before they made their incredible comebacks. It is important to see failure as a **discrete** event, not as a syndrome or part of a pattern. The next stop on the train could be Adaptation, then Adjustment, then Recovery, and then Triumph. You just never know.

- *You can't fail if you don't try.* Let's imagine that you're taking a science or math course without having had much of a background in those subjects. That's a real reach for you, and it's good to reach. But sometimes, when we reach, we fall. It's nothing to be ashamed. Pick yourself up and move on.

- *The secret is in the postgame analysis.* Okay, the fact is you've messed up. You've made mistakes. Let's face it—you've failed. It hurts and it's a setback in terms of your immediate goals. But, if you work at it, you can probably gain some valuable insights from the experience as well. Let's say you've been fired from the part-time job you've been holding down. You're smarting from the rejection, but nevertheless you sit down with your friends or family and you

discrete completely separate and unconnected

talk it through. You examine all the facets of what went on—what you thought you were doing right and what you might have been doing wrong—and with the input of those you trust, it's very likely that you can come away from the experience with a real perspective on what happened. That's called growth, and there's no substitute for it.

The first time you fail—that first time you're fired or get an F or have somebody break off a relationship with you—can feel very raw and painful. The next time something like that happens, it may be less raw, less painful. If you understand that failure isn't the end of the world, but merely the end result of a specific action, you can move on, toughen your hide, and be less *afraid* of failure. And being less afraid of failure will very likely increase your chances for success.

CASE IN POINT: TINA HOOVER

On her 21st try, Tina Hoover finally passed the California State Bar exam. Hoover graduated from American College second in her class in July 1991. Like many of her classmates, she assumed she would pass the bar exam on her first try, but she didn't ... nor did she on her second, third, fourth, or *20th* effort. Often she missed by only a few points, and once by only one point. She invested a considerable amount of money in different review courses until she finally found one that really worked for her. The morning of her 21st try, she opened the test book and her heart flipped. It was a monster! She was told that there were audible groans throughout the room, but she didn't hear them—she had her earplugs in. This exam looked harder than any of the 20 she had previously sat through. Her heart raced, but, as her most recent review course

had instructed her, she should just "work the process." Using all of her concentration, Hoover proceeded through each part of the exam. She noted that the last word she wrote for each section was just as legible as the first word—a good sign. For one of the sections, it took Hoover almost a full 20 minutes to prepare herself for what she was going to write. She nearly panicked, but she remembered what her review course taught her—that some sections might require more outlining than others. Immersing herself in the "process," she was able to proceed. When she finished, and put down her pen, tears streamed down her face. A woman in front of her tried to console her, thinking that Hoover was crying from being overwhelmed, but in fact she was crying with joy that she had come through the test feeling so much in control.

When the test results were posted on the Internet a few months later, Hoover had a heart-rending moment: it said that she had not passed. Something inside of her, however, told her to wait for the official results to come in the mail. The envelope that arrived was no different in size or shape than all the disappointing ones that had come so many times before. But when Hoover opened it and read the letter, her life changed in a moment. She actually had passed the exam, after 20 tries, and is now Tina Hoover, Attorney-at-Law, sole practitioner. "I was not always a good student," she admits, "but I am committed to being a good lawyer."

Source: An amazing story. Celebration Bar Exam Review. Retrieved December 2, 2005, from http://www.celebration-bar-exam-review.com/amazing.htm

Cheating

One surefire prescription for failure is cheating. Even if you don't get caught, cheating is still a form of failure, inasmuch as it represents a moral failing. The ironic thing about cheating is that those who cheat generally wind up cheating themselves most of all. To begin with, you place yourself in a situation of real jeopardy. Most colleges and universities exact severe penalties, even including expulsion, against students who are caught cheating. And most colleges and universities do a pretty fair job of catching people who cheat. Prepackaged essays swiped off the Internet have a way of advertising themselves to savvy professors. You should not be so naïve as to think that your **duplicity** will go undetected. Is it really worth the anxiety? Beyond that, you, the student, are cheating yourself out of the learning experience that you need and that you're paying a lot of money for. Substituting someone else's paper for your own robs you of the knowledge and skills acquisition that you are in college to get in the first place.

Unfortunately, we live in a society where cheating has become quite routine. In recent years, con man journalists who file fake stories have **sullied** the reputations of newspapers like the *New York Times*. The sports world is filled with tales of athletes who take steroids or other performance-enhancing drugs. Cheating on your income tax or expense account is regarded as standard operating procedure in some circles, and *not* cheating is even regarded as wimpy in certain corporate cultures. Donald McCabe, professor of management and global business at Rutgers Business School and founding president of the Center for Academic Integrity, has noted a rise in cheating in academic circles. Some of his surveys of college students have actually shown a 30 to 35 percent increase in some types of cheating during the 1990s. "Cheating is harmful," says McCabe, "because it betrays your responsibility to the community, and it can make community standards fall apart."

[*Source:* The Center for Academic Integrity. Retrieved June 15, 2005, from http://www.academicintegrity.org]

Cheating is like eating junk food. It can quickly become addictive, it appears to satisfy a need but it doesn't really fill you up, and you wind up paying the price for it. Even though it may seem like a quick solution, it's really a trap. Avoid it, and you won't be sorry.

duplicity the fact of being deceptive, dishonest, or misleading
sullied tarnished, damaged

What Did We Learn?

As we said at the beginning of the chapter, one predictor of doing well on tests is retaining the information you studied. Let's see how you do on this chapter:

1. Name a way of studying for a test that features an audio component. How about one with a visual component? Can you think of one with a motor activity connected to it?

2. Explain "chunking."

3. If cramming proves absolutely unavoidable, what are some steps you can take to make it a more productive experience?

4. Cite at least three general test-taking strategies that will help you with your testing performance.

5. What are some steps you can take to improve your handling of essay test questions?

6. True or False? Your first answer is usually the correct one.

7. Should you guess on an objective question test?

8. Name at least five of the Top 10 tips for overcoming test anxiety.

9. What are the four things you should never say when contesting a grade with an instructor?

10. What are five constructive things you can tell yourself when failure strikes?

Bibliography

Educational Testing Service. (2004). *Reducing test anxiety*. Princeton, NJ: Educational Testing Service.

Newman, E. (1996). *No more test anxiety: Effective steps for taking tests & achieving better grade*. Los Angeles: Learning Skills Publications.

Moving Right Along

So far in this book we've been looking at ways that you can boost your student performance—getting organized, managing your stress, improving your study skills, learning how to connect with your creativity, becoming comfortable in a test situation, and more. Now we'd like to move on to another area that all students and citizens of the world must develop—your social skills and the way you interact with people. As a student, you will be involved in group projects, you will be involved in challenging living situations, and you will need to foster positive relationships with your teachers, your advisors, and other important people in your life. In our next chapter, we will be looking at these issues to see where and how you can improve.

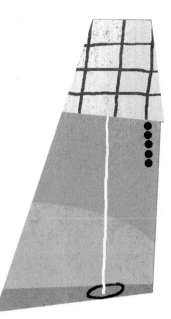

Rozakis, L. (2002). *Test-taking strategies & study skills for the utterly confused*. New York: McGraw-Hill.

Tobias, S. (1995). *Succeed with math: Every student's guide to conquering math anxiety*. New York: College Board.

Links

Mnemonics. Retrieved December 2, 2005, from http://www.happychild.org.uk/acc/tpr/mne/

Study guides and strategies: Cramming. Retrieved December 2, 2005, from http://www.studygs.net/tstprp7.htm

Test-taking strategies. Retrieved December 2, 2005, from http://www.d.umn.edu/student/loon/acad/strat/test_take.html

Test-taking strategies. Retrieved December 2, 2005, from http://php.unc.edu/ovcsa/caps/index.php?option=com_content&task=view&id=71&Itemid=0

Word Smart

Test yourself on these:

accretion

ballast

cogent

discernible

discrete

duplicity

germane

infallible

proverbial

rationale

sullied

umbrage

WORKS AND PLAYS
WELL WITH OTHERS

Remember back, if you will, to your very early school days. Your report card probably had a section that "graded" you on your interaction with other children. Can you recall what your teachers had to say? Did they find you aggressive? Did you hoard toys? Were you shy about joining into group play? Did you throw fits if you didn't get your way? Or were you a natural leader who invented games that other children found captivating**?**

Well, guess what? Just as you were assessed in kindergarten, so shall you be judged in college and beyond on how well—or how poorly—you interact with others. As a student, you have to be able to work cooperatively with teachers, advisors, coaches, and counselors. Is that a problem for you? Do you find authority figures threatening? What about your peers—how do you interact with them? If you're living away from home for the first time, dealing with a roommate may be an early challenge. If you're an older student, do you feel uncomfortable around those who are younger? Do you find yourself in classrooms marked by a diversity you have not encountered before? Being a student means being involved in group projects—reports, lab assignments, performances—and these all require cooperation, shared responsibility, and

captivating attracting and holding somebody's attention by charm or other pleasing or irresistible features

mutual respect. You can't afford to let your social issues get in your way.

And then, of course, looming in your future is your involvement in the work world, where a whole set of social challenges awaits you. So much of your personal success will be determined by how well you do as part of a team. Will you be able to convince others that you can make valuable contributions and be counted on to assume your responsibilities? Will you know when to talk and when to keep quiet? Will you be able to hear feedback and offer it constructively? These are big questions that lie ahead.

In this chapter, we'll be providing you with some very useful tools that can help you improve in this important area of your life. You should know, right at the top, that there is *always* room for improvement when it comes to getting along with others. As the world becomes more complex and more complicated, most of us could use some help with interpersonal dynamics, and we intend to offer that help.

Successful social interaction has much to do with good communication, and we will be focusing on that in the next chapter. In this chapter, however, we'd like to discuss such issues of social dynamics as assertiveness, anger management, conflict resolution, giving and receiving feedback, and diversity, but let's begin with personality and attitude, which will influence all of your interactions.

Personality and Attitude

In Chapter 1, we discussed issues of personality and behavior, including self-esteem and one's orientation toward optimism or pessimism. These issues naturally emerge all over again in the context of how a person interacts with others. As we said earlier, while we may not be able to essentially change the personalities we are born with, we can certainly alter our attitudes and actions—through introspection, the careful consideration of constructive input, and a desire to do better when it comes to interacting with others. We can learn how to manage our anger, how to resolve conflicts, how to give and receive feedback, and more.

One of the fundamental ways we have to classify human beings is to judge whether they are introverted or extroverted. It is inappropriate to assign either positive or negative values to either of these orientations. Extroverts don't automatically become back-slappers and introverts don't have to become shrinking violets that hide behind doors. Still, these *are* very different ways to approach the world, and so it is useful to understand how they work.

The following traits are characteristic of introverts:

- They don't mind (or may even prefer) to be by themselves.
- They need physical space and dislike being crowded.
- They need time to reflect on issues and questions.
- They prefer one-on-one interactions to larger gatherings.
- They are often mistaken for being shy or **aloof**.

Extroverts are characterized by these traits:

- They seek social interaction.
- Being around other people recharges and refuels them.
- They rarely choose to be alone.

aloof uninvolved or unwilling to become involved with other people or events, often out of a sense of lofty superiority to them

- They expect and offer immediate answers to questions.
- When faced with a problem, they will want to talk it out, seeking input and guidance from others.
- They do not feel the need for "processing" time and will want to share news and experiences immediately.

Understanding your personality orientation, enjoying your strengths, and accepting your limitations are important steps in your efforts to get along well with others.

FOOD FOR THOUGHT: SOCIAL ANXIETY

Being introverted is one thing; being painfully shy is quite another. Shyness is a handicap that afflicts millions of Americans. In fact, studies have shown that nearly 50 percent of the adult population in the United States is believed to be shy, and public speaking is the nation's number one phobia. Interestingly enough, some of the most famous people in the world and throughout history have identified shyness as a personal problem they've had to grapple with. We're talking about such individuals as Abraham Lincoln, Eleanor Roosevelt, Albert Einstein, Lucille Ball, Elvis Presley, Bob Dylan, Brad Pitt, Cher, Harrison Ford, Jim Carrey, Julia Roberts, Tom Cruise … the list goes on. Ask yourself the questions below to determine if shyness is a problem for you. If it is, check out the Internet links we have provided at the end of the chapter for ideas about where to get help with this problem.

If you've answered "Yes" to a fair share of the below, then your ability to enjoy the world around you may be seriously impaired. Don't allow that to happen. Social anxiety is hardly unique to you, and there are behavior modification techniques that are easy to learn and that can make a world of difference.

Source: Adapted from Painfully shy: No more. Retrieved December 5, 2005, from http://www.markway.com/quiz/shyness.htm

---

How Shy Are You?

☐ Yes ☐ No   Do you feel self-conscious in social situations?

☐ Yes ☐ No   Do you doubt your ability to interact with others?

☐ Yes ☐ No   Can certain situations—a party where you don't know anyone; a job interview—actually make you physically ill?

☐ Yes ☐ No   Do you think up excuses or even lie to avoid social situations that worry you?

☐ Yes ☐ No   Does giving a report in front of the class feel like torture?

JUST SAY "NO"

As you may have **surmised**, extroverts tend to be natural leaders while introverts are more likely to become followers—or, at least, quieter leaders. It is naturally easier for a leader to say no—to put his or her foot down and to call the shots. On the other hand, followers don't have to be meek or submissive, but often they run that risk. In either case—whether you're a leader or follower—the issue of saying "no" can be problematic. Leaders may be inclined to take on too much, while followers may find it difficult to assert themselves. Healthy assertiveness plays a very big role in how you interact with other people. So, you ask, what is assertiveness and how can you become good at it?

Assertiveness lies in between passivity, which connotes weakness, and aggression, which is characterized by self-centered, inconsiderate, hostile, and arrogant behavior. In other words, to be assertive means being able to stand up for yourself in such a way that you can get what you want and need without alienating those around you.

© Image 100 Ltd.

Developing a healthy assertive attitude can help you achieve the following:

- It will enable you to speak up for yourself, to ask for help when you need it, and to demand the respect you're entitled to as a human being of worth and significance.
- It will allow you to express negative emotions without anger or recrimination.
- It will help you to show positive emotions like pride and affection, and will enable you to give and receive compliments comfortably.
- It will empower you to question authority or tradition.

surmised reached a conclusion based on intuitive feeling

- It will foster your ability to deal with minor irritations before they become major aggravations.

One of the best ways we know to develop healthy assertiveness is to use the "I feel … I want … I will" system. Read the Student Talk section presented here to see how this worked for Greg.

Assertive responses to problems sound measured, dignified, intelligent, caring, and sturdy. Let's look at a couple of situations where assertive responses can save the day.

- *You've been introduced to someone at a party but you didn't catch the person's name*. A poor response would be, "You said your name so softly I couldn't hear you." This has the ring of aggression to it, as if you are attributing some fault to the other person. A better, more assertive response would be to say, "I'm sorry. I didn't hear your name. Could you tell it to me again?" No one will take offense at that, and, as soon as possible, you can make a point of using the person's name in a more natural context.
- *Your lab partner doesn't uphold his end of the arrangement*. A poor response would be to say, "You're such a screw-up. I don't know how I got saddled with you. If we get a bad grade, it'll be your fault." This kind of response doesn't offer opportunities for dialogue. A constructively assertive response—always using "I," instead of "you," which is a cardinal rule of assertiveness—would be to say something like, "I'm disappointed with your attitude and performance regarding this assignment. If we're going to continue to work together, you're going to have to pull your weight. Let me know if there's a problem with that or if there's anything else you feel I should know about." Such an assertive response is fair, to-the-point, tough-minded, and sets limits in an appropriate way.

Various factors can affect your capacity to be assertive. Socialization is one of the most significant of these factors. Women are often socialized as girls to *not* assert themselves. Culture and environment can also affect your assertiveness. People talk about "pushy" New Yorkers who seem to have no trouble making their way to the front of the line, while people from other parts of the country, like the South and the Midwest, may be much more **reticent** when it comes to expressing their feelings and their needs. And, of course, people from other countries who may have language difficulties or cultural differences can have special problems asserting themselves.

reticent reserved; reluctant to speak freely

STUDENT TALK: *THE THREE-STEP ASSERTIVENESS PLAN*

"My soccer coach in high school was a real mentor for me. He taught me how to stand up for myself, but in ways where I wouldn't look like I was some kind of crazy road-rage person. He taught me this three-step system, where the key phrases are 'I feel … I want … I will.' That's a way you can analyze and handle almost any situation. For instance, let's say you're on a team and you're not getting into any games. You say to yourself, 'I *feel* like I'm not being paid attention to.' So, right off the bat, you've established the situation in a clear, rational way. Next you go on to 'I want,' as in 'I *want* to have enough time on the field so that it feels fair to me.' Then you move on to 'I will,' as in 'I *will* tell the coach about my feelings and we'll see what happens.' That 'I feel … I want … I will' structure will really help you get a handle on almost anything."

—Greg A., 19, Albuquerque, NM.

The capacity to become constructively assertive does not develop overnight. Like some of the other issues of personal growth that we've talked about in this book, assertiveness will start to feel more natural the more you practice it. There are several important tips about assertiveness, however, that you should always keep in mind. Consider the following:

- Confront another person only when you feel that you are in control of your emotions. Do not confront anyone in the heat of conflict. If you do, you are liable to say things you will regret. Some wise person once said, "Speak when you're angry and you're sure to give the finest speech you'll ever regret."

- Stay away from the written word when you're feeling angry. Don't send the other person an E-mail or a letter "summing up" the situation. Such an E-mail or letter could very well become Exhibit A in the **dissolution** of your relationship.

- Threats are one thing, consequences another. If, for instance, you have a friend who is in the habit of standing you up, a threat might be, "If you do that one more time, I'll never speak to you again." But are you really ready to follow through on that threat? Don't make any statements you can't get behind. Perhaps a better response to the situation would be to present the offender with a natural consequence, as in, "I see that you're really having difficulty making plans right now, so why don't we hold off on getting together until you can let me know if things have cleared up and you can be a little more sensitive to my feelings?"

Handling Feedback

Another touchy subject regarding social dynamics is giving and receiving feedback. For the purposes of this discussion, it is important that we differentiate feedback from criticism. Too often, they are thought of as being one and the same. Feedback is meant to be positive, whereas criticism can carry a negative connotation. As a student, you are on a learning curve, and so it is completely normal for you to be regularly receiving feedback. Do you participate in class? Do you come to class prepared? Do you cut classes? Do you seem frivolous? Easily bored? Do you work to your full potential? Do you go the extra mile to make each assignment something special? Ask yourself these questions, for they

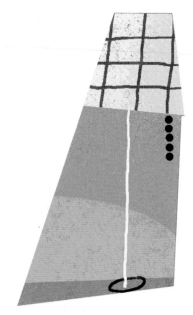

dissolution disintegration

will be asked of you, and, if you're just entering college, be prepared for the fact that the assessments you receive might be far more demanding than what you're used to. Oftentimes, students will enter college and, even though they've been getting A's and B's in Biology or French or English all through high school, suddenly they're looking at C's or even D's. This kind of shift can shake up a person, but you should also be aware that these low grades serve as a wake-up call to get you to work harder, in ways that are more creative, more thorough, and more engaged.

As a student, there are times when you may also be called upon to give feedback and criticism, usually to another student. In a writing class, for instance, it is quite customary for students to exchange papers and critique each other. You might also be asked to critique a student presentation, or you might receive a student critique of your own work. Approaching situations in which you give or receive feedback can be highly charged, depending on your history with such situations. For instance, family members or teachers may have hurt you at an early age by belittling your efforts, and so the issue of feedback is a sensitive one for you. Now is the time to learn constructive ways to give and absorb feedback and criticism. To that end, consider these principles when you are receiving feedback:

- *Start out by listening.* Make eye contact and ask questions in order to confirm that you're really hearing what you think you're hearing.
- *Don't rush to your own defense.* Always start by listening. Assuming a defensive posture can deflect potentially useful feedback. It's true that the feedback might not make you feel great at first, but, if you

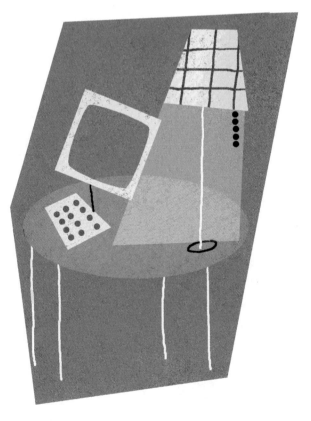

can hear what's being said, and if you agree with it, then perhaps you can incorporate these ideas and suggestions and achieve more than you would have otherwise.

- *Join forces with the person who's giving you the feedback.* Approach the situation as an opportunity for real collaboration. If you can come up with some ideas of your own as to how you can improve your work, you may very well impress the person you're conferring with.

- *Get a second opinion if necessary.* If you feel that the feedback is unfair, then you may want to check in with others to hear what they have to say. For instance, let's imagine that the manager of the store where you've been working calls you "disorganized" or "lazy." Instead of going into a funk or a fury, a better next step would be to have a conversation with someone you really trust. Then you can ask the tough questions: "Do you think I'm lazy? Disorganized? Is my manager off-base or should I be paying attention to this?"

While receiving feedback can be difficult, the act of giving feedback is no picnic either. It can be truly challenging to provide another person with feedback in a way that feels good to both parties. Keep these pointers in mind:

- *Ask first.* Unless you're in a tightly scripted classroom situation where the other party knows that you're going to be offering feedback, you should first ask the other person if it's all right to offer input on his or her work. If the person says no, then back off.

- *When giving criticism and feedback, focus on what the other person can realistically change.* If, for instance, you're giving feedback on an oral report that is being presented by another student, and if that student has a heavy foreign accent, it won't do a bit of good to say, "I couldn't understand a word you said because of your accent."

- *Try to be as specific as you can with your feedback.* If you're evaluating someone's stage performance, for instance, you might say something like, "I felt you were a little reluctant to go with the physical comedy in the beginning." That's a lot different than just saying, "You weren't funny."

- *Always include some positive comments.* Nobody wants to hear bad news alone. Temper your criticisms with some praise ... and usually there's *something* for you to hold up in a positive light.

- *Solicit a self-critique from the other person.* Asking something like, "How did *you* feel about the job you did here?" can be a much more fruitful and less painful way to initiate dialogue.

Anger Management

Sometimes situations break down to the point where we can no longer proceed in a calm, even way and, instead, we find ourselves in the grip of anger. Your so-called friend has just stood you up for the third time in a row. Your little brother got ink on your best shirt. Your girlfriend was flirting with one of your best friends. Whatever....

If you haven't developed certain important interpersonal skills, like assertiveness, you'll probably be more likely to find yourself in a situation where your anger is getting the better of you. Knowing how to deal with anger in a way that is not destructive to others or to yourself is very important. Some people repress anger and wind up suffering from headaches or stomach problems as a result. That's not good. Others go into a rage—those seizures when seemingly normal people flip out and start throwing around chairs and potted plants. So how can we manage anger in a way that is healthy and effective? Here are some good ideas:

- *An ounce of prevention is worth a pound of cure*. If you know what pushes your buttons, then don't allow those buttons to be pushed. Let's say you have a friend who always keeps you waiting. You agree to go to a movie with her. She keeps you waiting on a street corner, you miss the film, and you're seeing red. The alternative? Tell her that you'll each buy your own tickets, you'll wait for her in the lobby until 10 minutes before the show starts, and then you'll take a seat and save one for her for whenever she gets there.

- *Stop the action*. You've probably heard that old **bromide** about counting to 10 until your anger subsides. Hey—it's not such a bad idea. Breathing deeply can work too, as can going for a run, doing 25 push-ups, or whatever it is that will break the cycle of your anger.

- *Don't throw fat on the fire with words like "never" or "always."* Fights become ever so much worse when you start tossing around words like *never*—"You *never* hear me when I'm talking to you"—or *always*—"You *always* walk away from me when I'm talking to you." Try to avoid such words, and speak simply with honesty and genuine feeling instead.

- *Take your "angry" temperature*. How angry *are* you anyway? Some people grow up in families where everyone is always yelling about something. Other people grow up in families where, if someone raises their voice, it's a major event. If you have a fight with someone you love or even like, do a postmortem on it. How angry were

bromide a saying that lacks originality or significance

you really? How did it feel? You got over it, didn't you? Anger is a normal part of life. Being afraid of it—or being addicted to it—is unnecessary and counterproductive.

CONFLICT RESOLUTION

Anger happens … and then there's the making up. Knowing how to end an angry episode in a way that is graceful and that can maintain positive feelings between two or more individuals is a wonderful skill to possess. Here are some good thoughts about how to resolve conflicts as they come up:

- *Don't take it personally.* Even if you *have* taken it personally, try to get over it. You should realize that people say things because they're having a bad day or their car wouldn't start or they had a fight with their significant other or who knows what? It's not always about you—you might just have caught some flak because you were standing in the wrong place at the wrong time. Let it roll off you, if you can.
- *Walk it off … work it off … laugh it off.* Maybe you really *don't* have to have it out with the other person. Maybe that person has made you angry, but perhaps a walk around the block, a glazed doughnut, or a good laugh checking out *The Onion* on the Internet will do the trick. At least give it a try.…
- *Again, always use the "I" word, not "You."* As in the case of anger management, it is infinitely preferable to frame your discussion using a first-person point of view, not a second-person. In other words, a statement like, "I felt very upset when you said that to me" is a lot more constructive than saying, "You deliberately said that to hurt me." What's more, the other person can understand your feelings that way without feeling accused.
- *Try to hold on to whatever is good.* Before, after, and, if at all possible, during a conflict, try to share a good feeling with the opposing party. Telling somebody something good about him or her can totally alter the direction of a conflict. For instance, try saying something like, "Ralph, you always speak what's on your mind and I admire that about you, but I think you might have misunderstood what I was trying to say here." Ralph, if he's at all human, is going to respond to that positive thing you've said and will be much more inclined to mend fences.
- *Make a direct appeal for peace to the other person.* When wolves are fighting, one of them will expose his jugular to the other as a sign of submission. This immediately ends the conflict. We're not

suggesting that you do the same, but something akin to it wouldn't hurt. Saying to the other person, "I could really use your help to figure a way out of this problem," indicates that you aren't in it for the big win. And that is a message that goes far.

Dealing with Diversity

One aspect of your life that may change drastically when you enter college is that you will be exposed to many new kinds of people. If you come from a small town, let's say, where everyone looks and sounds the same, and you arrive at your big state university, you're bound to encounter people of different races, religions, and lifestyles, and that can take some getting used to. By the same token, if you come from a big city—or, particularly, an ethnic concentration within a big city—you may never have met a person who comes from a small town. The challenge and the excitement of college is meeting and becoming comfortable with all kinds of people.

© Digital Vision

The fact is that our society is becoming increasingly diverse. Looking into the future, the U.S. Census Bureau is predicting that Hispanics and Asians will increase their proportions of the overall U.S. population by almost 50 percent in the next 50 years. The non-Hispanic white population percentage in the United States is actually projected to decline during this period and will comprise just 50.1 percent of the total population in 2050, compared with 69.4 percent in 2000.

This is obviously a huge change in the world as we know it, and it will be a major topic in the lives of us all. Your experience with diversity will be an experience in growth. You're bound to make mistakes but, with basic good will, you should be able to enjoy meaningful and productive relationships with all kinds of people. Keep these key guidelines in mind:

- *Approach everything as a learning opportunity*. People coming to America from other cultures have a lot to learn about their adopted land, but remember: it's a two-way street. Meeting people from different backgrounds is a wonderful way for you to expand your horizons, to grow, and to become a real citizen of the world.

- *Be proactive about your learning*. Many schools have clubs that promote diversity, like clubs for Asian students, African-American students, and gay–straight alliances. Most of these clubs hold educational and/or social functions. Join in! Everyone is welcome, and it's a great way to become comfortable with people from different sorts of backgrounds.

- *Acknowledge your own stereotypical thinking*. Chances are, down the line, someone may accuse you of stereotypical thinking or bias. Don't just get your back up. Listen. There may be a lot of truth in what the other person is saying, and this is your opportunity to learn.

- *Seek common ground*. Sure, you may feel different from someone who comes from Malaysia or someone who's gay or someone who's Jewish or Muslim. But you should be able to find ample opportunities to share common ground with such people. Working side by side in a lab, playing on a field together, acting on a stage together … these are all situations that will allow you to form the kinds of bonds that break down barriers.

As we've indicated, becoming comfortable with diversity is a matter of growth. Growth doesn't happen overnight, except in fairy tales like Jack and the Beanstalk. Take your time, be open, and growth will happen.

Working with Teachers

Before we leave this chapter on working and playing with others, we just wanted to spend a moment or two discussing ways to get along with people who are very important in your life right now: your teachers. Perhaps at an earlier stage in your life you were intimidated by teachers or were resentful of their authority. Now it's time to correct that attitude and to view teachers as human beings with whom you are collaborating toward your educational goals. Consider these pointers to help you achieve rewarding relationships with your professors, teachers, and instructors:

- *Form personal connections with your teachers*. Talk about your interests with them. Maybe you'll find something in common—a love of fly fishing, Martin Scorsese films, yoga—that can serve as a building block for a more meaningful connection.

- *Be an active participant in the classroom*. Teaching is not easy, and one of the most difficult aspects of the job can be getting a roomful of students to come alive and take part in a discussion. Teachers are very aware of students who really involve themselves in classroom discussion and will usually reward them in some way for their efforts. The key is to be prepared ... and be awake!

- *Teachers are people too*. Like the rest of us, they have their good days and their bad days. If they seem irritable or distracted or **lackluster**, tell yourself that maybe they had a domestic quarrel or they're coming down with a cold or they're dealing with some aggravating work issue outside the classroom. It happens.

We could go on and on regarding the subject of social interaction ... and we have! We've covered a lot of ground in this chapter, and we hate to leave it, because there's a good deal more we could talk about. On the other hand, we're anxious to get on to our next subject: Chapter 11: Say It ... Hear It. Come to think of it, that subject also has a lot to do with social interaction.

lackluster lacking energy, excitement, enthusiasm, or passion

What Did We Learn?

Test yourself on the following questions to see what you remember from this chapter:

1. What traits characterize introverts?
2. What traits characterize extroverts?
3. What does it mean to be "assertive"?
4. Name four or five benefits that come with developing assertiveness.
5. What factors can affect a person's ability to develop assertiveness?
6. What's the difference between feedback and criticism?
7. Name four principles to keep in mind when receiving feedback.
8. Name four points to remember when giving feedback.
9. Cite four basic principles that can help you manage anger.
10. Name five fundamental concepts of anger management.
11. What guidelines should you keep in mind regarding your approach to diversity?
12. What are three things you can do to develop positive relationships with your teachers?

Bibliography

Bower, S. A., & Bower, G. H. (1991). *Asserting yourself: A practical guide for positive change*. Boston: Addison-Wesley.

Laney, M. O. (2002). *The introvert advantage: How to thrive in an extrovert world*. New York: Workman Publishing Company.

Littauer, F. (1992). *Personality plus: How to understand others by understanding yourself*. Grand Rapids, MI: Revell.

Markway, B., & Markway, G. (2003). *Painfully shy: How to overcome social anxiety and reclaim your life*. New York: St. Martin's Griffin.

Schiraldi, G. R., & Kerr, M. H. (2002). *The anger management sourcebook*. New York: McGraw-Hill, 2002.

Seashore, C. N. (1991). *What did you say? Giving and receiving feedback*. North Attleboro, MA: Douglas Charles Press.

Weeks, D. (1994). *The eight essential steps to conflict resolution*. New York: Jeremy P. Tarcher.

Links

Assertiveness training. Retrieved December 5, 2005, from http://mentalhelp.net/psyhelp/chap13/chap13e.htm

Controlling anger before it controls you. Information from the American Psychiatric Association. Retrieved December 5, 2005, from http://www.apa.org/pubinfo/anger.html

Diversity Web. Retrieved December 5, 2005, from http://www.diversityweb.org/

Giving and Receiving Feedback. Retrieved December 5, 2005, from http://www.selfhelpmagazine.com/articles/growth/feedback.html

SP/SAA. Social Phobia/Social Anxiety Association. Retrieved December 5, 2005, from. http://www.socialphobia.org/

The Conflict Resolution Information Source. Retrieved December 5, 2005, from http://v4.crinfo.org/

Word Smart

The following words can help to enrich your vocabulary:

- aloof
- bromide
- captivating
- dissolution
- lackluster
- reticent
- surmise

SAY IT ... HEAR IT

As we said in Chapter 10, the quality of your interaction with others will depend largely on your ability to communicate effectively. If you have a hard time hearing other people, or making yourself heard, then you really can't expect your relationships to be as meaningful or as satisfying as they should be. Your ability to hear other people and to express yourself will also play a critical role in your academic pursuits.

Your first experience with communication began as soon as you were born, with your parents. Mothers and fathers who understand how to communicate with their babies, starting in infancy with reflective cooing and "baby talk," prepare their children for rewarding interactions with others. Parents who block out their children's voices or who speak gruffly or abusively can inhibit healthy socialization. But no matter what kinds of lessons you received early in life, you can help make up for lost opportunities by educating yourself now about the fundamentals of communication. So let's look at those fundamentals to see what you can do to improve your communication skills.

NONVERBAL LANGUAGE

When we talk about "language," most of us immediately think of spoken or written language, but the fact is that human beings continually pour out reams of communication without speaking or writing a single word. Our facial expressions, our posture, and how we use our hands can be even

REFLECTIONS: *YOUR HISTORY*

When you were growing up, what was it like to communicate in your family? Did people actually sit down to talk with each other? Did they listen? Were books read to you as a child? Write a paragraph or two reflecting on the history of communication in your home. Consider the positives and the negatives. What could have been done to improve communication? How do you feel that your family's habits around communication have helped you or hindered you in the world at large? Even now, as you reflect on this subject, do you feel that the lines of communication with those you love are open enough to talk about these things?

OPEN FOR DISCUSSION: *SPEAKING UP*

In a short, honest, written assessment, rate your speaking skills. Do you speak too fast? Too slowly? Do you mumble? Are you **strident**? When you've finished with your assessment, exchange your writing with another member of the class. (It's probably best, in this situation, not to exchange with a friend, but, rather, with a more objective party.) Take turns reading each other's assessments out loud, and then write a very short critique of the other person's speaking skills. Don't be cruel and say something like, "You sound like a foghorn on a stormy night." Be honest but compassionate. After all, nobody's perfect.

more expressive of our feelings than our words. That said, it's important to watch our gestures just as closely as we watch our words. If you don't want to appear hostile or aggressive when you're talking to someone, then don't fold your arms across your chest or jut out your jaw. Similarly, to avoid seeming bored, don't twiddle your thumbs or tap on the table.

Given our multicultural society, you will also want to be sensitive to the differing styles of nonverbal communication that exist from one cultural group to another. Certain nonverbal communications are universally understood—a smile or a frown means the same in Albania as it does in Alabama—but other nonverbal communications are understood in entirely different ways across the cultural spectrum. For instance, crossing your fingers in the United States **denotes** a wish for good luck. In parts of Asia, however, crossing your fingers can convey a sexual connotation.

Verbal Communication

As important as nonverbal communication may be, we ultimately *do* open our mouths—for better or worse. So much of the impression we make on the world comes from the way we express ourselves with our spoken language. Think about how you express yourself. How do you sound to your own ear?

SPEECH PROBLEMS

Obviously, we're not all planning to go into the communications field and so we don't need to cultivate the polished speaking tones of a TV news anchorperson. Many people regard speech as just another

denotes acts as a sign or representation
strident harsh, loud, grating, or shrill

Researchers have identified four primary areas of nonverbal communication.

- *Kinesics.* Kinesics is a nonverbal behavior that is connected to movement. Researchers P. Ekman and W. V. Friesen describe five forms of kinesics: *emblems* (nonverbal messages that have a verbal counterpart, like the "V" for victory); *illustrators* (nonverbal movements that illustrate what is being said, as in hand gestures); *affective displays* (primarily facial movements that display emotions, as in frowns, smiles, etc.); *regulators* (nonverbal signs that regulate, modulate, and maintain the flow of speech during a conversation, as in nodding); and *adaptors* (changes in posture or other movements, like slouching or resting one's chin on one's hand).

- *Proxemics.* The term *proxemics*, coined by researcher Edward T. Hall, refers to the "perception and use of space." *Body space*—the distance deemed appropriate in social intercourse between two people—is one example of proxemics. Hall identified four bodily distances: *intimate* (0 to 18 inches); *personal-casual* (1.5 to 4 feet); *social-consultive* (4 to 10 feet); and *public* (10 feet and beyond). Hall noted that different cultures set different norms for body space, and that standing too close or too far away can lead to misunderstandings and even suspicion and disharmony, based on these cultural standards.

- *Occulesics.* The study of the way the eyes are used during communication, occulesics is also culturally determined. In the United States, we are suspicious of people who "don't look us in the eye." In other parts of the world, however, it is considered rude or **presumptuous** to establish eye contact with a person you don't know well, and thus, lowering one's gaze is a common sign of respect or deference.

- *Haptics.* Haptics, a nonverbal behavior identified by psychologist Richard Heslin, deals with manners of touching in different societies. One prominent example of a haptic action is the handshake, which can be interpreted in widely divergent ways depending on the cultural context.

Source: Stephan Dahl's Web site. Retrieved January 6, 2005, from http://Stephan.dahl.at/nonverbal/kinesics.html

expression of one's overall personal style, and they may think it's cool to mumble or to barely move their lips when they have something to say. While it's true that we're all entitled to adopt whatever personal style we choose, you should also recognize that your personal style could become a seriously limiting factor in your life. Covering yourself with tattoos, piercing yourself in unlikely places, wearing your pants halfway down your rear, slurring your speech … these are all manifestations of a personal style that can seem "cool" when you're 16 but considerably less so when you're 26. So when you choose the emblems of your personal style, be careful not to get trapped in a situation that you might wind up regretting. (Or, otherwise put, temporary tattoos have a lot to be said for them.)

The mumbling and "you know … like … uh" habits that **pervade** your speech today may become a handicap tomorrow. When you interview

presumptuous unduly confident or bright
pervade to be present throughout

© Image 100 Ltd.

for a job, for instance, you'll want the interviewer to be able to understand what you're saying. Ultimately, personal style aside, most of us cannot afford to have points taken off for speech problems or any other externals that limit the way people see us. Some of the more common speech problems, with suggestions for what you can do about them, are outlined here.

- *Poor enunciation.* This is a problem that will quickly drive your listeners to distraction. Think about it—have you ever found yourself in a situation where you've had to repeatedly say to the person who's speaking, "Excuse me. I didn't catch what you were saying. Would you mind repeating that?" Maddening, isn't it? Poor enunciation can take the form of mumbling or of sloppy speech, as when you continually drop the "g's" on verbs like "going," "thinking," or "walking." Closely related to poor enunciation is speech that is too rapid for the average person to decipher. Now we're not going to suggest that you do what the Greek orator Demosthenes did—practice enunciation with marbles in your mouth—but if, in fact, you are motivated to improve your enunciation, you can do so by studying your face in the mirror as you speak. Are your lips moving when you come to those final "g's" or are they so barely opened that you seem to be imitating a ventriloquist? You can improve your communication skills by asking a friend or family member to listen as you speak and then tell you where you went wrong. Keep in mind that poor enunciation can be a habit, and habits are never easy to break.

- *Over reliance on fillers*. One of the characteristics that people often note about Senator Hilary Rodham Clinton is that she can spool out entire paragraphs of seamlessly spoken language in perfectly formed sentences and even paragraphs. Most of us cannot do anything of the sort. We find it difficult to articulate our thoughts, and, as we proceed haltingly with what we have to say, we hem and haw and tend to rely excessively on "fillers" like "um" or "like" or "you know." Our goal, as we seek to become more assured, is to flush out these fillers and, if necessary, substitute blessed silence in their place. As with the enunciation problem, it's good to have someone listen as you speak **extemporaneously** on any subject—describing a TV show or even last night's dinner. That person can keep track of how many and what kinds of fillers you use.

- *Tone of voice*. Listen to any professional speaker—an experienced lecturer or a television commentator—and you'll see that one of the tricks of the trade is the ability to vary vocal tone and pitch. We're sure that somewhere in your experience you've had to sit through classes taught by teachers who drone on in a monotone. That's pretty deadly, isn't it? A person can be conveying the most extraordinarily fascinating information, but if the voice stays in one key the whole time, it doesn't matter how good the material is. One way to improve in this area is to practice saying things with more emotion. Choose any few sentences—"I'm going to the supermarket; I found a penny in the street; I am having tuna casserole for dinner"—and try saying them as if they were (1) situations that fill you with joy or (2) situations that fill you with despair. Just practicing this and listening to the sounds your voice can make depending on the emotional content of what you're saying can be a real revelation. Also related to tone of voice is volume. Thinking back to some classic TV comedies for examples, do you remember Janis, Chandler's ghastly ex-girlfriend, on *Friends* and the shrill tones she emits? Or, going to the other end of the spectrum, do you recall the classic *Seinfeld* episode when Kramer's girlfriend, the notorious "low talker," spoke so softly that she got Jerry to promise to wear the infamous "puffy shirt" on national television? Talking too shrilly or too low are **transgressions** found at either end of the scale.

- *Pronunciation*. Be careful how you say certain words. Even though President Bush gets away with saying "nucular" for "nuclear," it still

extemporaneously performed without preparation
transgressions an act or the process of overstepping a limit

makes a better impression to say a word as it was meant to be said. That means "library" instead of "liberry," "idea" instead of "idear," "drowned" instead of "drownded," and so on.

- *Stuttering*. Stuttering is a serious communication disorder in which the flow of speech is broken by repetitions, prolongations, or abnormal stoppages in which no sounds emerge. Over three million Americans suffer from this problem, or approximately 1 percent of the population. Some very successful people have stuttered and gone on to major careers, among them Winston Churchill, the actor James Earl Jones, singer Carly Simon, basketball player Bill Walton, and others. Stuttering can respond very well to speech therapy. For more information on this subject, visit the Web site of the Stuttering Foundation at http://www.stutteringhelp.org.

GRAMMAR AND VOCABULARY

One reason why we included the Word Smart vocabulary builder in this book is because we believe that a rich vocabulary enhances your ability to communicate with other people. As an example of what we're saying, think about colors. Let's say you want to describe a shirt you just bought. Telling your friend that the shirt is blue may be valid, but being able to describe the shirt as turquoise, cerulean, teal, or any of the many other precise shades of blue is a lot more **evocative**.

Grammar is another issue on which you may be judged. If you're talking to friends, and you say, "Him and me went to the mall last night," nobody is going to think twice, right? But if you're going on a job interview—depending on the sort of job you're aiming for—using "him and me" instead of "he and I" may cost you points. Working toward a solid understanding of grammar is a worthwhile goal for all of us, for even though grammatical mistakes may be forgiven in speech, they tend to be much more noticeable and unflattering in your written language.

Public Speaking

What is the nation's number one phobia? A fear that paralyzes Americans even more than snakes, spiders, heights, or even death? That's right—public speaking. Roughly 85 percent of the U.S. population confesses to "stage fright" when they are asked to speak before an audience.

© Digital Vision

evocative serving to bring to mind

The issue of African-American Vernacular English (AAVE), sometimes thought of as Black English Vernacular (BEV), African-American Language, or Ebonics, has become controversial in some school communities, as well as in the Black community at large. AAVE originated in the **pidgin** of the slave trade and Plantation Creole in the U.S. southern states, and has been **augmented** through the years with linguistic features from the world of blues, jazz, and, more recently, rap and hip hop. AAVE is "non-rhotic" or r-dropping. In other words, the r is not pronounced in words like *art*, *door*, or *work*. Other characteristics of AAVE—some going back to similar features in the root African languages from which it springs—include the following:

- The use of *d* and *t* instead of *th*, as in "dem" for "them" and "tree" for "three"
- *l*-dropping, as in "hep" for "help" or "sef" for "self"
- Dropping consonants at the ends of some words, like "wha" for "what" or "pas" for "past"
- Use of "in" for "ing," as in "runnin" for "running"
- Multiple negatives, as in "no way nobody can do it"
- Dropping the verb *to be* in some constructions, like "she sick" for "she is sick"

AAVE, while once thought "careless" or "lazy" speech, is now recognized as a dialect that has offered our culture a rich infusion of new language forms. Words like "dis" (to disrespect), "hang-up" (problem), 'tude (attitude), "make it" (succeed), and "bad" meaning "good," are all derived from AAVE and are all widely used now. Despite the recent recognition and respect that AAVE is starting to receive, however, it must be understood that it diverges widely from Standard English, and for those situations that may call for Standard English, as in drafting a business letter, for example, AAVE may create unwanted confusions and difficulties.

For further readings on AAVE, check the bibliography at the end of the chapter.

At some or even many points in your student career, you will be called upon to get up before a room full of your peers and your teachers to give a talk about something you have researched, something you have created, or some issue you've been asked to argue or debate. This is a prospect that strikes more fear in the hearts of many than sharing a tent with a black mamba would. So what to do about it? The good news is that there are many useful strategies that can wrestle your fear back into its cage. Here is some of our best advice on the subject:

- *Start with preparation*. The better prepared you are for a public speaking situation, the less nervous you'll be and the better you'll do. It's called doing your homework, folks. And a big part of doing this particular homework assignment is to practice—with note cards,

pidgin *a simplified language made up of elements of two or more languages, used as a communication tool between speakers whose native languages are different*

augmented *grown or increased in number, amount, size, strength, or intensity*

in front of a mirror, in front of friends and family, as much as you need to in order to feel crisp and comfortable.

- *Check out all physical arrangements in advance*. If you're speaking in an auditorium or even if it's just in your classroom, make sure that everything is as it should be before you get up to present. If you're using audiovisual equipment or props of any sort, check to see that everything works. The goal is for there to be no surprises.

- *Remember to breathe*. As in any anxiety situation, conscious breathing can be an excellent way to relax. Before getting up to speak, inhale deeply through your nose and hold the breath for a few seconds. Then slowly empty your lungs, exhaling through your mouth. This relaxes the muscles in your throat, your neck, your shoulders, and, in turn, relaxes your voice.

- *Start big and end big*. Your start and your finish will be the two parts of your presentation that most people will remember, so make them count. Don't squander your opportunities on stale jokes or hemming and hawing. Find a strong story, a strong statement, or a strong example to open and close with.

- *Visuals help*. Any speaker will tell you that visual aids can really boost your stock with your audience. Today, with PowerPoint being so popular, visual aids are more important than ever. Again, make sure that you are in full control of all technology *before* your presentation. Your audience will not be patient as they wait for you to figure out which buttons to push. Also, if you have handouts, make sure that they are well organized and be sure to have extras.

- *See the audience as your friend, not your enemy*. Sure, there's such a thing as a "hard room," but, in most cases, an audience wants to connect with a speaker as much as the other way around. After all, they're not looking to be bored for a half hour. Unless you have reason to think otherwise, assume that the audience is on your side and don't feel that, if you happen to drop your cards or lose your place, they're going to throw you to the lions. Don't apologize for any mistakes either. Just get on with the show. If you leave something out of your speech, for instance, and then you start to apologize for the oversight, you may simply be drawing attention to a minor problem that your audience might never have noticed in the first place.

- *Keep your gestures natural and restrained*. One thing that worries speakers the most is what to do with their hands. Don't keep them in your pockets. You don't want to look like you're just hanging out on a street corner, after all. Keep them to your sides when you're not using them to make gestures or, if possible, lay them gently on a podium or on a table in a relaxed manner. When you are gesturing, keep your hand movements simple, graceful, and flowing. Quick, jerky gestures suggest anxiety, which is exactly what you do *not* want to convey. Repetitive gestures also become quickly noticeable and monotonous, so vary your gestures or keep them to a minimum.

Like a lot of other things that people are initially afraid of—driving, swimming, flying in an airplane—public speaking can become a great and satisfying adventure once you get over your fears.

Communicating with Non-English Speakers

We so admire the courage of people who come to this country with the goal of learning a new language. And you have to be courageous indeed to set out to learn English, because it's certainly not an easy language to learn. Why is "through" pronounced "threw," for example, and why when you say "I threw a ball" is it not spelled "through"? Of course, there are so many people from so many different language backgrounds coming into the United States that nobody has to feel alone with this challenge. The complexities of learning English should be tackled in comprehensive classroom settings, but as you master English as a second language, here are a few good general ideas to keep in mind:

- *Use as much English as you can in school.* Speak it all day long. Maybe when you get home you'll be speaking Thai or Russian or Spanish or Arabic, but in school your first choice should always be English. And don't worry about mistakes. Just practice as much as you can.

- *Check out conversation clubs.* We know you're busy with school and work and family, but, if you have any time left over (yeah, right!), you might wish to check out a conversation club. These are offered in many big cities and provide opportunities for foreign speakers to congregate and practice what they've learned. Newspapers often have postings of such clubs, and they're usually offered free of charge.

- *Take your time in restaurants and stores.* When people are selling you something—food, a watch, an appliance, a service—they're usually very patient. Wouldn't you be, if you wanted to make a sale? So regard these encounters as opportunities for you to practice your newly found language skills with a captive audience.

• *Watch TV.* This is not advice we normally dispense, but watching a lot of English-speaking TV and going to English-speaking movies will definitely help you learn language and speech patterns.

In our increasingly multicultural society, it is very important that *native* English speakers understand how to best communicate with *non-native* speakers. Consider these suggestions:

• *Use short words in short sentences.* Think SWISS—(a mnemonic standing for Short Words in Short Sentences). "Nice to meet you" is going to translate a lot faster than "It's been a pleasure to make your acquaintance."

• *Avoid slang.* Some of the slang that native English speakers commonly use is not yet found in English dictionaries, let alone in translation dictionaries. Non-native speakers who try to look up words like "geek" or "techno-savvy" in their pocket translators are likely to come up empty-handed.

• *Avoid idiomatic expressions that won't literally translate.* It was reported in the *Wall Street Journal* that the familiar English expression "out of sight, out of mind" became "invisible, insane" in a Japanese translation. An expression like "Let's talk turkey" is going to have you discussing the virtues of poultry if you're communicating with a Laotian or a Pakistani.

• *Don't yell.* Raising your voice is not going to make it easier for any non-native speaker to understand what you're saying. In fact, it might only make him or her anxious. Speaking slowly, however, is bound to help.

FOOD FOR THOUGHT: LOST IN TRANSLATION

The following stories of marketing missteps, while in some cases perhaps **apocryphal**, convey the pitfalls and the amusements that come with translating from one language to another.

• In Taiwan, the translation of the Pepsi slogan "Come alive with the Pepsi Generation" came out as "Pepsi will bring your ancestors back from the dead."

• In Chinese, Kentucky Fried Chicken's "Finger-lickin' good" slogan became "Eat your fingers off."

• When Parker Pen marketed a ballpoint in Mexico, its ads meant to say, "It won't leak in your pocket and embarrass you." The company didn't realize that the word "embarazar" in its translation didn't mean "embarrass." To Mexicans, the ad said, "It won't leak in your pocket and make you pregnant."

apocryphal probably not true, but widely believed to be true

Listen Up

Picture this scene, if you will. You enter a doughnut shop and have the following exchange with the counterperson:

Server: May I help you?

You: Yes. I'd like a glazed doughnut, please.

Server: How many doughnuts did you say?

You: One, please.

Server: One powdered doughnut.

You: Glazed. A glazed doughnut.

Server: One powdered doughnut and one glazed doughnut—

You: No! One powdered ... I mean glazed ... doughnut. And a cup of coffee, with milk and two sugars.

Server: One glazed doughnut and one cup of coffee with cream ...

You: Milk!

Server: ... with milk and one sugar ...

You: Two!

Server: Two powdered doughnuts?

You: One glazed doughnut! One cup of coffee with milk and two sugars. Got that?

Server: Would you mind repeating that?

Been there? Done that? Sure you have. We all have. Why? Because a lot of people in our society simply do not know how to listen.

Why might that be? One reason is that technology—television and radio—encourages us to listen in terms of **sound bites** so that our capacity to listen to larger chunks of spoken material is becoming limited. This situation obviously can present problems for students who are expected to sit in a lecture for an hour or more.

As a student, how well you listen may be even more important than how well you speak. After all, this is a time in life when it really pays to listen, because your instructors will hopefully be people that have a lot of valuable information and knowledge to share. Here are some basic rules to be aware of when it comes to listening:

- *Apply motivation and discipline.* Listening is not a passive behavior. It is active. In other words, it's a job and, like any job, it helps for you to be motivated. Compare it to exercise, for instance. When you set out to exercise, you might give yourself a little pep talk, right?

sound bites short sentences or phrases that are easy to remember

> **STUDENT TALK:**
> **ARE YOU LISTENING?**
>
> "My mom says I don't listen. And I say, 'What?' No, seriously, I have to admit that I don't listen to my mom very much, or to a lot of other people I try to screen out. But that's the problem. When you get into the habit of screening people out, it can be hard to screen them *in*. Like my teachers—some of them say I don't pay attention in class or I look like I'm bored. In fact, enough of them have told me this that I guess I can't really deny it. Yeah, listening is hard for me, but I'm going to get better at it. That's my goal."
>
> —Ming-Cho L., 19, Bronx, NY.

© Image 100 Ltd.

Similarly, if you're going to a lecture in Economics, a pep talk might be in order too. "I'm going to pay attention. I'm not going to look all around the lecture hall at everyone else. I'm not going to doodle." (Unless, as a kinesthetic learner, doodling helps you concentrate).

- *Show yourself as an active listener.* Whether in conversation or sitting in the classroom, let the speaker know that he or she is being heard. After all, teachers are people too and they appreciate signs that you're listening just as much as your friends do. What are those signs? Eye contact. Nodding. Demonstrating that you are present and accounted for. An even more persuasive way to show that you're an active listener is to ask good questions—always appreciated by an instructor.

- *Use reflective listening.* One way to show you've been listening is to reflect a person's words back. For instance, if you're in a conference with an instructor and he or she tells you that you need to improve the quality of your written work, you might say something like, "Yes, I realize that I need to improve my writing." Indicating to the instructor that you've heard what he or she has to say will confirm your dialogue and help you foster a good relationship.

LISTENING IN THE CLASSROOM

We'd like to narrow the focus of our discussion on listening skills by looking at the special circumstances of the classroom, where you'll be spending so much time. Consider these ideas on how to maximize your listening experience:

- *Sit up front.* Many students dread sitting in the front row. Why? Because they think they may be called on. Being called on is only problematic in two cases: (1) you are unprepared and (2) you are phobic about speaking in front of others. In the first case, it is easy to solve the problem: prepare yourself. Do the work. That's what you're in school for anyway. In the second case, the first time is always the hardest. It gets easier. Jump in—it's like swimming. You'll find that you actually enjoy going to class more when you are actively engaged, and your instructor will certainly appreciate your contributions.

- *Anticipate and avoid distractions.* Come to class prepared with everything you need in order to be able to pay full attention to what's going on. If you get thirsty, bring water with you so that you won't be thinking about water instead of thinking about what's being said. If you get cold easily, pack a sweater and avoid drafty spots. Sitting away from distracting people also helps.

- *Be a critical thinker*. We've talked about being actively engaged, but that doesn't mean *just* listening. It means listening and thinking at the same time. When you read a book, you should be asking yourself questions. "Is this author convincing me? Should I trust what he or she has to say? How legitimate are his or her sources?" You should also exercise that kind of critical thinking when you're listening to your instructor. Remember—"critical" doesn't mean "hostile." It means that if you hear a point you don't understand or agree with, you get to ask a respectful question. No instructor is going to resent that. Far from it. He or she will appreciate your active engagement.

- *Get enough sleep*. If you are seriously, chronically sleep-deprived, either from working too hard or from partying too hard, you cannot expect to be a great listener. Aim for something in the neighborhood of 8 hours or so of sleep a night.

HEARING DEFICITS

Did it ever occur to you that you might be having difficulty listening because you're having difficulty *hearing?* If you think that's a possibility, by all means check into it. Perhaps the problem is as simple as a building up of earwax, or perhaps it's a more serious situation. Whereas one or two generations ago, noise-induced hearing loss usually didn't affect people until they were well into their forties or fifties, noise-induced hearing loss from loud music is increasingly afflicting much younger people. In fact, a study in the *Journal of the American Medical Association* reported that nearly 15 percent of school-aged children had hearing deficits at low or high frequencies.

These sorts of statistics suggest that it's never too early to take precautions with your hearing. One rule of thumb is that any environment, like a dance club or a concert, where you have to shout to be heard represents an unhealthy level of noise. You should also use personal music players responsibly. In other words, if the person standing next to you can hear the music coming over your headset, it's too loud. Earplugs should always be worn when you are working around loud noise (e.g., running a lawn mower or operating a string trimmer). To be effective, earplugs should block the ear canal entirely, creating an airtight seal. Cotton is essentially worthless for blocking out loud noises. Pay attention to what your ears are telling you. They will often warn you when you've been exposed to potentially damaging sound levels. Temporary hearing loss is one indication; ringing in the ears is another.

IN OTHER WORDS

"If speaking is silver, listening is gold."—Turkish proverb

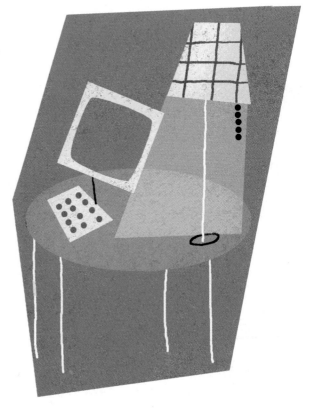

© Ingram Publishing

If you experience either of these symptoms after having gone to a concert, for instance, it is your ears' way of telling you that to repeat this experience too often will send you down the road to deafness. Got that?

Check out the Web site for the nonprofit organization Hearing Education and Awareness for Rockers (HEAR) at http://www.hearnet.com. This organization was founded by a rock musician who suffered hearing loss, and it's filled with valuable information that can open your eyes ... and save your ears!

CASE IN POINT: PRINCESS BEMPONG

Her name implies royalty, and in a sense, Princess Bempong is just that: clearly, a person who rises above others. In 2003, Princess Bempong was named valedictorian of Samuell High School in Dallas, Texas. Princess and her family emigrated from the West African nation of Ghana in the early 1980s. Her parents, deaf from birth, found modest hospital jobs and had four children, of whom Princess was the eldest. All were born deaf, too.

In her senior year, Princess took advanced classes in calculus, physics, English, Spanish, and U.S. government. Nothing below an "A" ever appeared on her report card. Her cumulative average of 95.12 placed her No. 1 in a class of 300. "She's endowed from God," says Michelle Hamm, Princess' interpreter and bus driver. "She's also a perfectionist. She eats up knowledge like Pac-Man eats up those dots."

Princess says she doesn't want to be identified as the first deaf valedictorian of a public high school in Dallas. She's just a regular girl who's proud of her parents for the sacrifices they made in coming to this country. "I want people to know that deaf people have the ability to do things and the potential to be successful," Princess says. "I want them to know that I'm a humble, intelligent, friendly, and fun-loving deaf person."

In 2004, Princess entered Gallaudet University in Washington, D.C., a comprehensive, multipurpose institution of higher education for deaf and hard of hearing citizens of the United States and the world.

Source: Deaf Today. Retrieved November 14, 2004, from http://www.deaftoday.com/news/archives/003503.html

A Final Word

It's just a small jump from speaking and listening to the written word. Our next chapter will be all about reading, spelling, grammar, sentence structure, writing blocks, editing, proofreading, and more. No matter what you do, writing is going to play a part in your life, so let's get to work on it.

What Did We Learn?

See how well you digested this chapter by sampling the following questions:

1. Name five of the more common speech problems.
2. What is African-American Vernacular English?
3. What is the nation's number one phobia?
4. Describe at least five ways to counter fear of public speaking.
5. What are some ways that non-native speakers of English can make themselves more comfortable with the language?
6. Name four ways to communicate better with non-native speakers of English.
7. What are the three basic rules for improving your listening skills in general?
8. Name four guidelines for improving your listening skills in a classroom setting.

Bibliography

Anderson, P. (2004). *The complete idiot's guide to body language*. Indianapolis, IN: Alpha.

Baker, A., & Goldstein, S. (1990). *Pronunciation pairs: An introductory course for students of English*. New York: Cambridge University Press.

Carnegie, D. (1990). *The quick and easy way to effective speaking*. New York: Pocket Books.

Dimitrius, J., & Mazzarella, M. C. (1999). *Reading people: How to understand people and predict their behavior—anytime, any-place*. New York: Ballantine.

Esposito, J. (2000). *In the spotlight: Overcome your fear of public speaking*. Southington, CT: Strong Books.

Garner, A. (1992). *Conversationally speaking: Tested new ways to improve your personal and social effectiveness*. New York: McGraw-Hill.

Green, Lisa J. (2002). African American English: A Linguistic Introduction. New York: Cambridge University Press.

James, A., & Kratz, D. (1995). *Effective listening skills*. New York: McGraw-Hill.

Jones, C. M., Jones, M., & Miculka, J. H. (1991). *Speaking American English for the non-native speaker*. Belmont, CA: Thomson Wadsworth Publishing Company.

McWhorter, John H. (1998). Word on the Street: Debunking the Myth of a 'Pure' Standard English. New York: Basic Books.

Links

Commonly mispronounced words. Retrieved December 7, 2005, from http://www .infoplease.com/ipa/AO907075.html

Give your ears a chance! Retrieved December 7, 2005, from http://www.youth.hear-it.org/

Loud music causes hearing loss. Retrieved December 7, 2005, from http://www .hearinglossweb.com/Medical/Causes/nihl/ loud_music.htm

Nonverbal communication. Retrieved December 7, 2005, from http://www .natcom.org/ctronline/nonverb.htm

Overcoming fear of public speaking. Retrieved December 7, 2005, from http://inin .essortment.com/overcomingfear_num.htm

The Stuttering Foundation. Retrieved December 7, 2005, from http://www .stutteringhelp.org

Toastmasters International: Making effective communication a worldwide reality. Retrieved December 7, 2005, from http://www.toastmasters.org

Word Smart

Speaking of words, how about these?

apocryphal	pidgin
augment	presumptuous
denote	sound bite
extemporaneous	strident
evocative	transgression
pervade	

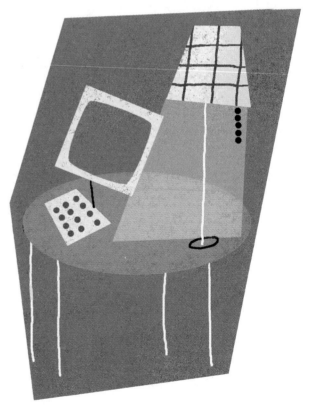

12

WORD PERFECT

We've all heard about the so-called death of the written word, but guess what? Words are still very much around. In fact, you're reading some at this very moment. While there may be a lot of people who spend a disproportionate **amount of time watching television, millions of others regard reading and writing as vital activities. In fact, reading achievement scores in the United States have actually been on the rise over the past 25 years.**

Interestingly enough, while it has become something of a cliché to say that American students are among the worst readers in the world, the fact is that testing conducted by the International Association for the Evaluation of Educational Achievement (IFA) shows that 9-year-olds in the U.S. rank second in the world in reading achievement, while 14-year-olds rank a respectable ninth out of 31 nations.

To be sure, there are distressing statistics as well. A 1990 Gallup poll on reading habits found that the proportion of Americans who failed to complete a book in the previous year had doubled to 16 percent in 1990 from 8 percent in 1978. That still shows, however, that 84 percent of Americans in 1990 *had* completed a book. Was it a "good" book? That's a whole other question. The point is that worrying about the death of the written word is a little bit like worrying about the melting of the polar ice cap—we all know it's happening, and we can never make it go back

disproportionate out of proportion with regard to size, form, or value

to what it was, but we still have to protect what we have. Seeing as the written word is not going to disappear in the near future, we would do well to increase our reading and writing proficiency instead of turning to worst-case scenarios as some kind of excuse.

This chapter will show you ways to improve your reading and writing skills and will offer ideas that you can build upon for new strength in these areas. So read on and see what you can learn.

The Joy of Reading

Anyone who's ever been an **avid** reader doesn't need to be told how powerful a good book can be. If you were one of those kids who stayed up all hours of the night, making a tent out of your blanket and using a flashlight to read Katherine Paterson's *Bridge to Terabithia*, Louis Sachar's *Holes*, Lois Duncan's *Killing Mr. Griffin*, or the Harry Potter books, then you fully understand what we're talking about. You know what it means to be in the grip of a "page-turner"—a book you really can't put down. People have been known to walk right smack into telephone poles when reading books like that, which makes reading an exhilarating if potentially dangerous activity ... a little like bungee jumping for the mind. So, then, why are there insulting names for people who like to read? Names like "bookworm" or "egghead" or "nerd"? Undoubtedly, it's because people who fling such insults really don't understand the passion that can fuel reading, and that's their loss.

Reading is wonderful on a lot of levels, and it's completely portable. Yes, so is an iPod, but reading a book lends itself ideally to just about any environment: a coffee house, the beach, the park, the bus, the subway, bedtime, lunchtime, you name it. Audio books, which we regard fully as a form of reading, are a terrific option for car trips—far better than listening to talk radio, one of the least welcome inventions of the last quarter-century. Reading has an extraordinary capacity to be calming and provocative at the same time. It can make you feel focused and productive. When you read, you're exercising your brain just the way you exercise the rest of your body when you're on a fitness machine. Try it and you'll see.

For a change, instead of watching reality TV, where bronzed bachelors review the **dubious** credentials of bleached blonde bimbos, try curling up with a great book. Maybe it's Ray Bradbury's *Fahrenheit 451* or Ken Kesey's *One Flew Over the Cuckoo's Nest* or John Irving's *The World*

avid eager for, dedicated to, or enthusiastic about something
dubious of uncertain quality or appropriateness

According to Garp. Any of these novels will surely grab and hold your attention. If you don't think you like novels, select a nonfiction work that explores an area of life that interests you. Whether it's dogs or cats or business or computers or sports or weather or film or military history, there are wonderful books out there on just about every subject you can think of. Consult with a librarian or check out the Web sites recommended throughout this chapter to find a good book to read. If you don't feel confident that you're a reader yet, try inching into reading with graphic novels. Though some people might regard this relatively new form of literature as glorified comic books, most serious critics give graphic novels the attention and respect they deserve. Books like Art Spiegelman's *Maus*, Marjane Satrapi's *Persepolis*, Harvey Pekar's *American Splendor*, Daniel Clowes' *Ghost World*, and Max Allan Collins' *The Road to Perdition* are not only significant creative achievements that can stand on their own, but they can also serve as stepping stones for readers who want to move on to more demanding forms of literature.

FOOD FOR THOUGHT: PICKING A BOOK

If you're having trouble finding something to read, try these tips:

- Consult with your librarian at school or at the public library for suggestions.
- Visit the recommended Web sites below for suggested titles.
- Browse through the displays in your school library's media center, at the public library, or at your bookstore.
- Read the summary of the book on the inside flap of the cover or on the back of the book to see if it interests you.
- Read through the first few pages of a book to see if they grab you.
- Check out readers' reviews of books on Web sites such as Amazon.com (http://www.amazon.com) or Barnes & Noble (http://www.barnesandnoble.com).

- Take out a few books at a time from the library and sample them at your leisure. Just remember to return them!

WEB SITES FOR READERS

The following Web sites are chock full of interesting ideas for books to read:

- American Library Association Notable Books http://www.ala.org/ala/rusa/rusaprotools/rusanotable/notablebooks.htm
- The Booklist Center http://home.comcast.net/~dwtaylor1/
- Hungry Mind Review's 100 Best 20th Century American Books http://www.bookspot.com/listhungry100.htm
- Modern Library: 100 Best Novels http://www.randomhouse.com/modernlibrary/100bestnovels.html

- 100 Favorite Mysteries of the Century http://www.mysterybooksellers.com/favorites.html
- 100 Great 20th Century Works of Fiction by Women http://www.literarycritic.com/feminista.htm
- Oprahlikes http://www.wakefieldlibrary.org/zraoprah.htm
- Who Reads What? Celebrity Reading Lists http://www.gpl.lib.me.us/wrwind.htm

Source: Devour a good book! Retrieved December 7, 2005, from http://www.whps.org/library/Selecting%20a%20Book%20to%20Read%20for%20Pleasure.htm

© BananaStock Ltd.

Joining or starting a book club or a reading group is also a great way to stimulate the reading habit. The imposed deadline of a book club meeting—whether it's once a month or once every few months—can help instill the discipline you're looking to bring to your reading. Connect with friends, classmates, or acquaintances to get something going—you only need a handful of readers to form a group—or find an established group that you can join. Your public library or local bookstore should be able to point you toward such a group.

Becoming a Better Reader

Reading is a way of life, it's a discipline … in other words, the more you do it, the better you become at it. If the very idea of sitting down to read a book feels overwhelming, that means you're a beginner. It doesn't mean that you have to remain a beginner, however. Let's compare reading once more to exercise. The first time you go for a jog, it can feel like climbing Mt. Everest. After a while, it becomes easier and more enjoyable. It's the same with reading.

The best way to improve your reading is to sit down and do it in chunks of time that feel manageable. Pick a period of the day when you would normally be zoning out in some kind of fashion. Then, instead of watching reruns of *Saved by the Bell* or playing video games or poker on the Internet, exercise the same sort of discipline you would apply to your fitness regimen and tell yourself that you will be sitting down to read for 15 minutes.

As we know from our earlier discussions on goals, you're more likely to achieve success when your motivation is clear. You jog because you're motivated to be healthy and maybe shed a pound or two. But what motivates you to sit down for even 15 minutes a day to read a book? Right now, you might not understand what would motivate you to read for pleasure, but trust us—the pleasure will come if the book is right. And, then, ultimately you'll come to see reading as a way to vastly improve your knowledge base, your cultural awareness, and your chances of achieving success in the world. By learning how to read for pleasure, you'll also be developing the discipline that will help you with your course reading.

Many students are concerned about their reading speed, and want to know how to become faster readers. Again, getting into the habit of reading will help immeasurably, but here are some "ground rules" that might make reading come more easily for you:

- *Have your eyes checked.* Perhaps there is some physiological reason why you're having difficulty reading. If you're far-sighted,

OPEN FOR DISCUSSION: READ ANY GOOD BOOKS LATELY?

As a group, compare notes regarding your respective histories with reading. Why do you think people *don't* read? What's special about reading that distinguishes it from other activities? What are your reading habits like? Do you have any favorite books that you think could turn on a nonreader? If you're a book lover, make a case for reading. If you're someone who never sits down to read a book, be open to hearing why you should.

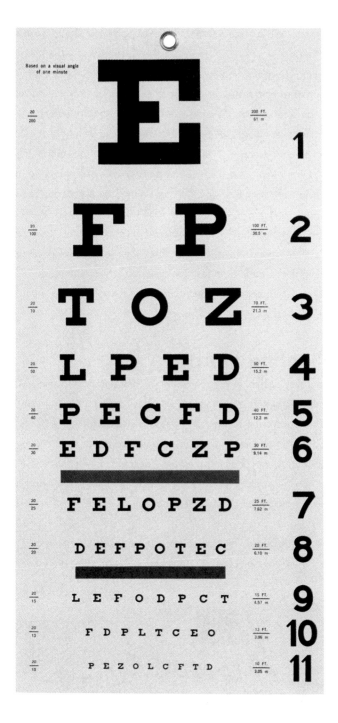

for instance, you may need prescription eyeglasses to correct the problem.

• *Read silently*. Some people read out loud as they go along, even if it's just in a whisper or a murmur. Resist the impulse. Generally speaking, silent reading will go two or three times faster than oral

reading. Whispering those words is a crutch you should learn to live without.

- *Avoid re-reading.* Readers are often tempted to go back over what they've read, but this tendency can significantly slow you down. Most readers can get the "big picture" without having to understand or absorb every word they read. Give yourself the benefit of the doubt.
- *Develop a wider eye-span.* In other words, see more than one word at a time. Try to see a whole phrase or even a sentence at a glance. Moving your finger or an index card along the text as you read can be a helpful way to develop this skill.
- *Find a position that's comfortable.* A lot of people flop down on a couch to read. Three minutes later, they're fast asleep. Sit up straight at a table or a desk for the entire 15-minute session you've set aside. Once reading becomes easier for you, then you can experiment with reclining options.

Collecting Words

To our way of thinking, there is always something astonishing when a person encounters an unfamiliar word and doesn't have the curiosity to find out what it means. Oh, we're sorry—is that *you* we're talking about? Are you really not interested in finding out what *mesmerize* means? *Kudos? Rococo? Imprimatur?* (**Mesmerize:** "Hypnotize." **Kudos:** "Praise, credit, or glory for an achievement." **Rococo:** "Overly ornate or fancy." **Imprimatur:** "Authority to do, say, or especially print something.")

Now you may ask, why do you need these words? If you know "hypnotize," then why do you need "mesmerize"? And when are you ever

going to use the word "rococo" in a sentence? We can only respond by saying that a rich vocabulary is like that top-of-the-line box of 100 crayons. Instead of making do with just the plain "brown" you'd find in the 10-crayon box, you get "sepia" and "burnt umber." Just as that kind of variety will enable you to draw a more vivid picture, greater variety with word choice allows you to write in a way that attracts more interest and attention.

Building a better vocabulary is not rocket science. Simply keep a dictionary on hand whenever you're reading a book. Just as you are developing a richer vocabulary from the Word Smart feature of this book (and kudos to you for doing so!), so, too, can you add to your vocabulary by maintaining your own index of words. When you find a new word that you regard as a "keeper"—and don't be overly choosy because, as we're suggesting, you never know when you'll need the precise word for something—jot it down on a 3 × 5 index card, along with its definition, and review your stack periodically. Obviously, another benefit of a good vocabulary is that it can boost your academic achievement. Your appropriate use of rich and varied words will distinguish your writing, and you will be better prepared for standardized entrance examinations that you may be taking later in your academic career, like the GREs, LSATs, or Praxis.

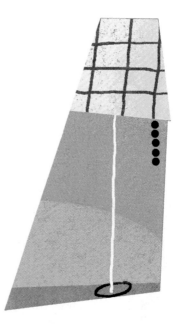

Spelling Tips

Spelling represents another area of mystery for many people. Fortunately, computer spell-checkers are commonplace in the 21st century, and so, with word-processed documents at least, you should be able to catch a lion's share of your mistakes. Nevertheless, you should have some basic understanding of how spelling works so that you don't embarrass yourself too badly when you find yourself without the support of your spell-checker. Here, in the brief space we've allotted to this subject, are our top hints on spelling:

1) *Forming plurals.* Adding *s* to a word—*dogs, cats, shoes*—is the most common way to pluralize something. When a word ends in *sh, ch, ss, x,* or *z,* add *es* to form the plural. Examples are *dishes, lunches, bosses, boxes,* and *fizzes.* If a word ends in a consonant followed by the letter *y,* then change the *y* to an *i* and add *es.* (For example, *babies, caddies, bodies.*) Then there are the nouns that end in a long o to which you add *es* for the plural. These include *tomatoes, mosquitoes, cargoes, volcanoes,* and *potatoes.*

A s you start to become more aware of your spelling, you may eventually tame those commonly misspelled words that are often referred to as spelling "demons." Take the following test and see how you do with these:

Circle the right choice

1) Accommodate/Accomodate

2) Independant/Independent

3) Irritible/Irritable

4) Accidentally/Accidently

5) Liason/ Liaison

6) Privilege/Priviledge

7) Exceed/Excede

8) Irresistable/Irresistible

9) Tyrrany/Tyranny

10) Harrass/Harass

11) Receive/Recieve

12) Sieze/Seize

13) Wierd/Weird

14) Judgement/Judgment

15) Seperate/Separate

1) accommodate. 2) independent 3) irritable 4) accidentally 5) liaison 6) privilege 7) exceed 8) irresistible 9) tyranny 10) harass 11) receive 12) seize 13) weird 14) judgment 15) separate

2) *Remember the ie-ei rule.* You probably know the mnemonic "I before E except after C." If you don't, learn it now, because it comes up often.

3) *Pay close attention to suffixes.* A suffix is a letter or letters added to the end of a word or root, to form a new word. For instance, the suffix *-ful* added to the word *faith* makes *faithful*. The suffix *-ance* added to the word *ignore* makes *ignorance*. As far as spelling goes, when a one-syllable word ends in one vowel and one consonant, that consonant is doubled before a suffix beginning with a vowel. (Examples: *bat + er = batter; bat + ing = batting*.) A word of more than one syllable ending in a single vowel and single consonant, which has the accent on the final consonant, doubles that consonant before a suffix beginning with a vowel. (Examples: *refer + ed = referred; occur + ing = occurring*.) When a word ends in e, drop the final e before adding a suffix that begins with a vowel. (Examples: *enrage + ing = enraging. Forge + er = Forger*.) When words end in an e, but the suffix begins with a consonant, retain the final e. (Examples: *excite + ment = excitement. Involve + ment = involvement*.)

There are obviously many more spelling rules, and generally, with English, most rules are made to be broken, but this is a start. For more tips on spelling, consult the links at the end of the chapter.

Word Usage

It would be impossible to fully probe the complexities of English grammar in the limited amount of space we have here. Fortunately, we don't need to—that's what you have composition classes for. We would like to take this opportunity, however, to address a few of the most common usage problems, with the hope that we can nip some of these problems in the bud. Here are our votes for the Top 10 problem areas to look out for:

1) *Lie/Lay.* This may well be the #1 usage problem in the English language, and it can confuse even **erudite** writers. You *lay* down a blanket on the grass, but you *lie* down on the blanket. The situation is complicated by whatever tense is being used. It really requires a chart to sort this out!

erudite learned, scholarly

Lie	First person	Third person
Present	I **lie** in bed.	She **lies** in bed.
Past	I **lay** in bed.	She **lay** in bed.
Perfect form	I **have lain** in bed.	She **has lain** in bed.
Participle form	I **am lying** in bed.	She **is lying** in bed.

Lay	First person	Third person
Present	I **lay** it down.	She **lays** it down.
Past	I **laid** it down.	She **laid** it down.
Perfect form	I **have laid** it down.	She **has laid** it down.
Participle form	I **am laying** it down.	She **is laying** it down.

Note the word *lain* as the perfect form of *lie*. You may never have seen this word before and, frankly, it is not a word that we can ever remember having used in common **parlance**, but at least now, if and when you see it, you'll know what it is.

2) *Affect/Effect*. There are four distinct words here. When *affect* has its accent on the final syllable (a-FECT), it is a verb meaning *to have an influence on*. "The cigarette smoke did not *affect* the dining experience." A much more rare meaning is indicated when the accent is on the first syllable (AFF-ect). This is a term that is mostly used by psychologists, meaning emotion, as in "The patient had little outward *affect*." This is not to be confused with the commonly used noun *effect*. "The *effect* of the medicine on the patient was astounding." Less commonly, *effect* is a verb meaning *to create*, as in "He was trying to *effect* change through education." For general purposes, however, just remember that *affect* is mostly used as a verb and *effect* is mostly used as a noun, as in "When you *affect* a situation, your actions have an *effect*."

3) *Alot*. One of the most common mistakes in the English language, this expression, which refers to *a great deal or a great amount*, should *always* be spelled *a lot*. Just as you would never write "alittle," so should you never write "alot." Just to confuse things, however, there is the verb *allot*, meaning to *apportion* or *grant*.

4) *I/Me/Myself*. Many people are unsure and uptight about when and how to use these pronouns. Let's see what we can do to clear this up. You would say, "*I* am going to the zoo." If you had a friend with you, you would say, "John and *I* are going to the zoo." (It's common to hear "John and *me*" or "*Me* and John are going to the zoo," and you're not going to get arrested for it, but it's not proper usage.) How about, "The card was signed by my wife and *I*"? Is that correct? In fact, no. You'll hear it a lot (not *alot*) because people are trying to sound "proper," but the correct English is "The card was signed by my wife and *me*." Substituting *myself* for *me* or *I* is another **gambit** used by people who are unsure of what they're doing, but it is not preferred English either. As a rule of thumb, remove the second party and then try the sentence. "The card was signed by *me*." That's correct … except that it's a passive, not an active, form, which we'll talk about in a bit.

parlance manner of speech, language
gambit a move or strategy

5) *Who/Whom.* Here's another killer for many people. *Whom* is essentially a dying word. It is rarely heard in speech, but is still used in formal writing. The distinction between *who* and *whom* is basically simple. *Who* is the subject form of the pronoun; *whom* is the object form. "*Who* gave you that black eye?" And: "His mother was so upset when he walked in with a black eye that she forgot to *whom* she was talking on the telephone." One of the few instances where you'll still see *whom* used regularly is in the salutation of a business letter that begins, "To *whom* this may concern."

6) *Good/Well.* *Good* is an adjective; *well* is an adverb. "He thinks *well* on his feet" is correct. "This cake tastes *good*" is also correct. Of course, people say, "I feel *good*" and "I feel *well*."

7) *It's/Its.* Here's one you'll really want to nail, because it's very simple to get the usage straight and so many people get it wrong. *It's* is a contraction of *it is* (for example, "*It's* nice to see you.") *Its* is a possessive form. "How the leopard lost *its* spots is an old folk tale." If you can substitute *his* for *its*, then you'll know that you shouldn't be using *it's* in that instance.

8) *Loose/Lose.* Check for proper usage by saying these aloud. *Lose* has a "z" sound to it and it's a verb. "Don't *lose* your gloves." *Loose* has a hissy "s" sound and is an adjective. "These gloves are too *loose* on me."

9) *Then/Than.* When comparing one thing with another, use *than*. "Jack is heavier *than* John." If you're talking about time, use *then*. "First, I'll go to the store, and *then* I'll meet Lisa for brunch."

10) *That/Which.* Common usage will dictate that these two are interchangeable. Your grammar-check on your computer, however, may highlight *which* and ask you to replace it with *that*. Make the grammar check happy and do as it asks, but otherwise don't worry about it.

Strengthening Your Prose

When it comes to determining what constitutes good writing, there is a great deal of flexibility. In general, however, we'd like to put forth the following ideas as guidelines to keep in mind when approaching any writing task:

1) *Passive/active voice.* Generally, active constructions are preferred to passive ones, as they make for livelier prose. For instance, "The

car ran over the deer" is livelier than "The deer was run over by the car." Your grammar-check will probably alert you to instances where you've used the passive voice and will urge you to change it to the active voice. Occasional use of the passive voice can be an effective aspect of style, as when one wishes to evoke a character in a novel that has passive tendencies, but, generally speaking, the passive voice is irritating to most people, sounds stuffy and ineffectual, and should be avoided.

2) *Sentence fragments*. Fine novelists can use sentence fragments effectively; students who use them generally expose their ignorance of sentence structure. For your purposes, your sentences should have a subject and a verb, at the very least. "I ate" is a complete sentence. "When I ate" is a fragment. You're waiting for the other shoe to drop—"When I ate, I ..." what? "When I ate, I got heartburn? When I ate, I felt better"? A fragment is an incomplete thought, and if you read your sentences out loud, you'll catch those that suffer from incompleteness.

3) *Vague reference*. It is important that your reader be able to track your thinking when you're using pronouns. Consider a sentence like, "Scientists and artists are both creative, but the public doesn't think of them that way." Who is "them" referring to in this sentence—the scientists or the artists? To keep your reader in the loop here, it would be best to rephrase the sentence as, "Scientists and artists are both creative, but the public doesn't think of scientists that way."

4) *Verb tense*. A wandering verb tense is a very common writing problem. Students describing plots of books often fall into confusing patterns around this issue. For example: "In *The Great Gatsby*, the character of Jay Gatsby lives in East Egg, Long Island, and was a mysterious millionaire." That sentence should all be in the same tense—past or present, your decision. In other words, it should read, "In *The Great Gatsby*, the character of Jay Gatsby lives in East Egg, Long Island, and is a mysterious millionaire" or "In *The Great Gatsby*, the character of Jay Gatsby lived in East Egg, Long Island, and was a mysterious millionaire." Pairs of verbs that go together should always be in the same tense. "Over the summer, Jack walked and feeds the neighborhood dogs" is obviously wrong. It should be, "Over the summer, Jack walked and fed the neighborhood dogs."

5) *Subject/verb agreement*. Here is another commonly encountered problem. "One of the boys likes the chemistry class" is correct English. "One of the boys like chemistry class" is not. "The boys likes chemistry class" is incorrect. "The boys like chemistry" *class* is correct. Keep an ear out to make sure that your subject and your verb match up.

BUT DON'T WORRY ABOUT THESE ...

There are so many rules when it comes to English that people sometimes feel like they're walking on eggshells when they sit down to write. In quite a few instances, you may be told that your usage is wrong when, in fact, you have actually been using Standard English. Here are some of the leading examples of usages for which you might be **chastised**, but that are actually technically correct:

- *Split infinitives*. Some people believe that a construction such as "to aimlessly wander" is incorrect and that it should be "to wander aimlessly." Most of the rest of the world could care less, and, in fact, there are instances where it is considered more graceful to split an infinitive. Most people don't even know what an infinitive is, so we certainly shouldn't spend a lot of time worrying about splitting them.
- *Ending a sentence with a preposition*. There's nothing wrong with that. To skewer this rule, Winston Churchill once wittily declared, "This is the sort of English up with which I will not put." Enough said.
- *Starting a sentence with a conjunction*. Another sacred cow that has gone down to defeat is the rule against starting sentences with conjunctions like *and* or *but*. To do so is not a mistake, but it will be up to you to decide whether it makes more sense to choose that route or to combine the sentence with the one before.

Issues of Process

We've been dispensing a number of rules about writing, but it's important to realize that writing is not principally about rules. In fact, it's often about *breaking* rules. (Take a look at a book by an author like James Joyce some time and you'll see what we mean.) That said, we're going to offer a few general guidelines to help you with the writing process. Remember that everything we've discussed in this chapter so far is just an *hors d'oeuvre*. The main course will be your composition and other

chastised punished or scolded

writing classes, where you will be writing on a regular basis and getting valuable feedback. But you can't go wrong with the following (note, too, that we just started a sentence with a conjunction):

- *Don't expect to get it right at the beginning*. Writing is all about going through a series of drafts. Nobody—that's *nobody*—gets it right the first time around. A writer working with a piece of text is like a sculptor working with a piece of stone. It's all about molding and chiseling and creating form and beautiful lines out of something that initially feels like an **unwieldy** mass.

- *Find your authentic voice*. Just as our fingers have thumbprints, so does our writing have its unique "voice." Some people are more formal; others remain relatively informal no matter what they're writing about. Some people use a lot of questions or adjectives, whereas others prefer a leaner sort of prose. You'll have to experiment in order to discover what really sounds like "you."

- *Read your writing out loud*. Everything you write should be read out loud. Oral readings provide that other dimension that allows you to "hear" your writing. Leaving out that step is a big mistake.

- *Discover where you write best*. Some people need absolute quiet and even isolation to produce their writing. Others write best in the amiable buzz of a coffee bar. It's all up to you. Discover too what works in terms of actual sit-down time. Can you write for a half an hour at a stretch? An hour? Do you need to break up your writing sessions with a walk or a talk with a friend? You decide.

- *If time permits, put it away and come back to it*. Writing always looks different in the morning. If you have the luxury of reflecting on your writing, you'll be sure to find things you'd like to change. Writers often bemoan that they see things in their published books they wish they could have done differently.

EDITING

Just as important as writing—if not *more* important—is rewriting or revising. We'll use the word *editing* to mean rewriting here. In the cardinal rules about process that we've already given you in this chapter, several refer to editing—*Don't expect to get it right at the beginning. Read it out loud. If time permits, put it away and come back to it*. Editing yourself is all about looking at your work with a fresh perspective and that's not

© Digital Vision

unwieldy difficult to move, manage, or control; awkward

an easy thing to do. You have to ask yourself a series of questions. Do you support your arguments? Is your evidence solid? Is your material well organized? Is your language lively and clear? We all tend to fall in love with our writing, and don't like to let go of things. A rather **macabre** adage that circulates in writing circles is that writing is all about "killing your babies." Sorry if that disturbs you, but there's priceless truth in it. You have to be ruthless when it comes to editing yourself. Even though a sentence may sound good and be chock full of wonderful words or images, is it really serving the text?

Here are our top tips for editing yourself. Just remember that self-editing is a learning process, and you'll only become better at it the more you do it.

- *Concentrate first on the big picture.* Some people think editing is all about taking out or putting in commas. That's the small stuff, and, as the big best seller advises us, don't sweat it. You want to assess the bigger issues instead. Do you stay on track for the entire paper? Is there a sequential logic behind it? Is your thesis strong?
- *Vet your information.* Are your facts accurate? Are they backed up, if necessary, with citations? Have you provided enough supporting evidence for your arguments?
- *Judge your conclusion.* Do you wrap things up too quickly at the end? Does your conclusion read abruptly? Does it need more work? (Introductions and conclusions are usually the parts of a paper that need the most fixing.)
- *Print out a hard copy.* You may think you can revise solely on your computer screen, but you'll find that you see things differently when you're looking at a hard copy. Paper and a red pencil still function as invaluable tools in the editing process.

Just in terms of writing style, here a few ideas worth keeping in mind:

- *Vary your sentence structure.* Check to make sure that you aren't starting all your sentences the same way. Some sentences should be simple, others complex.
- *Avoid repetitive words.* If the same words are cropping up from sentence to sentence, you will be boring your reader. Use a thesaurus to find new words as necessary, but don't go overboard in that direction either. A paper that sounds as if it were written with a thesaurus in hand—"I ambulated down the sidewalk with a

> ## IN OTHER WORDS
> "Rewriting is the essence of writing well—where the game is won or lost."—William Zinsser, author of the classic *On Writing Well*

macabre grim, gruesome

perspicacious expression on my face"—is usually a prime example of overkill and often has words that are used inappropriately, without a full understanding of what they really mean.

- *Avoid sentences that begin with* It is *or* There are. Usually you can dispense with these constructions entirely without any loss to your writing. For example, "It is my belief that the Native Americans were maltreated" is less desirable than "I believe that the Native Americans were mistreated" or, better yet, "The Native Americans were mistreated."
- *Review your pronoun references and verb-tense agreements.*
- *Review your tenses to make sure they are consistent.*
- *Avoid clichés and jargon.* Clichés are sure to lose you points. "As honest as the day is long," "Rome wasn't built in a day," "Living high on the hog"—these are all phrases that suggest a bankruptcy of original ideas. Jargon too is deadly. Phrases like "at this point in time" or "per your request" are sure ways to clog up your prose.

CASE IN POINT: JAY THIESSENS

Some people go through life without ever being able to read or write, and that is a human tragedy. For decades, Jay Thiessens hid his painful secret of illiteracy, even as he built his machine and tool company into a big business. By day, he was the harried executive, too busy to concentrate on contracts or other written documents. By night, he would sit with his wife at the kitchen table going over paperwork. His closest business associates had no idea that Jay was living with such a big secret. "I worked for him for 7 years and I had no clue," said Jack Sala, once his general manager. "He would bring legal stuff to me and say, 'You're better at legalese than me.' I never knew I was the only one reading them." Finally, Jay decided that he couldn't keep his secret under wraps any longer. At the age of 56, having resolved to learn how to read, he went public with his problem.

Jay's torment began in his earliest years of school in McGill, a small mining town in central Nevada. "A teacher called me stupid because I had trouble reading," he said. From then on, he was always the quiet boy at the back of the room. Somehow, he graduated from high school, mostly getting C's, D's, and F's. The day after graduation, Jay moved to Reno where, 10 years later, he started a small machine shop with his last $200. Today, his company —B & J Machine Tool Co.—specializes in welding, machine parts, and precision sheet metal. With 50 employees, it recently broke ground on a 54,000 square-foot expansion and brings in revenues of $5 million a year.

How did Jay stay afloat without being able to read or write? He compensated by being a good listener and by drawing on his strength with math and figures, a critical factor in the industry he chose. When Jay finally decided to do something about his illiteracy, he hired a tutor to instruct him for an hour a day, 5 days a week. Reading still does not come easily to him, but he continues to work at it. By making his story public, he hopes to encourage others to follow his example. "There is no shame in not knowing how to read," says Bonnie Thiessens, Jay's wife of 37 years. "The shame is in not doing anything about it."

Source: A 40-year secret. Retrieved December 7, 2005, from http://www.reviewjournal.com/lvrj_home/1999/Jun-11-Fri-1999/opinion/11345201.html

- *Make time for editing and visit your school's Writing Center.* These are the most important rules of all! As part of your writing process, you must set aside sufficient time for the editing stage. Rome wasn't built in a day, after all. (Just checking to make sure you were paying attention.) Most colleges and universities have writing centers that offer invaluable support.

Staying With It

If there is one point we'd like to leave you with from this chapter, it's that your reading and writing skills will evolve the more you work at them and the more you are committed to improving. Reading and writing are ongoing, lifelong activities. Even professionals never stop learning new ways to improve their writing. So put aside any of your old ideas about what kind of writer and reader you are, and concentrate instead on what kind of writer and reader you want to *become*.

What Did We Learn?

There was a lot to learn from this chapter. Test yourself on the following to see how you did:

1. Can you suggest some useful ideas for how to pick a book you might enjoy reading?
2. Name five "ground rules" that will help you to become a better reader.
3. Explain the difference between *affect* and *effect*.
4. Differentiate between *it's* and *its*.
5. When is it correct to use the word *alot*?
6. What is the difference between the passive and active voices and which should you use predominantly?
7. What are three examples of usage rules that are no longer really relevant and that you can break without worrying that you've made a mistake?
8. Name five vital guidelines regarding the process of writing.
9. What are the top four things you should remember about the self-editing process?

Bibliography

Adler, M., & Van Doren, D. (1997). *How to read a book*. New York: MJF Books.

Cook, C. K. (1986). *Line by line: How to edit your own writing*. Boston: Houghton Mifflin.

Fry, R. (2004). *Improve your reading*. Clifton Park, NY: Thomson Delmar Learning.

Funk, W., & Lewis, N. (1991). *30 days to a more powerful vocabulary*. New York: Pocket Books.

Goldberg, N. (1986). *Writing down the bones*. Boston: Shambala Publications, Inc., 1986.

Robinson, A. (2001). *Word smart: Building an educated vocabulary*. Princeton, NJ: Princeton Review.

Strunk, W., Jr., White, E. B., & Angell, R. (2000). *The elements of style*, 4th ed. New York: Longman.

Swan, M. (1995). *Practical English usage*. New York: Oxford University Press.

Truss, L. (2004). *Eats, shoots & leaves: The zero tolerance approach to punctuation*. New York: Gotham.

Van Doren, C. (1985). *The joy of reading*. New York: Harmony.

Zinsser, W. (2001). *On writing well: 25th anniversary: The classic guide to writing non-fiction*. New York: HarperResource.

Links

Building a better vocabulary http://grammar.ccc.commnet.edu/grammar/vocabulary.htm

Get it write: Usage tips. Retrieved December 7, 2005, from http://www.getitwriteonline.com/archive/tips.htm

How to edit your own writing: Self-editing. Retrieved December 7, 2005, from http://home.earthlink.net/~jdc24/selfEdit.htm

Spelling tips. Retrieved December 7, 2005, from http://www.askoxford.com/betterwriting/classicerrors/spellingtips/

The Writing Center: Revising drafts. Retrieved December 7, 2005, from http://www.unc.edu/depts/wcweb/handouts/revision.html

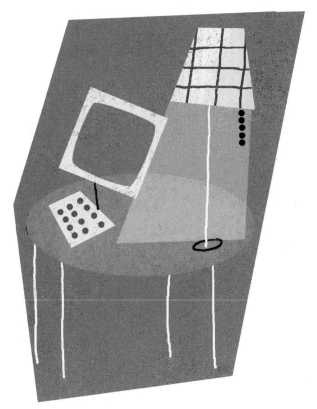

Word Smart

As we said, a rich vocabulary will strengthen your writing. There may come a time when you'll want to use one of the words below because it's really the right word.

avid

chastise

disproportionate

dubious

erudite

gambit

imprimatur

kudos

macabre

mesmerize

parlance

rococo

unwieldy

PART THREE

GETTING IT TOGETHER

13

THE WHOLE YOU

The student experience is generally not thought of as a portrait in healthy living. These hectic years evoke images of all-night study sessions, fast-food dinners, frequent periods of stress overload, and sometimes reckless ways of letting off steam. It would require a minor revolution to change the basic nature of this experience, and we understand that most younger college students wouldn't even want it to change. After all, many younger students regard these years as a time of liberation, experimentation, and breaking the rules, not a time to worry about eating high-fiber cereals and taking baby aspirins for your heart. So, rest assured, we're not going to come on like some pitchman in a late-night infomercial, trying to sign you up for "healthy living 12 ways." On the other hand, too much of a good thing runs the very real risk of becoming a bad thing. Liberation and experimentation is one thing, but there's still a job to be done—the job of being a student—and that's very hard work indeed. Making it across the finish line can present quite a challenge if there are too many obstacles in the way, like health risks and unsafe living.

Let's back up a moment to consider what your life is like right now. You're taking a heavy course load. You're encountering material that's stretching you academically. You're working to **defray**

defray bear the burden of

tuition costs or, at the very least, to earn money for your day-to-day expenses. Whether you're a son or a daughter or whether you *have* a son or a daughter—or a husband or wife or significant other—chances are you have relationship responsibilities. You may also have extracurricular responsibilities, whether they be team sports, musical or theatrical pursuits, community activism, or your involvement with a religious or other organization. In other words, your plate is very full.

As a student, you sometimes feel like you're running a marathon with hurdles all along the course—grade pressure; overdrawn checking accounts; housing issues; car trouble—and it requires enormous energy just to keep up. You wouldn't run a marathon without the proper physical conditioning, would you? So why would you think you could undertake the full load of enormous responsibilities that college demands without girding your energy and mustering your physical resources?

In this chapter, we will be discussing ways to achieve the physical conditioning necessary to reach your potential as a student. We're not talking about becoming supermen or superwomen. You're not going to have to go to the health food store and stock up on protein boosters and hormonal supplements. This chapter is dedicated to real people with real needs who are aiming to achieve *wholeness* and *wellness* in their lives so that they don't fall behind before they cross the finish line.

What do we mean by wholeness and wellness? Wholeness, which gives rise to the term *holistic*, as in holistic medicine, emphasizes the organic or functional relation between the parts and the whole of something. Wholeness, to our way of thinking, is closely connected to wellness, which acknowledges the connection of the mind and the body. In adopting a holistic approach to life, we take into account the mind, the body, and the spirit, and we examine how these spheres interact and impact on each other. To neglect the one will, over time, negatively affect the other. In this chapter, we will be looking at ways to hold all the parts of ourselves together in order to stay healthy and fit for achievement. Let's begin by looking at the subject of food.

You Are What You Eat …

… goes the old saying, and, as is the case with many old sayings, there's a lot of truth to be found there. What we put into our bodies has great bearing on what we can expect to get *out* of our bodies. If we strive for energy, stamina, and strength, we can't expect to get something out of nothing.

What is nothing? To start out with, it's junk food—pork rinds, potato chips, beef jerky, and all the rest of those salty, greasy, fat-laden, sugar-laden, highly-processed **comestibles** that fill us up with useless calories while they starve us of anything really useful.

American eating habits have become so wrongheaded that it's hard to know where to begin affixing the blame. The biggest problem may be that many Americans no longer recognize when they are hungry and when they are full. "Part of the way our brain gets the message we're full is **satiety**, but we're not getting it," says Dr. David Spiegel, associate chair of psychiatry and behavioral sciences at Stanford University.

We overeat, says Dr. Spiegel, because too much of the food we ingest is highly processed, inexpensive, loaded with calories. The trouble is that it's not really satisfying, and so we eat more and more in order to try to feel full. This state of affairs has created a national trend toward what is known as *portion distortion*—which means, essentially, not having any idea of the amount of food you're actually eating. "Super-sizing is a public health issue of the highest priority," testified Harvard Medical School's Dr. George Blackburn, a professor of nutrition and surgery, at a hearing of the Food and Drug Administration's obesity working group.

Super-sizing is, in fact, so unhealthy that some fast food franchises have eliminated the practice. One reason they have chosen to do so is to protect themselves against potential lawsuits. The Centers for Disease Control and Prevention has released a study predicting that obesity would eventually overtake smoking as the leading cause of preventable disease. In the year 2000 alone, about 400,000 Americans died as a result of bad diet and lack of exercise, a rise of 33 percent over the course of 10 years. Fast food providers are increasingly worried about being sued by consumer activists, who have had considerable success suing the tobacco industry.

Portion distortion began in earnest back in the 1970s, when McDonald's introduced its large portion of fries and food manufacturers realized that there was a windfall to be made from selling jumbo portions. Since then, foods like hamburgers and bagels have increased in size by two to five times. As a result, compared to eating habits of 20 years ago, women today are eating 300 more calories a day than they had been and men are eating 168 more. Since it's a nutritional fact that 100 extra calories a day will lead to a net weight gain of 10 pounds

comestibles things that are edible
satiety the state of being satisfied

within a year, you don't have to be a genius to do the math. Take the following quiz and see how well you do when it comes to portions:

Bagel

20 Years Ago   **Today**

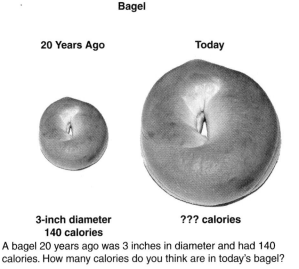

3-inch diameter   **??? calories**
140 calories

A bagel 20 years ago was 3 inches in diameter and had 140 calories. How many calories do you think are in today's bagel?

○ 350   ○ 250   ○ 150

Answer: Today's 6-inch bagel has 350 calories.
This is 210 more calories than a 3-inch bagel 20 years ago.

GETTING CONTROL OF YOUR EATING

Not only do many Americans overeat, but also a great many Americans *undereat* … to the point of seriously endangering their health. Two eating disorders that are particularly prevalent in young people are *anorexia nervosa* and *bulimia nervosa*. Anorexia nervosa is characterized by both an extreme fear of becoming overweight and by excessive dieting that can lead to **manifold** physical issues and sometimes even death. Bulimia nervosa is a condition in which bouts of overeating are followed by undereating, use of laxatives, or self-induced vomiting. Television and print advertising showing super-thin models creates an unrealistic desire and pressure to be thin in individuals whose body size will never allow them to wear a size 4 or 6. Going down this path is not only dangerous but, as we've said, even deadly. It is important to get back to healthy, normal attitudes toward food.

In this chapter, we will be sparing you the usual discussion of food pyramids and other such things you've studied over and over in Health

manifold of great variety, numerous

REFLECTIONS: *YOUR HISTORY*

Spend a few moments reflecting on your history with food. Have you struggled with any weight issues over the years? Have you always craved "forbidden" foods? What are your favorite foods, how often do you eat them, and how guilty do you feel about eating them (if at all)? How is the issue of food treated in your family? Do you come from a long line of dieters? Were food and meal times a source of pleasure in your home? Do you know how to cook? Do you enjoy it?

Ask yourself any or all of these questions, and see where your reflections lead you.

classes through the years. By now, most Americans realize that a banana beats out a brownie and tuna trumps Tootsie Rolls every time. Of course, every now and then all but the most devout among us will reach for a candy bar or an ice cream cone or a chocolate chip cookie or a bucket of popcorn *with* butter. The most important guideline to keep in mind is moderation. Few foods have the potential to cause serious damage if they are consumed in reasonable amounts.

Food and weight have become something of a national obsession in the United States, spawning a multibillion-dollar dieting industry. So many books on the subject of food and eating have been published that you could get a stomachache just thinking about them. So we're not going to attempt to comprehensively cover this issue here, but we would like to share some thoughts on this topic that we think are quite valuable. Following these food tips will help point you on the road to wellness:

1) *Drink water.* As you may know, the human body is made up of 60 to 70 percent water. Much of that water is lost from the body in a variety of ways and needs to be regularly **replenished**. Eight glasses of water a day is what physicians recommend, so always have some handy. Bring bottled water to class, and drink *before* you get thirsty. Playing the catch-up game *after* you become thirsty doesn't work nearly as well. And when we say water, we mean water. Water has a lot going for it: it's noncaloric, it has no sugars, salts, chemicals or additives, and it's either free or relatively low-cost. It's always the better choice than sodas, caffeinated drinks, or high-priced, high-calorie juices.

replenished filled again

2) *Look for real food.* "Real" food—also called "whole" food or "slow" food—is food that's been tampered with as little as possible. Think real cheese instead of "cheese food" or rolled oats instead of some sugar-coated, rainbow-colored cereal. Even a piece of plain semisweet chocolate is a better choice than something that's packed with nougat, marshmallow, and Krispy Crackles. Do you really need all those artificial ingredients?

3) *Eat less meat.* You've probably heard about the "Mediterranean diet." Many physicians believe that this diet represents one of the healthiest ways to eat. The Mediterranean diet features a high consumption of fruits, vegetables, breads, grains, beans, nuts, and seeds. More than half the fat calories in the Mediterranean diet come from olive oil, a monosaturated—i.e., healthful—fat. Wine is taken in moderation, eggs, dairy products, fish, and poultry are consumed in low to moderate amounts, and there is very little red meat on the menu. In fact, meat is almost always regarded as an "extra," which is how more Americans should learn to regard it.

4) *Stop fearing fats and carbohydrates.* Suddenly, in our culture, "fat" and "carbohydrates" have become dirty words. Nonsense! There are good fats, such as the olive oil, nuts, and seeds mentioned previously with regard to the Mediterranean diet, and there are bad fats (like, uh, pork rinds?). There are good carbohydrates, such as whole grain breads and pastas, and bad carbohydrates, like doughnuts and spongy white breads. As we said earlier, most foods that are consumed in moderation—yes, even fats and carbohydrates—won't harm you.

5) *Read labels.* Becoming a healthy eater is very much linked to becoming an educated consumer. Reading product labels will tell you pretty much all you need to know about what deserves to go into your mouth and what doesn't. Peanut butter packed with sugar (if it's listed on the label as the second or third ingredient then you know it's a major player) is far less desirable than peanut butter that's made from 100 percent pure peanuts.

6) *Don't forget fiber.* The word "fiber" in this context may bring to mind some old geezer on a TV commercial, looking pained and unhappy on account of "irregularity." It's true that younger colons don't have quite so much to worry about as older ones do, but, whatever your age, it's never too early to establish healthy eating habits that set you up for better health later in life. Fiber, which your grandma might refer to as "roughage," is an indigestible complex carbohydrate found in plants. It has no calories because the body cannot absorb it. High-fiber foods like fresh fruits, vegetables, and bran and whole grain breads and cereals are low in fat and low in calories and give you larger, softer stools. If you're watching your weight, you should know that fiber takes up space in your stomach, thus giving you a feeling of fullness, without adding calories to burn. When increasing your fiber intake, be sure to increase your water intake accordingly.

7) *Don't eat when you're not hungry.* As we discussed earlier in this chapter, Americans, to the astonishment of most of the rest of the world, have a hard time *knowing* when they're hungry. We suggest that you pay attention to your hunger in a very conscious way, perhaps even by keeping a log for a week. If you're eating because you're stressed or bored, try doing something else, like going for a walk or riding a bike. You'll be amazed how much easier it is to keep your weight under control when you eat only when your stomach tells you you're hungry, and not when you eat just for the sake of putting something in your mouth.

8) *Chew your food* … like your parents always told you to. You don't necessarily need to chew each piece 100 times, but you should chew your food enough to experience the pleasure of eating so that you're not running ahead of yourself and eating more than you should in order to feel satisfied. This habit is good for the digestion as well.

Staying Fit

Along with a healthy diet, you can "condition" yourself for your demanding student lifestyle by incorporating a regular fitness routine into your schedule. The most important thing to remember when you launch yourself on a fitness regimen is that you needn't aim to look like Mr. or Ms. Universe. If you wind up a contender for such an honor, that's nice, but most of us are not in that league, and never will be. In fact, most of us are in the position where we have to make some kind of peace with our bodies—their shortcomings, their imperfections, and their "realities."

BODY IMAGE

As distorted as portions have become in the 21st century, so too has body image gone out of whack for a great many people. As we've said, advertising that shows super-thin models puts pressure on average people to conform to some kind of ideal that they might never realistically be able to achieve. In fact, the average American woman is 5'4" tall, weighs about 143 pounds, and wears a 10 to 12 dress size. That might be slightly overweight, but it's far from obese. Still, so many people who aren't overweight *feel* overweight, and, beyond that, so many people who are overweight are made to feel bad about their bodies. Here are some things to remember about body image and weight:

- *Few diets work.* Fad diets—all cabbage, all steak, all anything— are particularly notorious for their failure rates. According to the National Association to Advance Fat Acceptance (NAAFA), an advocacy group dedicated to improving the quality of life for fat people, fewer than 5 percent of all people on weight-loss diets succeed in losing a significant amount of weight or are able to maintain their weight loss over a 5-year period. Ninety percent of all dieters regain some or all of the weight originally lost, and at least one-third wind up gaining even more. In recent years, an increasing body of research has shown that genetic and physiological factors determine body size, not food intake. (By the way, according to NAAFA, "fat" is not a four-letter word. It is an adjective, like short, tall, thin, or blonde. While society has given "fat" a derogatory meaning, NAAFA believes that when people use the word "fat" to describe themselves, they are taking an important step in shedding the shame that they have been taught to feel about their bodies.)

- *Different cultural groups and different eras determine different standards of beauty.* We're living in the era of The Thin. At other times in history, thinness was not considered desirable and, in fact, was thought to be an indication of illness or poverty. Different cultural groups also have different ideas of what constitutes beauty. Don't be ruled by what you see on commercials. Think bigger ... in every way.

- *Focus on fitness.* No matter what size you are, you can still enjoy the benefits of a healthy, fit body. Concentrate more on your cardiovascular rate than on your waist size.

- *Think about which people history has deemed "great."* When you're feeling bad about yourself because you can't get into a pair of skinny jeans, just stop for a moment and think about the people in history who have achieved greatness. Dr. Martin Luther King,

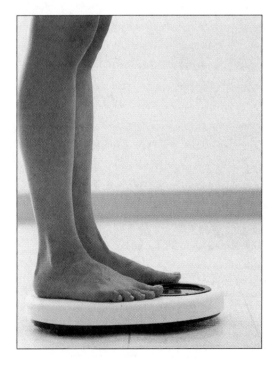

Gandhi, Golda Meier, Albert Einstein, Louis Armstrong, Mother Teresa … they came in all sizes and shapes, but none of them would be hired to walk down a runway.

In a perfect world, everyone would look as they wished to look. In a perfect world, no one would go to bed hungry, there would be no war, and the air we breathe and the water we drink would always be safe. We don't live in that world. We have to make the best of what we have … including the bodies we've been given.

CASE IN POINT: MORGAN SPURLOCK

Filmmaker Morgan Spurlock—33, a tall, rangy New Yorker—shocked audiences across the nation with his film *Super Size Me*, a look at America's addiction to fast food. Spurlock made himself the guinea pig in a daring experiment. He decided to eat exclusively at McDonald's for a solid month—three meals, every day—and took along a camera crew to record his experience. The deal was that if a counterperson offered to supersize his portion, he was compelled to say yes … and would then have to eat everything on his plate, including the pickles.

Neither Spurlock, nor his three attending physicians, were prepared for anything like the ravages caused by this diet. Within days, he was vomiting up his burgers and battling headaches and depression. He bid farewell to his sex drive, too. By the end of 1 month, his liver, overwhelmed by saturated fats, was in revolt. "The liver test was the most shocking thing," said Dr. Daryl Isaacs, one of the attending physicians. "It became very, very abnormal." Spurlock piled on 25 pounds during this period, and his cholesterol spiked from a healthy 165 to 230. "I got desperately ill," Spurlock told the *New York Post*. "My face was splotchy and I had this huge gut, which I've never had in my life … It was amazing—and really frightening."

The idea for *Super Size Me* came to Spurlock on Thanksgiving of 2002, as he watched TV after a dinner that had left him overly full. He saw a news item about two teenage girls in New York who were suing McDonald's for making them obese. The company responded by saying that their food was nutritious and good for people. Skeptical, Spurlock set out to test their claim.

All the while that *Super Size Me* was a hit on the art house film circuit, generating much press attention, McDonald's maintained a stony silence on the film, finally addressing it with a formal comment. "Consumers can achieve balance in their daily dining decisions by choosing from our array of quality offerings and range of portion sizes to meet their taste and nutrition goals," a McDonald's spokesman said. In fact, many people in low-wage jobs live in situations where they have no refrigerator, no microwave, no oven, no hot plate, and, for lack of any other options, their food comes from convenience stores and fast-food outlets. So Spurlock's "adventure" is really a way of life for a lot of poor people who are not only suffering from bad nutrition, but are literally paying a high price for it.

Spurlock claims that his goal was never to attack McDonald's as such. Among the issues he highlights in his film is the willingness of schools to feed students nothing but burgers and pizza. "If there's one thing we could accomplish with the film, it is that we make people think about what they put in their mouth," he said. "So the next time you do go into a fast-food restaurant and they say, 'Would you like to upsize that?' you think about it and say, 'Maybe I won't. Maybe I'll stick with the medium this time.'"

Source: Big Mac—not so nutritious. Retrieved December 7, 2005, from http://www.laleva.org/eng/2004/02/big_mac_not_so_nutritious.html

DEVELOPING A FITNESS REGIMEN

As you know, exercise is a great form of stress relief and has highly beneficial effects on your general body function. Many people, however, attempt to institute a fitness regimen but can't manage to stay with it. Here are some good ideas on how to make exercise fit into your life:

- *Take reasonable aim.* You don't have to be Lance Armstrong, Marion Jones, or anything even close to an Olympic hopeful. All you need is to complete a set amount of exercise in a set number of times a week. Even if your regimen is not as challenging as the ones being followed by your friends, the fact that you maintain discipline will have an enormous impact on your attitude and possibly, over time, on your appearance.

- *Find an activity that you enjoy.* Exercise doesn't have to be boring. In fact, it shouldn't be. It's all a matter of figuring out what you like to do. Some people are water babies; others like to bike; some like to dance. You choose. Just make sure that it's something that gives you enough basic pleasure to carry you through those periods when you really don't feel like doing it.

- *Remember that there are fitness opportunities everywhere.* You don't have to drape yourself in Spandex and join an expensive health club to get into shape. As you start to get into a fitness frame of mind, you'll find that there are opportunities wherever you look. Taking stairs instead of the elevator and then taking those stairs two at a time, for instance, is one way to turn a **mundane** moment into a fitness opportunity. When you go to the mall, instead of spending a half an hour looking for a spot closest to the stores, park as far away as you can and spend 20 minutes walking to and from your car.

- *Line up an exercise buddy.* The support of another individual—someone who can encourage you, praise you, and nag you—is an excellent spur toward further fitness.

- *Stay on schedule.* People who stick with their fitness regimens over the long haul have generally been able to do so because they exercise at certain times on certain days of the week. In other words, barring some emergency, they know that they'll be available at 4 o'clock on a Tuesday to go to the gym. If your fitness regimen is floating all over the place, you may be more likely to shunt it to second place when other matters come along.

mundane commonplace, not unusual, and often boring

- *Train—don't strain*. There's no point in setting the bar so high that you become discouraged almost as soon as you begin. Proceed at a sensible rate, and, if exercise is new to you, make sure to have a physical first.
- *Track your progress*. You may want to keep a chart of your fitness activities from day-to-day, week-to-week, month-to-month. Your satisfaction in seeing your progress can overcome the feeling of burnout that often threatens to take over.
- *Remember to breathe*. Deeply, that is—several times a day. A lot of us are so busy running around that we never allow ourselves a real inhalation. Deep breathing aerates your lungs and increases your workout capacity.
- *Hydrate*. Once again, drink water—lots of it. As you exercise, you lose water so replenishing it is vital.

Fitness is a lifelong proposition. Just visit any gym and you'll see people in their late sixties or even seventies whose workouts can put a twenty-something to shame. But don't be ashamed—be inspired! These folks serve as great role models.

And Then There's Sleep ...

Sleep—its quantity and quality—is as important as anything we've talked about so far in this chapter. Scientists don't really understand *why* human beings need to sleep; they just know that they do. Research has shown that after as few as 6 days of reduced sleep (4 hours or less a night), the body's ability to metabolize carbohydrates is diminished. In other research experiments, it has been shown that laboratory rats deprived of sleep will die in 2 to 4 weeks.

While the need for sleep is programmed into all humans, different people have different sleep patterns. The vast majority of humans either sleep in one long stretch of 6 to 8 hours or perhaps a period of 5 to 6 hours with a short snooze in the afternoon. The timing of sleep is profoundly connected to the cycles of light and dark. Humans are a **diurnal** species that chooses to sleep at night, in the dark, whenever possible.

Some of us need a good 10 hours of sleep to feel rested the next day; others do fine with just 5 or 6. Whatever your needs, your sleep habits can benefit by avoiding the don'ts below and following the do's:

SLEEPING DON'TS

If you're looking for a restful sleep, observe these guidelines:

- *Be sensitive to your caffeine intake*. That means chocolate, colas, and tea, as well as coffee. If sleep is your goal, eliminate all caffeine intake after 4 in the afternoon, and, if your sleep has been fitful lately, eliminate caffeine altogether … at least for a while.
- *Avoid alcohol late in the day*. To which, obviously, you are replying, "So when should I be drinking alcohol?" We're just giving you the facts, folks. The decision is yours. Alcohol, or a large meal, consumed late at night causes an increase in cortisol, a hormone secreted by the adrenal glands, and this increase can lead to sleeplessness.
- *Be careful about what you eat at night*. A bucket of greasy chicken wings or some hot and spicy tacos can rob you of a night's sleep. Are they worth it?
- *Establish an exercise routine that is consistent with your sleep needs*. Although exercising late at night might fit most easily into your work and school schedule, the overstimulation can wreak havoc on your sleep schedule. Late afternoons or early mornings are better times to exercise.
- *If sleep problems persist, seek medical advice*. You don't want to fall too deeply down the hole of sleep deprivation. Visit your physician or health facility to see what they advise.

SLEEP DO'S

If you're looking to establish better sleep habits, try these suggestions:

- *Stay on schedule*. This is probably the most important rule if you want to better your sleep. Wild variances in sleeping habits—staying

diurnal active during the day rather than at night
deleterious harmful

FOOD FOR THOUGHT: SLEEP DEPRIVATION

Sleep deprivation is a serious medical condition that affects over 47 million Americans. Although it can cause any number of **deleterious** effects, here are two of its most significant dangers:

- *Driver fatigue*. According to the National Highway Traffic Safety Administration, sleep-deprived drivers are involved in over 100,000 automobile accidents each year. Research studies have shown that driving while sleep-deprived is as dangerous as driving while intoxicated. Researchers in Australia and New Zealand have found that people who go 17 to 19 hours without sleep have more trouble operating their motor vehicles than people with blood alcohol levels of greater than 0.05 percent—the legal limit in most Western European countries.
- *Impaired glucose tolerance*. Sleep deprivation studies at the University of Chicago have shown that sleep deficits can quickly alter the body's ability to produce insulin, thus mimicking the symptoms of impaired glucose tolerance. The studies suggest that impaired glucose tolerance as a result of sleep loss could eventually lead to diabetes, obesity, and hypertension.

Source: The dangers of long term sleep loss. Retrieved December 7, 2005, from http://www.sleep-deprivation.com/html/dangers.php3]

up until 4 in the morning two nights a week, let's say—will pitch you headlong into a game of catch-up that you might not win.

- *Be careful about napping.* While a short nap of even 15 minutes can be restorative, you should try to schedule naps for the same time every day, if you're planning to incorporate them into your daily routine. Otherwise, you can interrupt your sleep cycle and wind up more tired than before.
- *Consciously relax before going to bed.* This may seem obvious, but a lot of people don't factor in any cool-down time before they retire to bed. Watching a raucous television show and then turning off the lights to go to sleep is a lot less effective than reading a book, listening to Celtic lullabies, or doing other quiet, contemplative activities that set you up for the quietest activity of them all—sleep. Nature has a natural "dusk" phase when the lights dim. We should simulate that phase by gradually lowering lights as the evening progresses, either by using the dimmer switch on the lighting fixture or by bringing out the candles. Simulating this "dusk" phase helps ease us into sleep.
- *Make sure your environment is conducive to sleeping.* If you're having sleep problems, perhaps your room is too warm or too cold. Or maybe you're sensitive to some detergent that you've been using to launder your sheets. Do your best to discover what's keeping you up at night.
- *Don't panic.* If you do have bouts of insomnia, take a deep breath … literally. Conscious breathing may lead you back to sleep. Whatever you do, try not to get up and start watching TV or playing solitaire or starting some other activity. You'll want to stay with your normal light/dark schedule as much as possible, so getting out of bed and turning the lights on will just confuse your body further. Try to stay in bed to ease yourself back into sleep.

Body Woes

One last subject we'd like to discuss in this chapter is the physical stress that people put on their bodies. If you are younger, you may not have experienced real musculoskeletal stress yet, but by adopting certain habits now you can save yourself a lot of pain down the line. If you are older, you know exactly what we're talking about. Here are some good thoughts to keep in mind:

STUDENT TALK: CATCHING THE ZZZZ'S

"I was having trouble sleeping, so I went to a sleep clinic. I think the most valuable piece of advice they gave me was to save my bed for sleeping purposes only. Now I know that's hard in a dorm room, where you're cramped for space, but, instead of doing all my reading and studying and stuff on my bed, I made a point to go to the library or the lounge instead, so that I could really try to keep my bed for what it was intended for: sleeping. It worked. My brain got the message: Bed = Sleep. So far, so good."

—Raven F., 20, Terre Haute, IN.

- *Sit the right way.* When you're working at your desk, keep your back straight and the soles of your feet on the floor. Don't cross your legs or your feet at the ankle. Keeping your soles on the floor lends you support. Also, when you sit, slide your rear to the rear of the seat. It takes discipline to do this, as many of us like to sprawl out, but your body will be grateful if you observe correct sitting habits.

- *Break up sitting with stretching.* Long hours of sitting at a computer takes its toll. Break up your sitting time for 10 minutes every 50 minutes with standing, stretching, and walking around.

- *Wear decent shoes.* As a student, you're going to be on your feet a lot, walking from class to class. If you have a job that requires standing, that's significantly more vertical time. Make sure you wear a pair of shoes that gives you support. High heels for women are one of humankind's worst inventions and can cause a host of musculoskeletal problems. Select shoes that are sufficiently wide, low-heeled, and that give your toes the room they need.

- *Be careful how you carry your books.* Backpacks are getting heavier and heavier, and potentially run the risk of posing serious hazards to those who carry them. According to the American Physical Therapy Association, backpacks should never weigh more than 15 percent of the carrier's total body weight. If your back or neck starts to bother you from carrying around a backpack, you might want to try a backpack on wheels. All right, it might not be the coolest-looking thing, but neck braces aren't exactly high style either. *Source:* Wellness Junction. Retrieved October 31, 2004, from http://www .wellnessjunction.com/athome/ergonomics/backpk3.htm

What Did We Learn?

Valuable information to remember was featured in this chapter. Test yourself to see what you remember with the following questions:

1. Explain the terms *wholeness* and *wellness*.
2. What is "portion distortion"?
3. Explain *anorexia nervosa* and *bulimia nervosa*.
4. What is meant by "real" food?
5. What are the staples of the Mediterranean diet?
6. What are nine tips that you should keep in mind when you're trying to establish a fitness regimen?
7. Name five sleep "don'ts."
8. Name five sleep "do's."
9. Describe the proper position for sitting in a chair at a desk.

Bibliography

Cloutier, M., & Adamson, E. (2004). *The Mediterranean diet: Newly revised and updated*. New York: Avon.

Dement, W. C., & Vaughan, C. (2000). *The promise of sleep: A pioneer in sleep medicine explores the vital connection between health, happiness, and a good night's sleep*. New York: Dell.

Hirschmann, J. R., & Munter, C. H. (1996). *When women stop hating their bodies: Freeing yourself from food and weight obsession*. New York: Ballantine.

Novak, J. (1999). *Posture, get it straight!* New York: Perigree Books.

Sapolsky, R. M. (2004). *Why zebras don't get ulcers*, 3rd ed. New York: Owl Books.

Schlosberg, S., & Neporent, L. (1999). *Fitness for dummies*. Hoboken, NJ: John Wiley & Sons.

Weil, A. (2001). *Eat well for optimum health: The essential guide to bringing health and pleasure back to eating*. New York: Collins.

Aim for Good Habits

The best time to establish healthy habits for your body is when you're young and still feel like you have infinite possibilities. It is much easier to acquire healthy lifelong habits *before* you do a lot of damage than *after*. Of course, nobody's perfect, and slip-ups do happen. Knowing the difference between good habits and bad habits is at least a step in the right direction. In our next chapter, we're going to focus on bad habits and what to do if you, or someone you know, are in their grip.

Willett, W. C., & Skerrett, P. J. (2002). *Eat, drink, and be healthy: The Harvard Medical School guide to healthy eating*. New York: Free Press.

Links

Body image. Retrieved December 7, 2005, from http://www.edreferral.com/body_image.htm

Dr. Andrew Weil, M.D.—health visionary. Retrieved December 7, 2005, from http://www.drweil.com

Ergonomics.org. Posture, movement and ergonomics. Retrieved December 7, 2005, from http://ergonomics.org/

Food and Nutrition Information Center. Retrieved December 7, 2005, from http://www.nal.usda.gov/fnic/

Mediterranean diet. Retrieved December 7, 2005, from http://www.americanheart.org/presenter.jhtml?identifier=4644

National Sleep Foundation. Retrieved December 7, 2005, from http://www.sleepfoundation.org/

The President's Council on Physical Fitness and Sports. Retrieved December 7, 2005, from http://www.fitness.gov/

Word Smart

Some of these are less likely to be encountered in your day-to-day living than others, but all are useful to know:

comestibles
defray
deleterious
diurnal
manifold
mundane
replenish
satiety

BREAKING BAD HABITS

In the last chapter, we talked about the importance of establishing balance in your life. In this chapter, we'll be looking at how bad habits can throw your life off balance in drastic ways. No matter how much you try to establish good habits, you'll be fighting a losing battle if you allow your bad habits to continue. Good habits like eating well, exercising, and getting enough sleep quickly fade in the face of bad ones. A drinking binge, for instance, creates a health risk that will far outweigh a few weeks of steady healthy living.

The college years—for younger students, in particular—are often a time of exploration and experimentation. Experimentation demands **prudence**, however. While self-experimentation has played an important and sometimes even heroic role in the history of science, it also evokes the image of the "mad scientist" who recklessly ignores the value of a controlled setting. When you experiment with yourself—how many drinks you can down in how short a time, for instance—you run the risk of joining those mad scientists whose experiments blew up in their faces. When you experiment, you want to be able to stay in control. Otherwise, the price may be too high.

In this chapter, we're going to look at bad habits, and we're going to be as frank and open-minded as we can be. Can you promise to do the same?

Let's start with that familiar force that lies at the root of so many bad habits—peer pressure.

prudence cautious wisdom

Peer Pressure

We first mentioned peer pressure all the way back in Chapter 1, when we cautioned that it doesn't disappear upon entering college. In fact, peer pressure often intensifies at this point. You're thrown into a whole new social grouping, and you may feel compelled to do things you wouldn't do otherwise in order to make a positive impression. Peer pressure is generally a problem for younger students, but people of any age can succumb to social pressure. A 45-year-old individual who gets a new job in a strange city can also be very susceptible to drinking too much or gambling too much at a "social" poker game or indulging in any number of other negative behaviors in order to gain admittance to "the club."

Peer pressure is usually associated with obviously destructive behaviors, like binge drinking, which we will be discussing later in this chapter. Peer pressure can show its negative effects in more subtle ways, however—as in fiscal irresponsibility. It's not unusual for college students to drive up large credit card bills in the hopes of keeping up with more affluent peers. Credit card companies are aware that they have good targets in college students, and their marketing objectives have shifted rapidly over the last 5 years from young professionals to college freshmen and high school seniors. In fact, 80 percent of teens between the ages of 18 and 20 use credit cards and, according to a survey conducted by George Washington University, three out of five students maxed out their accounts during their freshmen year at college. This disturbing statistic suggests that peer pressure comes in many different guises, and so it is very important to develop an awareness of how it works its destructive ways.

Peer pressure is usually thought of as a negative force, but it can be a positive force as well. In fact, a number of schools today are discovering a powerful tool: positive peer pressure. They are using "social norms" marketing to combat alcohol abuse, smoking, and at-risk sexual behaviors. Colleges are now hanging up posters, giving away key rings and T-shirts, and using their Web sites to convey the message that, contrary to popular belief, it's entirely normal and even "cool" to engage in healthy behaviors.

A number of quantitative studies back up this kind of "social norms" marketing. For instance, a 1999 survey showed that 61.5 percent of students at Virginia Commonwealth University had not smoked cigarettes for 30 days and that only 15.9 percent smoked daily. Another survey, conducted in 1999 at the University of Hawaii-Manoa, revealed that

How has peer pressure operated as a force in your life? Break up into small groups, appointing one group member as the reporter, and exchange your thoughts on the subject. Is peer pressure really as significant a force as it's reputed to be? If so, what can a person do to resist it? Do you think it operates in college as much as it did in high school? What kind of advice could you offer to someone who is struggling with this issue? After there's been time to talk in the small groups, re-form into one group and then, going around the room, let the reporters share the highlights from your small group discussions with everyone.

94 percent of its students reduced their risk of sexually transmitted diseases, including HIV, through abstinence, condom use, or by choosing to be in a monogamous relationship. "College students tend not to realize they are as healthy as they are," says Michael P. Haines, coordinator of health-enhancement services at Northern Illinois University and one of the pioneers of the social-norms movement. "It's certainly been my hypothesis that some of the reason for this underappreciation of their health is because authorities on college campuses have focused on their problems and identifying all the ways they get into trouble."

While peer pressure can work positively or negatively, the important thing to remember is that it doesn't simply go away as soon as you enter college. In many cases, it intensifies, with stakes as high, or even higher, than ever.

The Evil Weed

So many bad habits—where to begin? Smoking seems a good place, as it's so **prevalent**. The question is, with all that we know about smoking, *why* is it so prevalent? The answer is on account of the same old reasons—because people think it makes them look cool or more mature, because it calms them in certain stress situations, because it curbs the appetite, and because their friends are doing it. As well, a huge amount of very intense marketing drives home the message that smoking is the thing to do. It's no surprise that Joe Camel is more familiar to many young people than Donald Duck.

It is now common knowledge that smoking is an enormous health issue that can lead to lung problems, heart problems, bowel and bladder problems, and, of course, all sorts of cancer. As if these health problems weren't reason enough to kick the habit, consider the following reasons to cease and desist:

- *It smells bad*. Sometimes you have to get away from tobacco before you realize how much your clothes, house, and car stink of it. Your breath is no bed of roses either.
- *It's socially stigmatizing*. Why has smoking been banned from restaurants and public places in so many states? Because nonsmokers really don't want to be around the stuff. Not only does it smell bad, but second-hand smoke is also harmful. When you smoke, you run the risk of creating distance and disharmony with all those people who don't smoke. Can you afford that?

prevalent occurring, or accepted and practiced, commonly or widely

- *It detracts from your stamina and your appearance.* Even if you don't develop a major illness from smoking—although research indicates that in time you will—it can still cause breathing problems and fatigue. Heavy smoking will stain your teeth and fingers—not an attractive look—and can cause premature wrinkling of the skin.

- *It's expensive.* Is it ever—about $1,000 a year to support a pack-a-day habit. That may be more than all your school books, your gas money, and your food expenses put together. Is it worth the expense for something that's so bad for you?

Smoking is a notoriously difficult habit to break. Canada's cigarette pack warning, put into place in 2000, says, "Cigarettes are highly addictive. Studies have shown that tobacco can be harder to quit than heroin or cocaine." Smokers develop a psychological dependence on nicotine that has a real physiological basis. Within 8 seconds of an inhalation, nicotine releases a flood of dopamine into the brain. Dopamine is a neurotransmitter that is commonly associated with the brain's "pleasure system." The "aaah" release is similar to that brought on by cocaine and heroin, and is one reason why people keep smoking: to sustain this high dopamine level.

Even though smoking is such a hard habit to break, people are still managing to get the job done—these days, only 23 percent of all adults over the age of 18 smoke. That figure is down considerably from 42 percent in 1965. Heartening statistics regarding the health benefits of smoking cessation also provide good motivation for kicking the habit. Consider the following:

- Risk of heart disease is reduced by almost half just 1 year after a person stops smoking. Following 15 years of abstinence, ex-smokers suffer the same degree of risk for heart disease as people who have never smoked.

- In 5 to 15 years, the risk of stroke for ex-smokers becomes the same as that for nonsmokers.

- Male smokers who quit between the ages of 35 and 39 will add an average of 5 years to their life expectancy. Females in this age group who quit add 3 years.

Heartening statistics aside, it is still extremely difficult to quit smoking. Once you have made the decision to do so, you will find yourself bombarded with a dizzying array of nicotine replacement options—from patches to chewing gum, lozenges, sprays, inhalers, and more. Controversy swirls around all of these. Essentially, quitting smoking is a two-step process that involves: (1) overcoming the physical addiction to

nicotine, and (2) breaking the smoking habit. Nicotine replacement therapy may help with the first step, but should not be relied on exclusively.

Quitting smoking is a challenging affair that is different for each person. These top 10 tips should prove useful.

1) *Keep a log of your smoking habits.* It's important to understand the triggers that set off your habit. If, for instance, if you can't sit in a bar without lighting up, then you may have to stop going to bars—at least for a while.

2) *Seek the advice of medical professionals.* When you're ready to quit, consult your doctor or a physician's assistant. They will know more about the subject than you do, and may have some valuable ideas about how to make the process easier.

3) *Be clear on why you want to stop.* Make a list of all the reasons why you're ready to kick this habit. Just the expense alone might be enough of an incentive to get you to stop.

4) *Set a stop date.* Never underestimate how hard it is to quit smoking. Some people do it cold turkey—on a moment's notice—and that works for them. Most people, however, do better with some planning. Post your stop date in a place where you'll see it often—a refrigerator memo board is ideal—and carefully prepare yourself for what lies ahead.

5) *Find support wherever you can.* Let your family and friends know what you're doing. Ask them to reinforce your good behaviors and not tempt you with bad behaviors.

6) *Experiment with substitutes.* Some people find it useful to munch on carrots or suck on hard candies, chew on a pencil or a straw, or snack on sunflower seeds; some don't. You won't know until you try.

7) *Fight the cravings.* Cravings, on average, generally last 3 to 5 minutes. Knowing this can help you get through them.

8) *Drink water.* Lots of it! It will help flush the nicotine from your system, not to mention giving you something to do instead of smoking.

9) *Exercise helps.* Exercise is another useful way to keep your mind off smoking. As you watch your stamina and breathing begin to improve, you'll be even more motivated to stay with the program.

10) *Join a quit-smoking program.* Why go it alone? Studies show that people who join together with others who are trying to stop are generally more successful. The American Lung Association offers their excellent Freedom from Smoking programs all over the country. The Internet site http://QuitNet.com is another great resource for finding support programs. Consult the links at the end of the chapter for even more information.

It's important to remember that most people who quit smoking have to try at least more than once. Don't look at these episodes as failures. Cast them in a more positive light as "practice" and keep on trying. More than 45.7 million Americans have kicked the habit—so can you.

Under the Influence

The issue of drinking in our culture is simply monumental. Here are a few quick and sobering statistics:

- More than 100,000 deaths are caused by excessive alcohol consumption each year in the U.S. alone.
- More than 18 percent of Americans experience alcohol abuse or alcohol dependence at some point in their lives.
- Underage drinking costs the United States more than $58 billion each year—enough to buy every public school student a state-of-the-art computer.
- Alcohol kills six and a half times more youth than all other illicit drugs combined.

annals history or records

FOOD FOR THOUGHT: SMOKELESS TOBACCO AND CLOVE CIGARETTES

In the **annals** of bad ideas, smokeless tobacco ranks high. Some people switch from cigarettes to smokeless tobacco to get around smoking bans in restaurants, at the office, and in public buildings. They may also be under the illusion that they have picked a healthier alternative. Surprise—they haven't.

Smokeless tobacco comes in three forms: (1) chewing tobacco (loose leaf, plugs, or twists); (2) snuff; and (3) betel quid. All of these significantly increase the chances of developing oral cancer, which encompasses cancers of the mouth, tongue, throat, cheek, gums, and lips. Surgery to remove the cancer from any of these areas can result in severe disfigurement, and only 56 percent of people with mouth or throat cancer survive 5 years beyond their diagnosis. Smokeless tobacco also puts you at risk for cancers of the esophagus, larynx, stomach, and pancreas. It leads to severe gum disease and contributes to high blood pressure and cardiovascular disease. It's a disaster for your breath as well.

Smoking clove cigarettes, also known as bidis, is another habit that should never be taken up. While clove cigarettes are marketed as a safe alternative to tobacco, nothing could be further from the truth. According to the December 2000 issue of *Archives of Pediatrics and Adolescent Medicine*, clove cigarettes produce *three times* as much nicotine and carbon monoxide as regular cigarettes and *five times* as much tar.

When you think about drinking, what kinds of images come to mind? Do you see drinking as a glamorous activity? A kind of ongoing party? Does your family have a painful history with drinking? Take a few moments to explore your fundamental feelings about drinking—what confuses you, interests you, excites you, repels you. This will serve as a baseline to return to as you learn more about the subject.

"People see me as Little Miss Perfect. I've always been at the top of my class, I play varsity basketball, the clarinet, hold down a job at campus food services—the whole nine yards. Sometimes though, the pressure gets to me. Sometimes, it gets to me so bad that I'll go out on a Saturday night and get wrecked. When I'm doing it, it seems like fun, but the next day I'm still wrecked and it's no fun at all. In other words, I don't think it's working."

—Sandy T., 21, Towson, MD.

So why are so many people doing something that is potentially so destructive to their health? Good question.

People drink for a variety of reasons. In the short term, drinking releases tension and makes one feel more socially at ease. As you become dependent on drinking at certain times and in certain situations, your body will come to expect what it has come to rely on and there you go … you have a habit. Drinking is not genetically hereditary, but children who grow up with alcoholic parents are more likely to take up the habit. Finally, people drink because the culture tells them to. More money is spent promoting the use of alcohol than any other product. A recent study by the Center of Alcohol Marketing and Youth (CAMY) at Georgetown University showed that while advertising on television decreased overall by 11 percent between 2002 and 2003, the number of alcohol ads continued to rise, reaching 298,054 in 2003. The rate of ads for distilled spirits on national cable networks has exploded, from 513 in 2001 to 33,126 in 2003. That's a tidal wave of advertising, and tidal waves, as we know, are hugely destructive.

Alcoholism, like any disease, has its warning signs. Take a look at the following list. Do any of these indicators strike too close to home for you or someone you know?

- Getting drunk on a regular basis
- Avoiding others so that you can get high
- Giving up activities that were once of interest, like sports, music, drama, hobbies, and so on
- Lying, particularly about substance abuse
- Exchanging old friends who don't drink for new ones who do
- Expending energy in planning when, how, and with whom you can drink
- Complaining of hangovers
- Engaging in risk-taking activities, like combining drinking with driving or unprotected sex
- Experiencing blackouts, when you can't remember anything
- Suffering from depression and suicidal thoughts or fantasies

Identifying and treating bad habits is a complex process. In the space we have available in this chapter, we can only touch on these subjects. If you feel that you have a problem with alcohol, or any other illicit substance, a good place to begin seeking help is with the Student Health Services at your school, where you can discuss the issue with a counselor. Your visit will be held in confidence, and you should come away with a good sense of what your options are.

BINGE DRINKING

Binge drinking—which can be defined as drinking five or more drinks in a row for men and four drinks for women—is fast becoming one of the most notorious campus problems. According to a recent Harvard School of Public Health College Alcohol Study, approximately two out of five college students are binge drinkers.

Binge drinking has been very much in the news lately. In 2004, two tragic incidents in Colorado attracted widespread media attention. At Colorado State University, 19-year-old incoming freshman Samantha Spady, homecoming queen of her high school, went on a binge where she consumed 30 to 40 drinks and was found dead on the floor of a fraternity house. Just 12 days later, at nearby University of Colorado, freshman Gordie Bailey, 18, was found dead, also on a frat house floor, after drinking massive amounts of alcohol in a hazing ritual.

The dire effects of binge drinking are **unarguable**. Students who binge drink are 21 times more likely than nonbinge drinkers to damage property, miss classes, engage in unprotected sex, or be otherwise hurt or injured. Alcohol is involved in 90 percent of all campus rapes, according to Columbia University's National Center on Addiction and Substance Abuse. In short, binge drinking is tantamount to playing Russian roulette. Actually, your chances of surviving binge drinking may be even worse than your chances of surviving Russian roulette. You don't need a medical degree to know that putting 30 to 40 drinks into your body is going to be deadly, every time.

To avoid getting caught up in any binge drinking episodes, follow these tips:

- *Understand the physiology of drinking.* You should begin by knowing exactly how alcohol works on your body, how much (or how little) is required to cause inebriation, and what the effects of being drunk are.

- *Understand why you drink.* Explore the subject, either by yourself or with some trusted friends. Often, people drink to mask feelings of low self-esteem. Do you drink because you feel insecure in social situations? If that's the case, what else might you do that will help you feel more secure going into a party? For that matter, do you even need to go to that party?

- *Learn to resist.* Think before you act and ask yourself what's at stake. What do you stand to gain and what do you stand to lose?

unarguable cannot be argued with

What will it mean to your life to be in a car accident, to seriously injure a friend or yourself, or to be arrested for driving under the influence?

- *Keep your distance.* Until you feel stronger in terms of resisting peer pressure, perhaps you should forego certain situations where you know there are going to be activities that aren't good for you. Now may not be the right time for partying. That doesn't mean you have to stay home alone. You can join a club or some other group that offers social activities that don't emphasize alcohol.
- *Keep your stress level under control.* Review our chapter on stress for some good ideas.

Binge drinking exacts the highest price there is. You have too much ahead of you to risk such a tragedy.

Intervening with Friends

We're not going to be looking at the entire range of illicit substances that confront your average college student today. Unfortunately, there are simply too many of them. In addition to alcohol—the drug of choice for most college students—there is marijuana, amphetamines, barbiturates, club drugs, cocaine, steroids, and even heroin to choose from. But we do want to make room in this chapter to talk about the difficult subject of intervening with friends if you see them falling into destructive patterns of behavior. Here are some guidelines to follow:

- When picking a time to have your big talk, make sure it's when your friend is sober or straight and when you know you won't be interrupted.
- Discuss *your* feelings, not your friend's mistakes. Starting out with something like, "Lee, I'm worried about you" is far preferable to "Lee, look what you're doing to yourself."
- Be prepared to give specific examples. "What about that time, Lee, when you couldn't even remember that we had gone to Jack's party?" Or, "Let's look back to New Year's Eve, when you ran over my parents' outdoor furniture."
- Pay strict attention to your tone. You want to sound caring—not accusatory, not pitying.
- Expect denial and even anger from your friend. If it becomes too intense, suggest you take it up again at another time.
- Before you talk to your friend, try to gather information about resources that can help with the problem. It helps all around if you're informed.

Any way you look at it, it's a hard job to intervene with friends who are having serious problems. It's even harder, however, to just stand by and watch people endanger themselves or the lives of others. Do the hard deed, and, however it turns out, feel good about the fact that you did what you could.

Safe Sex

Let's look at the progression of this chapter. We started out talking about smoking—a bad habit any way you look at it. Then we turned to drinking—not, by definition, a bad habit. After all, millions of people obviously are able to control their drinking and can enjoy wine, beer, or a cocktail without hurting themselves or anyone else. But while we can't state that alcohol is a *bad* thing, we wouldn't go so far as to say it's a *good* thing either. Essentially, it is what you make of it. Sex, on the other hand, is innately good. Sex is one of life's great pleasures … under the right circumstances. Understanding the right circumstances will determine whether sex is a positive force in your life or a negative one.

Like most things that come with real maturity—spending money, driving a car, drinking—sex must be approached responsibly. As we indicated earlier, in the section on binge drinking, there is a direct correlation between alcohol impairment and unsafe or unwanted sex. That's just one example of approaching sex irresponsibly. In this section, we are going to present the parameters of safe sex and clear up a few key questions you may have. Your sexual life is an evolving entity and we can only offer some **rudimentary** advice. The rest is up to you, and we suggest that you educate yourself on the subject. A good place to begin is by exploring the books and Web sites listed at the end of this chapter.

rudimentary introductory

Safe sex is easily defined. It means to take precautions during sexual activity in order to decrease the potential for transmitting or acquiring sexually transmitted diseases (STDs). An STD is a contagious disease that is transferred not only through intercourse, but also through other sexual contact. The **pathogens** that can cause STDs are present in the mucous membranes that line the urethra, vagina, anus, and mouth. Some pathogens can also live on the skin. STDs, which can be transferred through oral, vaginal, or anal intercourse, are an issue for straights and gays alike. The following are the most commonly encountered STDs:

- *Gonorrhea*. If untreated, this infection of the genital mucous membranes can cause sterility in both men and women. Gonorrhea can be cured with antibiotics.

- *Chlamydia*. An infection of the genital and urinary tracts that is milder than gonorrhea but manifests similar symptoms. Left untreated, Chlamydia can cause severe pelvic inflammatory disease in women and can lead to sterility in either sex. Antibiotics can cure Chlamydia.

- *Genital herpes*. Caused by a virus similar to that which causes cold sores, genital herpes come and go. Although it cannot be cured, there are drugs that will control the symptoms and reduce the frequency of occurrence.

- *Syphilis*. A grave disease caused by bacterium and once the **scourge** of millions, syphilis can be treated successfully with antibiotics. Untreated, syphilis will seem to disappear on its own, sometimes for years, only to reappear, in its devastating final stages, with blindness, paralysis, insanity, and, ultimately, death.

- *HIV infection*. The human immunodeficiency virus (HIV) gradually destroys the immune system, resulting in infections that are hard for the body to combat. People who become infected with HIV may be without symptoms for up to 10 years, but they can still transmit the infection to others. During this time, their own immune system weakens until they are diagnosed with AIDS (*acquired immune deficiency syndrome*), the fifth leading cause of death among persons between the ages of 25 and 44 in the United States. About 47 million people worldwide have been infected with HIV since the start of the worldwide epidemic in the early 1980s.

- *Hepatitis B* and *Hepatitis A*. These forms of hepatitis, both of which can be fatal, are caused by viruses found in blood, semen, and feces and are spread in the same manner as HIV. Hepatitis B virus

pathogens disease-producing organisms
scourge any means of causing suffering or death

(HBV), which attacks the liver, is easier to catch than HIV because it is 100 times more concentrated in an infected person's blood and can exist on surfaces outside the body. There are vaccines available that offer protection against both of these disease strains. Check with your health care professional or your local public health department for more information.

These illnesses are frightening, but the good news is that people can fully enjoy sex as long as they avoid high-risk behaviors and do what they can to promote safer behaviors. High-risk behaviors include:

- Having sex with an unknown partner without the use of a condom.
- Having multiple sex partners.
- Using drugs or alcohol in a situation where sex might take place.
- Having sex with a partner who is an IV drug user.
- Having anal intercourse, which is a particularly high-risk sexual activity.

Safer sex practices you can follow include:

- Knowing your partner well enough so that you can have a dialogue about sex that includes such topics as your own and your partner's current health status and previous experience with STDs.
- The use of barriers to avoid contact with semen, vaginal fluid, or blood. It is crucial that you understand the correct use of condoms—male or female condoms. (The female condom has an effectiveness rate of only 75 percent to 82 percent, as compared to the male condom, which has an effectiveness rate of 98 percent.) Note that only water-based lubricants should be used in conjunction with condoms. Oil-based lubricants or petroleum-type lubricants may cause latex condoms to weaken and tear. Note, too, that "natural" or "sheepskin" condoms, while protecting against pregnancy, are ineffective in preventing STDs and HIV/AIDS.
- Stay sober and maintain your independent judgment at all times.

Perhaps the most important piece of advice that we can offer about safe sex is that it's safest when you share an experience with someone you trust. It may take a while to know whether you do trust a person. Don't rush. There's time.

Date Rape

Along with binge drinking, date rape has tarnished the college image in the minds of many people. Date rape is a very serious issue that all students should be made aware of. Date rape is forced or coerced sex between partners, dates, friends, friends of friends, or general

acquaintances. The coercion can be physical or emotional, in terms of threats to one's reputation if you don't "put out" or other kinds of blackmail. Date rape is the most common form of rape, accounting for 78 percent of all rape incidents. Looking for another sobering statistic? One in four women are expected to fall victim to rape or attempted rape before they turn 25, while three out of five rapes occur before a girl reaches 18. And rape doesn't just happen to women. Men can be raped, too. Approximately 1 in 14 men is a rape survivor.

It must be universally understood that rape is a capital crime. If a person says no to sex, regardless of his or her degree of emphasis, and you go ahead with it anyway, you are committing rape. Legally speaking, you are also committing rape if you have sex with a person who has had too much to drink or is on drugs and cannot consent to having sex. The average prison sentence for a rape conviction is 14 years and 8 months.

Date rape often occurs after a victim has been drugged with one of the so-called "date-rape drugs." These drugs may render a person unconscious and limit memory. Using these drugs on a person, even without carrying out a rape, is a federal crime that can potentially result in a 20-year prison sentence.

The three most prevalent date-rape drugs are:

- *Rohypnol*. With street names like Rophy, Ruffles, Do-U, Forget It, and Mexican Valium, Rohypnol is a prescription sedative/depressant produced worldwide by Hoffmann-La Roche, Inc. This drug is not manufactured or approved for use in North America, but it is easily obtainable as a street drug. It is tasteless, colorless, and can be crushed and added to any drink, including water, without detection.
- *Gamma hydroxy butyrate (GHB)*. Among its street names are Easy Lay, Liquid Ecstasy, Get-Her-to-Bed, and Liquid X. This colorless, odorless liquid, banned in the United States and Canada, acts on the central nervous system as a depressant/anesthesia. It can be easily concocted in home labs.
- *Ketamine hydrochloride*. With street names like Special K, OK, KO, and Kid Rock, this legal drug, sold as a veterinary sedative, goes under the brand names Ketaset or Ketalar. It has an anesthetic effect on humans, rendering them vaguely aware of but comfortably detached from bodily sensations.

Date-rape drugs not only make a person vulnerable to rape, but they can also kill. GHB has been linked to more than 60 deaths in the United States between the years 1992 and 2001 alone. In most of these cases, alcohol was also a contributing factor to the mortality *Source:* Greater Dallas Council on Alcohol and Drug Abuse. Retrieved February 11, 2005, from http://www.gdcada.org/statistics/ghb.htm. It should be remembered, however, that the most prevalent date-rape drug, and one of the most devastatingly effective, is alcohol.

How can you protect yourself against date-rape drugs? Follow these guidelines:

- Don't accept drinks from strangers.
- Don't accept open drinks—either alcoholic or nonalcoholic. Drink only from a can, bottle, or tetra pack that you open yourself.
- When you're in a bar or a club, take your drink directly from the bartender and watch carefully as it is poured.
- Never leave your drink unattended or turn your back on your table. Take your drink with you if you move around.
- Avoid open beverage sources like punch bowls, pitchers, or tubs.
- Use the buddy system. Watch out for your friends and make sure they watch out for you in case any of you seem too intoxicated too quickly. Get help immediately if you suspect foul play.

Source: Retrieved February 11, 2005, from http://teenadvice.about.com/library/weekly/aa062502b.htm

If you know or suspect that you've been drugged and sexually assaulted, take the following steps:

1) Go directly to a hospital, medical facility, or Student Health Services.

2) To avoid destroying valuable physical evidence, do not shower before you go or wash the clothes you were wearing.

3) Explain to the personnel at the medical facility what you believe has happened to you. They will most likely have a routine in place to handle the situation. They will probably call in the local authorities. If they don't, you will need to report the incident to the police yourself—the sooner, the better.

4) Seek counseling. Rape is a traumatic event that can take its toll, psychologically and emotionally. The medical facility that treated you will probably be able to recommend a counselor or support group that can help you.

5) Remember that you have done nothing wrong and that you are not alone. Rape is a terrible crime that unfortunately happens to a great many people. Among the national hotlines that you

What Did We Learn?

This chapter is filled with genuinely life-saving information. Test yourself on how well you remembered it.

1. Is peer pressure a positive or negative force?
2. Cite at least five reasons why a person should stop smoking.
3. What is dopamine and how does it relate to nicotine use?
4. Describe the two-step process involved in stopping smoking.
5. Cite at least five of the top 10 tips for stopping smoking.
6. What is smokeless tobacco? What dangers does it present?
7. True or false? Clove cigarettes are a healthy alternative to tobacco.
8. Cite at least five warning signs of a drinking problem.
9. Define binge drinking.
10. Describe six guidelines to observe when intervening with friends who are having substance abuse issues.
11. Define safe sex.
12. Define a sexually transmitted disease (STD).
13. Name the six most commonly encountered STDs.
14. Name five high-risk sex behaviors.
15. Name three safe sex practices that should always be observed.
16. What are the three most prevalent date-rape drugs?
17. Cite at least five guidelines that can help protect you against exposure to date-rape drugs.

can call in times of crisis are the Rape, Abuse, and Incest National Network (1-800-656-HOPE [4673]), the Youth Crisis Hotline (1-800-HIT-HOME), and Ask-a-Nurse (1-800-888-5551), which offers free medical advice.

Play It Safe

In a perfect world, there would be no rape, no drug abuse, and no bad habits to wreak havoc on peoples' lives. We don't live in a perfect world, however. Our world is highly imperfect, but also full of wonder and joy. The operative word, once again, is "balance." Proceed with caution ... but proceed. Life is meant to be lived, even with all its dangers and pitfalls. Remember: the odds are with you.

Bibliography

Eisenberg, A., Eisenberg, H., & Mooney, A. J. (1992). *The recovery book.* New York: Workman Publishing Company.

Farquhar, J., & Spiller, G. A. (1991) *The last puff: Ex-smokers share the secrets of their success.* New York: W. W. Norton & Company.

Fisher, E. B. (1998). *American Lung Association 7 steps to a smoke-free life.* New York: Wiley.

Holmes, P. (1992). *Out of the ashes: Help for people who have stopped smoking.* Minneapolis, MN: Fairview Press.

Institute for Advanced Human Sexuality. (1999). *The complete guide to safer sex* Fort Lee, NJ: Barricade Books.

Tighe, A. A. (1998). *Stop the chaos: How to get control of your life by beating alcohol and drugs.* Center City, MN: Hazelden Press.

Warshaw, R. (1994). *I never called it rape: The Ms. Report on Recognizing, Fighting, and Surviving Date and Acquaintance Rape.* New York: Harper.

Links

Alcohol. Retrieved December 8, 2005, from http://www.gdcada.org/statistics/alcohol.htm

American Cancer Society Guide to Quitting Smoking. Retrieved December 8, 2005, from http://www.cancer.org/docroot/PED/content/PED_10_13X_Quitting_Smoking.asp

Acquaintance/date rape resources. Retrieved December 8, 2005, from http://www.vachss.com/help_text/date_rape.html

Binge drinking turning deadly. Retrieved December 8, 2005, from http://www.cbsnews.com/stories/2004/10/14/earlyshow/living/parenting/main649375.shtml

College drinking: Changing the culture. Retrieved December 8, 2005, from http://www.collegedrinkingprevention.gov/

Colleges use peer pressure to encourage healthy behavior. Retrieved December 8, 2005, from http://www.hws.edu/news/update/showwebclip.asp?webclipid=24

Enjoying safer sex. Retrieved December 8, 2005, from http://wso.williams.edu/orgs/peerh/sex/safesex/

Quit smoking. Retrieved December 8, 2005, from http://www.quitnet.com/

Surgeon General's Guide to Quitting Smoking. Retrieved December 8, 2005, from http://www.surgeongeneral.gov/tobacco/consquits.htm

Television alcohol ads bombarding teens continue to rise. Retrieved December 8, 2005, at http://camy.org/press/release.php?ReleaseID=24

Word Smart

Building a better vocabulary is a *good* habit.
Remember these:

- annals
- pathogen
- prevalent
- prudence
- rudimentary
- scourge
- unarguable

15

MONEY MATTERS

It certainly does—matter, that is. Surely there are ways to be happy in this world without a lot of money, just as there are ways to be profoundly unhappy with a great deal of the stuff, but there's no getting around the fact that, however you look at it, money is going to play a major role in your life. While money can create enormous opportunities, the lure of lucre **can also seduce you into devastating misjudgments. The bottom line is that the subject of money is never neutral.**

In this chapter, we'll be examining the fundamentals of money: budgeting, banking, credit, and more. You may already be familiar with much of this information, but other aspects might be new to you, particularly if you are among our younger readers. In any event, this overview will provide a good introduction to the subject, but that's all it is—an introduction. If you want to be smart about money, you have to keep on learning, because change is happening continually—both to you and to the culture around you.

With each new stage of life, your relationship to money will shift, and there are always new tax laws, new investment possibilities, and other developments that only an informed individual can take advantage of. Right now, as a student, you may be more concerned about your day-to-day money matters than you are about any long-range planning issues. So that's what we'll

lucre money or riches

235

be focusing on—those day-to-day matters. It's never too soon, however, to cast an eye toward the future, so we'll be allotting some space in this chapter as well to a discussion of longer-range money matters.

The Psychology of Money

As we said previously, money is never neutral. It carries a positive and a negative charge. When we have money, the possibilities seem endless. We can buy things, go places, and feel secure. But do we? If money makes people feel secure, then why do some people pursue it to such an extent that they incriminate themselves and wind up in prison?

As we've suggested elsewhere in this book, the existence of certain **dualities** help us organize our understanding of the world. Such dualities as introvert/extrovert or pessimist/optimist can be thought of as magnetic poles, with most people being more attracted to one pole or the other. A similar kind of duality exists around money. The compulsive nonspender, living in dread that expenses may exceed income, represents one pole. At the other pole is the compulsive spender whose buying sprees completely disregard economic realities. The pull we feel toward one or the other of these poles may be influenced largely by the values we learned within our families.

Compulsive nonspenders are often people who have lived through a period of great deprivation, like the Depression, for instance. For them, money in the bank—or, in extreme cases, under the mattress—is the only thing that can offer any kind of feeling of security. Ironically, these nonspenders often fall prey to conmen who tantalize them with get-rich-quick scams, promising them the only kind of happiness they can really relate to—a happiness symbolized by a sudden and dramatic increase in monetary reserves. The compulsive spender, on the other hand, may be out to buy love. Often, it's the love that was never given in childhood. Compulsive spenders turn to buying in order to feel better about themselves. When depressed, they may go on a buying spree, using a $500 pair of shoes or a $400 cashmere sweater as a "pick-me-up."

A person's relationship to money will be most balanced and healthy only when it is understood that money is a means to an end, not the end itself. Money provides a certain degree of freedom to do as you like and to avoid what you'd rather not do, but money is *not* the answer to all problems. As we've said, it is often the beginning of major problems.

IN OTHER WORDS

"Money frees you from doing things you dislike. Since I dislike doing nearly everything, money comes in handy."

—Groucho Marx

dualities states or parts that are complementary or opposed to each other

MONEY IN AMERICA

Not only do we all carry around the personal baggage that we've inherited from our families on the subject of money, but we also have to consider how the culture at large deals with this issue. That fact is that we live in a very material culture. For most people, the American dream means owning your own home or two cars or a plasma television set or titanium golf clubs or a platinum watch or diamonds or furs or … well, there's no end to it. That's the nature of materialism. The more you buy into it, the less you ultimately feel that you have. A kind of shark-like hunger for *things* begins to rule your life.

Our culture is set up to reinforce this hunger. Consumer items are churned out, and these have to be sold. To continuously stoke our desire for *things*, vast amounts of money are spent on advertising. We come to believe that in order to attract a mate we have to wear designer clothing, drive an expensive car, or spend money on cosmetic surgery. Our television shows are increasingly about "reality," as if reality were about winning big prizes—who can make a million dollars by lasting longest on a desert island or being the most devious member of an office crew? What we viewers may not realize is that these shows are just another form of advertising that has been put into place to convince us to *spend*. And so the system goes round and round, with too few of us escaping its clutches.

It's up to you to decide how much you're willing to buy into the culture of consumerism. One way to resist all this pressure is to recognize that we—not the vendors around us—are in control of our finances and our lives. The best tool in the shed for gaining that control is careful, conscientious budgeting.

Budgeting

Older students know all about budgeting—or at least they should—but if you're on the younger end of our readership spectrum, perhaps this subject is still fairly new to you. You may already have had some significant conversations on this subject with important people in your life, but, if you haven't, don't despair. Budgeting is actually a very easy concept to grasp. A budget is a blueprint that shows you how to use the money that is available to you. It should address your goals—short-term, intermediate, and long-term—and help you maintain control over your finances.

A budget will not only show you what's coming in and what's going out, but it will also help you achieve your goals. If, for instance, you want to take a vacation in the spring, your budget will help you attain that goal by showing you that you won't have the money if you spend it on CDs, poker, a bar tab, and fancy running gear in the winter. A budget doesn't lie. It's made up of hard numbers, and it forces you to make choices.

Let's see what a budget worksheet might look like for someone who is currently enrolled in college:

I. Monthly Income

Estimated monthly salary	0
Minus taxes *(approx. 28%)*	0
Net income	0
Financial aid award[s]	0
Other income	0
Total	0

II. Semester Expenses

Tuition and fees	0
Books	0
Deposits	0
Transportation/Moving	0
Total	0

III. Monthly Expenses

Rent	0
Combined utilities	0
Groceries	0
Auto expenses	0
Student loan(s)	0
Other loans	0
Credit cards	0
Insurance	0
Medical expenses	0
Entertainment	0
Miscellaneous	0
Total	0

IV. Discretionary Income

Monthly income	0

IV. Discretionary Income

Expenses (Semester + Monthly)	0
Total	0

You'll notice two kinds of expenses on this budget worksheet: *fixed* and *flexible*. A fixed expense is one that doesn't change. If you've signed a 2-year lease for an apartment to the tune of $800 a month, then your rent under the Expenses column will show $800 as a fixed expense. On the other hand, your Entertainment allotment is highly flexible. After all, you don't *have* to go to the movies every Saturday night, do you?

MAKING YOUR BUDGET WORK FOR YOU

Once you've totaled up your income and expenses, your budget worksheet should give you a pretty good picture of where you stand. When you subtract your expenses from your income, if less than 5 percent of your income remains, or if the sum is below zero, then you know it's time to trim your sails. Not only are you going to have to forego the movies every Saturday night, but you'd better not buy that pair of shoes and you might want to consider cooking up some spaghetti tonight instead of ordering in Chinese.

In addition to these stopgap actions, you might want to explore some ongoing ways to save money. For example, you might try shopping around for cheaper car insurance. Or how about looking for a better rent deal? You might start turning out lights, as your parents always told you to do. Once you start thinking economically, you'll see that it becomes a habit … a very good habit indeed.

Speaking of good habits, you'll also want to start saving some money —if not for the future, then at least to get into the savings habit. Ultimately, of course, as you get older, you will be saving for the future—for your kids' education, your retirement, and such. While you're still young, however, you'll want to establish the habit of saving by putting away money for a car, a vacation … something that you can work toward and feel good about achieving. Start out by trying to save 5 percent of your net income. You'll be surprised by how **doable** that is, and how quickly your nest egg will grow.

Here are some good ideas to keep in mind when it comes to budgeting:

- *Keep records*. As best you can, keep track of what you spend. Scrupulously maintain your bank and credit card statements. These will help you identify your spending patterns, and you'll need them for tax purposes, student loans, and so on.

doable able to be done or achieved

- *Look into automatic deposit and payments*. If you're in a job, see if your paycheck can be automatically deposited into your account. You might also want to see if you can make certain regular payments, such as phone bills and utilities bills, directly from your bank. That way, you won't be late and your credit rating will remain healthy.
- *Factor in special circumstances*. When you're considering your savings needs, take into account any special situations that may be coming up. They could be joyful (somebody's special birthday, anniversary, wedding) or difficult (an unforeseen medical expense or a trip to visit a sick relative).
- *Watch your withdrawals*. Try to withdraw all your money *for the week* at one time. Don't go running to the ATM every 5 minutes for those $20 fixes. It's hard to stay on top of your spending habits that way.
- *Don't put your head in the sand*. If you feel yourself moving into difficult financial straits, don't ignore it. That's like ignoring the tooth pain that you think is going to go away but is actually only getting worse. Seek advice as soon as possible. Your school's Financial Aid office is a good place to start. If necessary, they can refer you to the appropriate channels to help you get on top of your spending.

Banking 101

In this section, we're going to be walking you through checking and savings. You may already be familiar with many aspects of this material. If so, bear with us. Who knows? You may learn some things that are new to you as well.

CHECKING

Checking accounts probably do not represent an area of great mystery to most people, but, year-to-year, their features change, due to ever-advancing technology. Essentially, when you select a checking account, you want to weigh certain features, to see which bank can most closely meet your needs. Among these features are the following:

- *Fees*. What does the bank charge per check? Are there monthly fees associated with the account? Are there any ATM fees you should know about?
- *Convenience*. Is there a branch conveniently located near your home, school, or workplace? Do the hours of operation suit your schedule?

- *Interest*. Here you're looking at the rate earned, the minimum deposit that's necessary to earn interest, and how the interest is compounded. (More about compounding in a moment.) You'll want to know what happens if you fall below the necessary balance. Do you incur a fee?

- *Charges and restrictions*. Sometimes you'll find out, after the fact, that a checking account has features you really don't like. We're talking about things like holding periods for deposited checks and stop-payment fees. Know what you're getting into.

- *Bells and whistles*. These days, in their competition for customers, banks are offering a lot of attractive "extras." Among these are direct deposit options (allowing your earnings or government payments to be automatically deposited into your bank account), automatic payments (payments automatically made to utility companies, lending institutions, and other businesses), online banking (also known as cyberbanking, which allows customers to check balances, pay bills, transfer funds, and apply for loans on the Internet), and discounts or even free checking for students. Another feature that is very attractive, if you can get it, is overdraft protection. This provides you with a line of credit to write checks for more than the actual account balance. Instead of being charged $25 or even more for a bounced check, the overdraft protection, in a sense, provides you with an instant loan to see you past your shortfall. Some banks will charge a fee when the account balance falls below a certain level, but it's usually much less than the fee that you would incur for a bounced check. Ask your bank about overdraft protection and any of the other special features we've mentioned.

A Penny Saved …

… is a penny earned. So goes the old saying, but what exactly does it mean? After all, if you save a penny, you haven't *earned* it. Or have you? What we believe the saying means is that old-fashioned values like thrift and frugality promote savings, which, as you'll soon see, can earn money for you in a big way.

Let's imagine, for the moment, the kind of savings you could realize if you only bought one double mocha latté per day instead of your usual two. If the latté costs $2.99, then you would save $20.93 a week by foregoing that extra luxury. In one month, you would have saved $92.69. In one year, the savings would amount to $1,091.35. In 10

FOOD FOR THOUGHT: *RECONCILING A CHECKING ACCOUNT*

For many people today, reconciling a checking account is some kind of quaint, bygone activity, like making homemade jams or darning socks. In fact, the need to reconcile a checking account is just as relevant today as ever. Certainly, banks haven't stopped making mistakes, and reconciling your checkbook is your opportunity to be a watchdog over your account. Here's how it works:

1) When you get your bank statement, look at your current balance.

2) Add any deposits that you have entered onto your check register but that do not yet appear on your statement.

3) Subtract any outstanding checks that are not reflected in the statement.

4) Compare your result with the balance as shown on the bank statement.

If you discover a discrepancy, consult a bank representative. Don't be shy. As we said, mistakes *do* happen … a lot.

years, it would be $10,913.50. And that's all *without interest*. Have a look at the following table to see what happens when interest enters the picture.

The Impact of Interest		
Amount saved	**At % interest**	**In 10 years you'll have**
$7.00	5%	$4,720
$14.00	5%	$9,440
$21.00	5%	$14,160
$28.00	5%	$18,880
$35.00	5%	$23,600

As you can see from the chart, the roughly $21 a week you saved by giving up that second latté will earn you, in 10 years, approximately another $4,000 if you save it in an interest-bearing account.

This is a good time to explain how simple and compounded interest are calculated. With simple interest, you multiply your dollar amount by the interest rate and the length of time in order to calculate the amount earned. In other words, if you had $100 in a savings account that paid you a simple 6 percent interest, you'd earn $6 in interest during your first year. In 2 years you'd have earned $12, and so on. The account would continue to grow at a rate of $6 per year, despite whatever interest you've accumulated. With compounded interest, the interest is paid not only on the original amount of the deposit, but on the accumulated interest as well. So if you deposited $100 in a savings account that paid 6 percent compounded annually, in the first year you'd earn $6 in interest. You'd then have $106 dollars. In your second year, your interest calculations would look like this:

$106 (original amount + earned interest) × 0.06 (interest rate) × 1 (length of time) = $6.36.

Now that might not seem like a lot, but, as you'll see, it adds up dramatically over time.

TYPES OF SAVINGS ACCOUNTS

Once you decide to start saving—a decision we hope you'll come to sooner than later—you'll find a range of savings options to select from. These include:

- *Passbook account*. The depositor receives a booklet in which all deposits, withdrawals, and interest are recorded.
- *Statement account*. Essentially the same as a passbook account, except that the depositor receives monthly statements instead of a passbook.
- *Interest-earning checking account*. Combining the benefits of checking and savings, these accounts earn the depositor interest on any unused monies kept in the balance.
- *Money-market deposit accounts*. These are checking/savings accounts in which the interest rate is computed according to the size of the balance and current levels of market interest rates. A depositor can access money from this account through an ATM, in person at the bank, or by writing a limited number of checks per month (usually three). A minimum balance of $1,000 to $2,500 is usually required.
- *Certificates of deposit (CDs)*. Here the bank pays a fixed amount of interest for a fixed amount of money over a fixed amount of time. CDs are risk-free, there are no fees involved, and they pay a higher interest rate than savings accounts. The flip side of the coin is that your access to your money is restricted and there is a penalty if you withdraw funds before the expiration date.
- *Bonds*. Among the safest investments you can make, a bond is essentially an "IOU." It certifies that you've lent money to an institution—a government entity, let's say, or a public utility—and that you will be repaid in time. The bond has a fixed rate of interest for a fixed amount of time. When the time is up, the bond is said to have "matured," and then you can redeem it for full face value.
- *Mutual funds*. These are professionally managed portfolios made up of a diversified mix of stocks, bonds, and other investments. Your profits are returned to you monthly, quarterly, or semi-annually in the form of dividends.

In choosing the type of savings account that works best for you, you will be taking into consideration the following: the interest rate; any fees, charges, or penalties you may incur; and the balance requirements. For help in selecting a savings vehicle, consult with a responsible family member, a friend, a bank professional, or a financial professional whose references you have carefully checked out.

Credit and Debt

As a college student, you'll find yourself being aggressively courted by credit card companies. Why? Because these companies know that a lot of people in your situation live on borrowed money, and that's how *they* make money—by getting people to borrow it from them. Are credit cards to be avoided? Only if you can't handle them responsibly. To find out how to deal responsibly with credit, read on.

CREDIT PROS AND CONS

In olden days, the idea of using credit instead of paying cash for items was frowned upon. In the words of a Spanish proverb, "A pig bought on credit is forever grunting." Today, however, attitudes about credit have changed. It is not unusual for people in this day and age to view credit as a way of life. In fact, credit has its pros and its cons, as most things do. What's good about credit? Consider the following pros:

- You don't have to carry as much cash around.
- Resources are available to you in case you have to buy some kind of necessity right away that you can't afford to pay cash for—like new tires, for example.
- You get a record of your purchases, thus enabling you to see your buying patterns.
- Certain credit cards are accepted virtually everywhere and are excellent for getting you out of a jam, where an out-of-state check just won't do.
- Credit cards are ideal for Internet shopping.

© 2005 Jupiterimages Corporation

And the downside?

- You're paying for borrowing. It's called interest, and it can quickly add up to **stupefying** levels.
- You may fall into impulsive buying patterns—never a good idea.
- Your credit rating can become endangered if you can't pay your bills on time.

If and when you do decide to get a credit card—and the overwhelming majority of Americans go for the plastic—keep these ground rules firmly in mind:

1) Read the fine print of your credit card contract. You may find that there are **punitive** finance charges or other drawbacks.

2) Try to borrow only as much as you can pay back in a reasonable amount of time, according to the repayment schedule you've set up in your budget.

3) Pay your bill—at least the minimum—promptly.

4) Check all charges on your statement, for some may be erroneous. If you find mistakes, **rectify** them by contacting your credit card company immediately.

5) If you're having difficulty meeting your payments, notify your credit card company. Don't try to hide—they'll find you.

6) Report a stolen or lost card immediately.

7) Do *not* give your credit card number over the phone to anyone unless you're the one who's made the call or you are absolutely certain of who's on the other end of the line.

SELECTING A CREDIT CARD

When choosing a credit card, consider the following factors:

- *APR*. The Annual Percentage Rate is the rate of interest that you pay on an outstanding balance.
- *Special introductory rates*. To attract new customers, credit card companies often offer attractive deals on signing up, like a 0% interest rate for a limited time.

stupefying stunning, amazing
punitive inflicting punishment
rectify correct

- *Balance transfer rate*. Credit card companies compete fiercely for customers, and may offer excellent incentives for moving your balance from another company to theirs.
- *Cashback and rewards*. Some companies offer incentives, like reward points for purchases, as part of their credit card package. If you're lucky, you might be able to find a really nice perk, like accumulating points toward air mileage when you go grocery shopping.
- *Minimum repayment*. Be absolutely clear about the minimum you need to repay every month. Depending on your plan, failure to meet your minimum payment could result in harsh penalties. Late payments can incur extra charges as well.
- *Annual fees*. Some firms—like American Express—charge an annual fee simply to use their card. You'll have to decide if it's worth it.
- *Exceeding your limit*. Let the buyer beware—if you max out, you could be looking at extra fees as well.

CREDIT CARD TROUBLE

Debt can be an exhausting load to carry around. For the average student, credit cards represent the most dangerous form of debt. While it's true that student loans are also a form of debt, they are not structured to be oppressive. Credit card debt, on the other hand, can quickly spiral out of control. Here are some warning signs that can indicate credit card trouble:

- You avoid paying your bills, often sending them in late.
- You only pay the minimum amount.
- You don't even *know* how much you owe.
- You secure a new loan in order to pay off old loans.

How can you avoid this kind of trouble? One way is by observing a general rule for borrowing money known as the 20/10 rule. The 20/10 rule states that you should never borrow more than 20 percent of your annual net income (after taxes). For example, if your annual net income is $6,000, your maximum safe debt load would be $1,200. Similarly, your monthly debt payments should never exceed 10 percent of your monthly income. So then, if your monthly income is $500, your monthly loan and bill payments should not be more than $50.

If you're having a problem dealing with your credit card bill, try trimming your expenses wherever you can. Don't go out to eat as much ... or at all. Don't buy expensive makeup or shampoo or clothing. Make do with less. Rent a movie instead of paying $10 to see one at the mall. Notify your credit card company of your problem, and try to work out some kind

of payment schedule that you can stick to. In most cases, the credit card people will try to cooperate with you so that you can get out of the hole. After all, if you're in the hole, they're not going to be seeing any money.

If the problem continues, consider credit counseling. (You will find resources for this at the end of the chapter.) A credit counselor may advise you to consolidate your debt—meaning that you would put all your debt under one roof and only make one payment a month, instead of a lot of smaller ones. Be sure to use one of the **reputable** counseling services, such as the ones we recommend at the chapter's end, and not some shady "credit repair" company, like the ones that pepper the Internet with promises they can't keep.

YOUR CREDIT RATING

As you make your way through the world, you are building up a *credit history*. A good credit history will allow you to borrow money when you need it—like when you're looking for a car loan or a home mortgage. A tarnished credit history will prevent you from taking advantage of these financial opportunities.

Your credit history is reflected in a *credit report*. Such a report will include the following:

- Identifying information (your name, Social Security number, address, previous address, phone number, and employer)
- Credit history (previous and current types of credit, credit providers, payment patterns, outstanding obligations and debts, and credit lines)

reputable having a good reputation; honorable

In a frank and honest exchange, share your thoughts on the use of credit. When you were growing up, what kinds of messages did you get about credit and debt? Have you gotten into trouble around the issue? What advice do you have on the subject? Of course, if you don't want to get personal, then you don't have to join in the discussion. But you may find that many of you are in the same boat, and good ideas are meant to be shared.

- Public record information (tax liens, judgments, and bankruptcies)
- Prior requesters (names of those who have requested credit reports on you in the recent past)

The Fair Credit Reporting Act stipulates that you have the right to review your own credit report. To receive a copy of your credit report, contact any of the following:

- *Experian Consumer Assistance Center.* 1-888-397-3742. http://www.experian.com
- *Equifax Credit Information Services.* 1-800-685-1111. http://www.equifax.com
- *Trans Union Consumer Relations.* 1-800-916-8800. http://www.transunion.com/index.jsp

Credit reports are notorious for their mistakes. There may be records, for instance, that confuse you—John P. Adams—with someone named John P. Addams, who passes bad checks. If, however, you discover that your credit history is not what it should be—and you own up to the fact that you haven't been the most solid citizen when it comes to financial matters—then you'll want to start to remedy the situation immediately. The best way to start building up a better credit history is by increasing your income as you can, paying your bills on time, and reapplying once you feel you're in a better position.

STUDENT LOANS

One form of debt that you may have to assume is a student loan. Student loans make a college education possible for millions of people, and you should never be afraid of them. On the other hand, you must fully understand how they work and should recognize the nature of the responsibility you are taking on. A recent study titled "Big Loans, Bigger Problems" conducted by the United States Public Interest Research Group (US-PIRG) found that most students who take out loans do not have a clear understanding of their cost. Indeed, up to 78 percent of those college students surveyed underestimated the cost of their loans by more than $4,800.

The first place to turn when you want to familiarize yourself with the different types of student loans and how to apply for them is your school's Financial Aid office. For now, however, we'd like to make a few key points on this subject.

- *Shop around.* Even though the interest rate on federal student loans is set by the government and will be the same from every lender, the lenders themselves may offer different payment incentives that can result in significant savings for the borrower. For instance, some lenders will offer a quarter-percent deduction off your interest rate if you make electronic payments. Others will "reward" you by knocking off points on your interest rate if you pay on time for a certain amount of months. See what's out there before you make your decision.

• *Ask questions.* As with any borrower/lender agreement, it's important to read the fine print when you're taking out a student loan. You'll want answers to questions like: What is the interest rate? Is it variable or fixed? Is there a cap? What origination fees are charged? Will you need a co-signer? Is there a penalty for prepayment?

• *Be familiar with the repayment terms of your loan.* Student loans *must* be repaid! Some students don't seem to realize that. With federal loans like the Perkins or Stafford, repayment begins either 6 or 9 months after you graduate, withdraw, or attend school less than part-time. Ignorance is no excuse for not meeting the terms of your loan.

With college costs being what they are these days, loans are essential for millions of students. The U.S. Department of Education alone provides more than $67 billion a year to help students and their families pay for postsecondary education. Be proud that you qualify … but be an informed and responsible consumer as well.

GAMBLING

Gambling is insinuating itself into the lives of many college students today. While most people who gamble can manage to keep it in perspective, gambling clearly has the potential for becoming a full-blown addiction. Gambling—or *gaming*, as the industry prefers itself to be known—involves an exchange of approximately $30 *trillion* a year just in

STUDENT TALK:
THE POSSIBLE DREAM

"I went back to school when I turned 27. I already had a 3-year-old son, and I was working as a garage mechanic. It was okay, but I wanted more out of my life. I wanted to be an engineer. Some of my friends couldn't believe it. You'll be over 30 when you graduate, they said. So what? I told them. I'll be over 30 however you look at it—so I might as well be over 30 with a degree. I took on a whole loan package, my wife started cutting people's hair in our living room, and somehow we're getting through it. Sometimes it feels really tough, but, when you think about it, it's really not such a long time, you know?"

—Greg G., 29, Amarillo, TX.

its legal forms alone, from lotteries, casinos, and horse and greyhound racetracks to professional and collegiate sports, riverboats, and, most recently and explosively, online betting.

Why do people gamble? For any number of reasons. Because they think it's fun … and it can be. Because they think they might win … and it's possible. Because they don't know how easy it is to lose or because they just can't stop. As gambling opportunities have **proliferated** in our society, so have the number of people who suffer from a gambling problem. Approximately 2.5 million people or 3 percent of the adult population are said to be compulsive gamblers. Gambling is even more of a problem among younger people. According to research conducted over the last 5 years and presented at the 10th Annual Convention of the American Psychological Association, between 5 and 8 percent of young Americans and Canadians have a serious gambling problem. The research also shows that young people are more likely to become addicted to gambling than they are to alcohol, smoking, or drugs.

An addiction to gambling can turn a person's life into a living hell. Take the quiz below to see if you're prone to this problem.

Twenty Questions About Gambling

Gamblers Anonymous—a fellowship of men and women who share their experiences, strengths, and hopes with each other so that they may solve their common problem and help others to recover from a gambling problem—offers this "diagnostic" quiz:

1) Did you ever lose time from work or school due to gambling?

2) Has gambling ever made your home life unhappy?

3) Did gambling affect your reputation?

4) Have you ever felt remorse after gambling?

5) Did you ever gamble to get money with which to pay debts or otherwise solve financial difficulties?

6) Did gambling cause a decrease in your ambition or efficiency?

7) After losing, did you feel you must return as soon as possible and win back your losses?

8) After a win, did you have a strong urge to return and win more?

9) Did you often gamble until your last dollar was gone?

proliferated to create or reproduce in rapid succession

10) Did you ever borrow to finance your gambling?

11) Have you ever sold anything to finance gambling?

12) Were you reluctant to use "gambling money" for normal expenditures?

13) Did gambling make you careless of the welfare of yourself or your family?

14) Did you ever gamble longer than you had planned?

15) Have you ever gambled to escape worry or trouble?

16) Have you ever committed, or considered committing, an illegal act to finance gambling?

17) Did gambling cause you to have difficulty in sleeping?

18) Do arguments, disappointments, or frustrations create within you an urge to gamble?

19) Did you ever have an urge to celebrate any good fortune by a few hours of gambling?

20) Have you ever considered self-destruction or suicide as a result of your gambling?

If you've answered "yes" to at least seven of the above questions, a visit to Gamblers Anonymous, at http://www.gamblersanonymous.org, may be warranted.

Your Money or Your Life ...

As we said at the top of this chapter, money will play a central role in your life. Whether you dedicate yourself to making money or deemphasize it, money will always be a force to reckon with. The way you deal with money is very personal and very important. However you feel about money, it is important to educate yourself about it, so that you can make the right decisions in its regard. The learning is life-long, and, no doubt, you'll make your share of mistakes, but the good news is that money mistakes rarely last forever. History is filled with stories of men and women who made and lost and then re-made lost fortunes. It's not a habit we would recommend, but fortunately there is some margin for error and most of us will be able to learn from our mistakes and move on through life.

What Did We Learn?

There is much to learn about money, and, as we've said, this chapter was only a start. Let's see, however, how you did on this "start."

1. Explain the difference between a *fixed* and a *flexible* expense.

2. Name five important guidelines to keep in mind when you're budgeting.

3. What factors should you consider when you're selecting a checking account?

4. What is overdraft protection?

5. What is the point of reconciling a checkbook?

6. Explain the difference between *simple* and *compounded* interest.

7. What is the safest form of savings?

8. Name some of the pros of having a credit card. The cons?

9. What are the seven most important rules when it comes to opening and maintaining a credit card account?

10. What is an APR?

11. Name some warning signs that can indicate credit card trouble.

12. Explain the 20/10 rule.

13. What is a credit history?

14. What are the components of a credit report?

Bibliography

Eades, J. M. (2003). *Gambling addiction: The problem, the pain, and the path to recovery.* Ventura, CA: Vine Books.

Lawrence, J. (2004). The budget kit: The common cents money management workbook. Chicago, IL: Dearborn Trade.

Mundis, J. (1990). How to get out of debt, stay out of debt, and live prosperously. New York: Bantam.

Needleman, J. (1994). *Money and the meaning of life.* New York: Currency.

Stockwell, A. (1997). The guerilla guide to mastering student loan debt: Everything you should know about negotiating the right loan, paying it off, protecting your financial future. New York: HarperCollins.

Twist, L. (2003). *The soul of money: Transforming your relationship with money and life.* New York: W.W. Norton & Company.

Tyson, E. (2003). *Personal finance for dummies,* 4th ed. Hoboken, NJ: John Wiley & Sons.

Links

Consolidated Credit Counseling Services—nationally recognized nonprofit organization. Retrieved December 9, 2005, from http://www.consolidatedcredit.org/

Federal Reserve Board FAQs: Banking information. Retrieved December 9, 2005, from http://www.federalreserve.gov/generalinfo/faq/faqbkinfo.htm

Financial sense and smart savings. Retrieved December 9, 2005, from http://usa.visa.com/personal/student/index.jsp

National Council on Problem Gambling. Retrieved December 9, 2005, from http://www.ncpgambling.org/

Personal budgeting and money saving tips.
   Retrieved December 9, 2005, from http://
   www.personal-budget-planning-saving-
   money.com/
Practical money skills for life. Retrieved
   December 9, 2005, from http://www
   .practicalmoneyskills.com
The I.O.U. Degree: FAQs about student loans.
   Retrieved December 9, 2005, from http://
   hffo.cuna.org/story.html?doc_id=247&sub_
   id=12433

Word Smart

The following vocabulary words are money in the bank:

doable

duality

lucre

proliferate

punitive

rectify

reputable

stupefy

LIFE SKILLS 101

This chapter is not intended to teach you everything you need to know in order to get along in the world. Obviously, that would be impossible, and you don't need us for that anyway. You do fine on your own. There is definitely a value, however, in collecting useful information wherever you can get it, and that's our goal here. You should come away from this chapter with a good general sense of how to deal with some of the practical issues in your life and how to avoid the pitfalls that often accompany these issues.

A Place of Your Own

If you're a younger college student, you may soon be getting your own place for the first time. If you've started out living in the dorm or at home, there may come a time when you're ready for off-campus (or away from home) housing. This is an exciting step, but it comes with a serious load of responsibility.

The first thing to consider is the impact that this move will have on your finances. Obviously, you'll have to pay rent, and, if you've been living rent-free at home, or even contributing a small amount toward the family fund, taking on such a significant monthly expenditure can be a very big deal indeed. Once you decide that you can handle the rent, you will then have to consider all

the other expenses that are involved. For instance, you're going to have to absorb the cost of moving. Many people underestimate these costs, so you should have a clear idea as to what they are. They can include the following:

- Rent in full for the first month.
- Rent in full for the last month. (Less common, but sometimes required.)
- Security deposit. (The amount of money you give the landlord upon signing the lease to cover unpaid rent, damage to the premises, or cleaning charges. This amount should be refundable, according to the terms of your lease.)
- Cleaning deposit. (Sometimes required in addition to or in lieu of a security deposit, this is money that you pay in advance for cleaning the rental property before and after you move in. This deposit is normally nonrefundable.)
- Utilities deposit. (An amount determined by the utility company to be paid and kept on deposit with the utility until a good credit rating is achieved or service is terminated.)
- Telephone deposit. (Similar to a utilities deposit.)
- Cost of renting a moving truck or van.
- Cost of hiring movers, if necessary.

Assuming that you are not **dissuaded** by this list, and are already envisioning how you're going to set up your kitchen, your bedroom, and your houseplants, then it would help to know a few things about the landlord-tenant relationship.

dissuaded persuaded not to do something

© 2005 Jupiterimages Corporation

UNDERSTANDING YOUR RIGHTS

Sadly but truly, many students are compelled to move into housing that is distinctly subpar. This is what they can afford. The ceiling may be stained, the windows won't stay open, and the bathtub doesn't invite a long soak. While you may be willing to put up with certain things that are not **aesthetic**, you certainly don't have to sit by quietly if your landlord is exposing you to conditions that are unsafe or unsanitary. Broken windows or damaged plaster, insect or vermin infestation, excessive noise, lack of garbage collection, heating problems, broken locks on your door or the lobby door are all situations that call for action.

As a tenant, you have both clear-cut rights and responsibilities. You are entitled to:

- Safe and sanitary living conditions.
- A lease that stipulates the conditions and length of your tenancy.
- The right to withhold rent if your landlord refuses to make necessary repairs in a reasonable amount of time.

By the same token, a tenant must fulfill the following responsibilities:

- You have to pay your rent on time.
- You can only use the rental space for the purposes specifically stated in your lease.
- You must maintain your rental space as it was rented to you and pay for any damages you incur to the walls, floors, or furniture. (If you don't, you stand to lose all or part of your security deposit once you vacate the premises.)
- You have to notify the landlord if any major repairs are necessary. (After all, *you're* living in the apartment—not the landlord. If the toilet tank is overflowing, you're the one who's going to know about it.)
- If a roommate moves out, you have to find a replacement or else you have to pay for the ex-roommate's share of the rent. It's not the landlord's job to find you a new roommate.
- If you change the locks, you have to give the landlord a new set of keys. He or she needs to have access to the apartment.
- Notice is required if you vacate the premises before the end of your lease. The landlord may be open to your leaving, as this can allow for the rent to be raised, but if a new tenant cannot be found, you will have to assume the remainder of the lease.

aesthetic pleasing in appearance

That pretty much takes care of your responsibilities as a renter. Let's see how things look from the landlord's perspective. The landlord's rights include:

- The right to charge an additional fee if the rent is late. (This additional fee will be specified in your lease.)
- The right to keep the various securities and deposits if you don't live up to your end of the lease agreement.
- The right to enter the apartment if he or she thinks there is a problem of safety or sanitation.

The landlord's responsibilities include:

- Making necessary repairs in timely fashion.
- Ensuring that the premises, including the exterior grounds of the building, are kept safe and sanitary.
- Paying interest on deposit monies.
- Entering the premises only at an agreed-upon time to make repairs (unless there is an emergency) or to show the apartment to potential renters if you have given notice that you are moving out.

The relationship of landlord and renter doesn't have to be **adversarial**. A cooperative feeling between the two parties will make everyone's life easier and will help you enjoy your new freedom and independence.

Car Talk

More people lose more money on cars than on probably any other single purchase. If the word "lemon" sends a chill down your spine, read on to find out how to protect yourself when it comes to car ownership.

BUYING A CAR

As with renting an apartment, your first step when considering the purchase of an automobile is to go back to your budget to see what you can afford. To make an informed decision, you must be able to understand the costs involved. Some of these costs are fixed and some are flexible. The fixed expenses, which you can think of as ownership costs, include:

- The depreciation, which means the decline in the car's value over the course of its life. A standard rule of thumb is that a car loses 15 to 20 percent of its value each year.
- The interest on the loan, if you've chosen to take one out.
- The insurance costs.
- The various fees for registering the car, your license, taxes, etc.

adversarial relating to conflict

Flexible expenses are best understood as operating costs. Among these are:

- Gasoline.
- Oil changes.
- Tire maintenance, purchase of new tires, and snow tires, if necessary.
- Regular maintenance and repairs.
- Unexpected repairs.
- Parking and tolls.

As you can see, a car doesn't come cheap. But then what's the alternative? Taking three buses to school every day? So you spring for it. You decide to extend yourself. You can cut out smoking—a wonderful place to start economizing. You can increase your job hours, or take on some other kind of extra work. When people are motivated to make money, they can usually find a way.

Now you have to ask yourself the various questions connected with making such a significant purchase. What does a car mean to you? Do you see it as a status symbol or more as a way to get around? Do you have the expertise to service a car yourself? Do you know someone—a family member, a friend—who can help you, or do you have to rely on professionals for everything? Do you know what kind of car you want? New? Used? Do you know anyone who drives that kind of car? Are you going to take out a service warranty? What do the consumer guides have to say about the car that you have your eye on?

That's a lot to think about, but then a lot of money is involved. Can we assume that you're going to be buying a used car? Most likely, we suspect.

USED CARS

Many car experts advise *only* buying used cars. Even a car with a few thousand miles on it will be markedly less than that same car brand new. After all, people pay a premium for that "new car smell." Follow these two steps when you're planning your mode of attack on the used car problem:

1) *Lay the groundwork.* Whether you're buying used or new, you'll be following the same initial steps when you decide to buy a car. First, you have to figure out how much you can afford, what kind of car you want, and how to determine if you're getting a good vehicle at a good value. To figure that out, check out the model you've targeted in the various consumer guides and consult with

a service garage that handles this kind of car to see how much repairs generally run. To determine what kind of asking price you should anticipate for the model and year you're considering, consult the *Kelley Blue Book*, which you can find in the library or online at http://www.kbb.com.

2) *Know your dealer*. Do we need to point out that "used car dealer" has become synonymous in our language with swindlers? This public perception is not necessarily fair, as there are certainly many used car dealers who are honest and upstanding. Indeed, most used car dealers offer well-inspected vehicles with at least some kind of limited warranty. Unfortunately, those dealers who aren't so honest have given the field its bad name. One nasty trick they've become notorious for is "adjusting" the odometer. A very low mileage reading on a used car could be a warning sign of such dishonesty. Check with friends and family to see which dealers they recommend. Once you've zeroed in on a car and a dealer, secure your financing from a bank before you go any further. Generally, the bank's financing will be better than the dealer's. Before signing anything, *read the fine print*. Better yet, have someone who knows more than you—a family member or a friend—read it too.

Of course, in addition to used car dealers, you can also buy a used car from a private individual, at auction, or from a used car superstore. Let's look at those options.

- *Private individual*. A lot of people have had great experiences buying used cars from private individuals. There is always the appealing prospect of finding some little old lady in tennis shoes who's only driven her car back and forth to the drugstore and who doesn't have a clear idea of its worth. If you've gone to someone's residence to view a car, glance around to see if the place appears to be in good repair overall. A ramshackle house usually predicts a ramshackle car. Check out the car carefully. Are the lights working? How does the motor sound? Always ask to see the maintenance records on the vehicle. If the seller hesitates, your antennae should go way up. Take the car on a test drive, making sure that you try it out on different types of road surfaces and on the highway, where you can check its pickup. And make sure to have the vehicle thoroughly inspected by a private mechanic. If all looks good, then you can begin your negotiations.

- *Auctions.* Buying a used car at a government auction of repossessed vehicles can seem like a good opportunity, but there are risks. Usually, you don't know exactly what you're getting—auctions cars may have been previously damaged in an accident or some other mishap—and it's often difficult to get any sort of warranty in this situation.

- *Used car superstore.* One of the safer avenues for a used car purchase, the superstore differs from the usual used car dealership in that the salesperson is not operating on commission and the sticker price is for real. You won't have to worry about negotiations, even though you can try if you want to.

- *Car rental agencies.* A very good source for used cars, rental agencies probably maintain their cars better than most owners do. The agencies most often take their cars out of commission after 1 or 2 years and factory warranties are often still in effect.

Buying a used car is a scary business, but it can also be a terrific opportunity to save a lot of money. The excellent Web site http://www.carbuyingtips.com, lists the following as its top four ways to avoid used car scams:

1) Get a mechanic to put the car up on a lift for inspection and to check for accident damage.

2) Check the car's history. Run a Carfax Vehicle History Report to see if the car was ever totaled, salvaged, rebuilt, flooded, failed inspection, was stolen, or had signs of odometer fraud. (For information on how to order such a report, visit http://www.carfax.com.)

3) Never sign a paper at a used car dealership with the "As Is" box checked off. Always ask for a 30-day warranty.

4) Have your own financing and loan approvals ready *before* you go shopping, not after.

MAINTAINING YOUR VEHICLE

As your car represents one of your most important investments, you won't want to drive it into the ground before its time. Normal depreciation aside, you can preserve the life of your vehicle by following these basic tips:

- *Get to know your vehicle.* Learn about it. Read your user's manual, cover to cover. Find out about your car's engine, tire size, instrument panel, and all the rest. You don't have to become an authority, but you can't afford to be a know-nothing.
- *Establish a log book.* Get organized. Know when and where you brought your car in for service.
- *Change your oil and check filters every 3,000 miles.* How many cars have been ruined by running them dry? Way too many. Don't become another statistic.
- *Find a service shop you can trust and stay with it.* It may take some looking around to locate a garage you can trust, but it's worth the effort.
- *Check your tire pressure.* You can easily do this yourself with a tire gauge. Find out how, and always keep your tires inflated to the pressure recommended by your manual.

restitution the act of making good for injury or loss

"Lemon" is a word that strikes fear in even the most stout-hearted of individuals. Here's what to do if you think you've been had:

1) Find out if the car has ever been reported as a lemon before. You can do this through the Carfax Web site, http://www.carfax.com.

2) Check into the lemon laws in your state through the Web site Lemon Aid at http://www.lemonaidcars.com. Note, however, that few states have lemon laws for used cars.

3) Make sure all your documentation is present and accounted for. You'll need every bit of proof if you're looking for **restitution**.

4) If all else fails, make a stink. Tell the car dealership that you're going to report them to the Better Business Bureau. Call your state Attorney General to report them. Threaten legal action. Don't take bad treatment sitting down!

"When I bought a car, I didn't know anything about anything. I decided though that I was going to learn how to do an oil change on my own. I think garages tend to take advantage of women anyway, so I wanted to have some position when it came to my vehicle. I took a course at an adult education center, and now I have no problem changing my oil myself. I save a lot of money that way, but, even more important, I feel like I have some sense of how a car works. Without it, I'd be totally at the mercy of others."

—Jill E., 20, Little Rock, AR.

- *Rotate tires as necessary*. Tires are expensive. Rotating them at recommended intervals preserves the life of the tire and offers more driving stability.

- *Be a wary consumer*. Follow an established protocol even with people you basically trust. Always ask that old parts be saved so that you can view them after the work is done. Even if you're bluffing, the mechanic will most likely think you're an informed consumer. Get all guarantees in writing, and never sign a blank work order. Ask pointed questions about the necessity of the repair and expect a full and patient explanation. If you don't get it, go elsewhere.

Remember—you're in the driver's seat. You—and not your mechanic—will have the final say over repairs.

Being an Informed Consumer

By now, you've probably picked up on a major theme of this chapter: how to become an educated and informed consumer. We've been exploring that topic in relation to renting an apartment and owning a car, but it's important that you apply that kind of thinking to all of your consumerism. Here are our top tips for shopping the right way:

1) *Ask yourself the big question*. "Do I really need this item?" should always be your first line of thought. Do you really need that electric foot bath? Does anyone? At the heart of informed consumerism is the ability to parcel out impulse from need. It can take practice, but it's worth the effort.

2) *Comparison shop*. There's always someone selling something cheaper—you just have to look around. Online auction houses like eBay can offer extraordinary values. Online shopping bots—search engines that look for best prices and values—are also worth checking. These bots include PriceScan, Biz.Rate, DealTime, MySimon, and PriceGrabber.

3) *Know the market*. To get a really good buy, you need to do some preliminary general research. For instance, if you're going to purchase a diamond, you should understand something about how diamonds are priced. You'll find out that color, gem quality, and other factors affect the market value. With other items, factors like rarity, seasonality, and public demand can influence the price.

4) *Take your time*. Never let a salesperson rush or intimidate you. If that's what they're trying to do, then they're in the wrong. You'll come to a decision when you're ready. Until then, they'll just have to sit by and wait.

5) *Keep your receipt*. Always … for whatever you buy. Getting into the habit of keeping and filing away your receipts offers an excellent form of insurance against getting burned if the goods turn out to be the bads.

6) *Be skeptical*. Read the fine print. Ask the hard questions. If something sounds too good to be true, it probably is. Don't expect miracles. You're not going to be able to buy a pair of fine leather shoes for $15, unless you stumble upon them at a yard sale on the luckiest day of your life.

7) *Know the return policy*. Thinking that you can return an item for a full refund and then discovering that you can only get store credit is a distinctly unpleasant surprise. When you're considering making a purchase, ask about the return policy and if you don't like the terms, move on.

8) *Get it in writing*. As far as promises, claims, and warranties go, they should always be in writing. By the same token, if you're having an item repaired, get a written estimate *before* the fact, not afterwards.

This is just a start on a complicated subject, but it's a good start. Remember—we all get burned now and then. Learning from our mistakes is the real key to becoming a better consumer.

The Lost and Found of Time

If you're a younger student—moving into an apartment for the first time—you're looking at a host of domestic responsibilities that you may never have had to deal with before. Cooking, cleaning, laundry … Mom! Where are you? There are a great many books written on household tips, and we're not going to attempt to compete with those, but we

primordial primitive; fundamental
exult to rejoice in, as in a triumph

REFLECTIONS: *YOUR HISTORY*

Shopping calls upon some of the **primordial** skills we honed way back when we were all hunters and gatherers. We have to use our eyes, our ears, our noses, and our sixth sense to make a killing. How do you see yourself as a consumer? Does the subject interest you? Do you consciously work at improving your skills? Have you ever really negotiated for something? Have you ever been "taken"? Reflect on this topic, and see where you can **exult** and where you can improve.

© Ingram Publishing

do feel that we should take a few moments right now to deal with the lost and found of time. After all, successful housework is about getting the job done in as little time as possible, right? So here is a brief whirlwind of good ideas to get you going:

- Keep a small memo board or a pad on the fridge so you can write down your grocery needs as you remember them.
- Try to shop at the same supermarket all the time (assuming you've found one with good values). That way, you won't have to relearn the grid every time you shop.
- Shop with a friend or roommate. Tear the list in half and meet back at the checkout counter.
- Figure out eight or ten meals that you really like and that are easy to make, and keep the ingredients for making them on hand at all times.
- Prioritize your cleaning responsibilities on a daily, weekly, monthly, or yearly basis. Your daily tasks might include making your bed or taking out the garbage. Weekly tasks could be vacuuming or cleaning the bathroom. Monthly could be changing the linen … it's up to you. And yearly? Well, that's reserved for stuff like turning the mattresses or cleaning the bathroom grout—stuff you'll probably never get to.
- Wear two basic styles of socks in white or black so you don't have to spend time sorting out these items when you do the laundry.
- Create a stationary drawer with scissors, tape, stamps, pens, envelopes, and all the rest of those things that you spend too much time looking for. Also, always keep your keys, wallet, and eyeglasses in the same place at home, so you're not wasting time looking for these items.

Following these tips is no guarantee against the kind of unanticipated and time-consuming problems that beset us all now and again, but being aware of timesavers is a good way to start to get some control over your life.

Street Smarts

Before we leave this chapter on life skills, we'd like to look at some ways that you can develop your capacity to survive in a challenging urban environment. Unfortunately, many students live on very tight allowance and this means that they have to live in neighborhoods that may not be all that safe. This section is designed to help you learn some good, solid, self-protective habits.

SAFE AT HOME

People tend to become **complacent** in what they regard as the safety of their homes. Unfortunately, their homes may not *be* that safe, especially if safety issues are not clearly kept in mind. While at home, observe these safety measures:

- Never hide your keys outside. Putting keys under the mat, or over the lintel of the door, is hardly original.
- Lock your doors—that's what locks are for! Even if you're just running down the hall for a minute, lock the doors anyway.
- Know your neighbors—they'll be your safety net.
- Check to see who's at the door before you open it—that's what the peephole is for!
- Do not let strangers into the building. If people are visiting someone, they should be admitted by using the intercom or by having their hosts come down to meet them. If they're not visiting, they have no business being in your building. Don't worry about hurting their feelings.
- Keep your windows locked and block sliding doors with a pole in the bottom track. If you wish to sleep with your bedroom window open, install a safety guard.
- Unless you personally know the repair people who show up at your door, ask to see their credentials and/or identification. If you have any doubts, call your landlord or building superintendent to make sure that the service was requisitioned before you admit the repair person.
- Don't leave your house dark. Install timers so that people will think someone is home, and so that you can come back to a house that is well lit.
- When coming home, check your doors before entering to make sure there are no signs of forced entry.
- Before entering an elevator, look to see if anyone is in it. Some states require that a mirror be installed in one corner of the elevator to expose the hidden corners. Check the mirror before entering.
- If you have any reason to suspect trouble upon returning home, call 911 from a safe location. Do *not* enter your home if you suspect trouble. You're really not equipped to deal with it.
- If you receive an obscene phone call, hang up immediately. Do not engage with the caller. If the problem continues, report the calls to the police and the telephone company.

complacent smugly self-satisfied

Following the guidelines we've provided to stay safe while out and about are good ways to protect yourself, but you may want more. Here are two options:

- *Mace and pepper spray.* Mace is essentially a form of pepper spray, which is an inflammatory device that can cause temporary blindness and can incapacitate an attacker. In most states, it is legal to possess and carry pepper spray. You should, however, check with your local police headquarters or your state's Attorney General's office to find out if there are any regulations regarding its use in your area. The use of pepper spray is justified only in cases of attack. Note that it is a *crime* to use pepper spray maliciously—as in zapping an ex-boyfriend or girlfriend just for the heck of it.
- *Self-defense courses.* A course in self-defense is an excellent idea for anyone, and this option has become particularly popular with women. You might find a good course sponsored by your school, your local police department, or your town's park and recreations department. You might also choose to go to a martial arts school. This may be costly but, depending on the school's reputation, it could be one of the best investments you'll ever make.

Source: Frequently asked questions about pepper spray. Retrieved December 9, 2005, from http://www.peppersprayinc.com/faq_about_pepper_spray.htm

- Keep photos and descriptions of your valuables, along with serial numbers of your computer and any other electronics. These will be necessary if you have to report theft.

SAFE IN YOUR CAR

Make your car safer by following these guidelines:
- Always lock your doors—that's what the locks are for!
- Crack your window by about an inch. It's harder to break a window that's slightly open.
- Keep all valuables out of sight, in a locked trunk or glove compartment.
- Keep your gas tank filled. Running out of gas makes you extremely vulnerable.
- Service your car regularly to protect against breakdowns. In case of a breakdown, tie a white flag or handkerchief to your antenna and wait for help. Obviously, if you have a cellphone and reception, call a car service, like AAA, or, if you can't get through, call the police. Call a friend or family member too, to tell them your situation and whereabouts. Never go with a stranger who offers to drive you somewhere.
- Know how to change a tire.
- Need we tell you never to pick up a hitchhiker? If you're thinking of it, you've obviously never seen that horror movie....
- Always park in a well-lighted area.
- Check inside, around, and *under* your car before you get into it.
- Once you're in your car, drive away from the parking lot immediately. Don't sit in your car leafing through your CDs, making a phone call, or whatever. Someone could be watching.
- Stay away from ATMs at night. Plan your withdrawals more carefully, to be done during the day, when things are much safer.

SAFE WHILE OUT AND ABOUT

Of course, you want to go for walks, jogs, and have the freedom you're entitled to. Here are some ways to protect yourself in these circumstances:
- Choose well-lit, busy places for your outdoor exercise.
- Wear brightly colored clothes and walk or jog while facing traffic. That way, you can see approaching cars.
- Do not walk alone, especially after dark. Most campuses have programs where they can match you up with an escort for walks home from the library or to your car. *Take advantage of these programs.*

- Familiarize yourself with emergency campus phones—what they look like and where they're located.
- Trust your instincts. If you get a bad vibe, you probably are getting it for good reason. If you suspect that you're being followed, duck into a store or a restaurant, and call a friend or family member to come and escort you home. If you're not near a store, just go up to the next person you see, explain the situation, and enlist that person's help.
- Walk assertively. Look like you're alert and aware. Give off strong, assertive body language. If you're in doubt as to what kind of body language you're giving off, ask a friend to assess you and give you pointers.
- When riding a bike, always use a bike light at night, wear a helmet, and use a U-lock to secure your bike.

A Balancing Act

This chapter has been full of practical suggestions. We'd like to leave you with a more holistic message, however. When it comes to life skills, the real key is to try to achieve a kind of balance that feels right for you. Some people only feel content if their beds are made up with hospital corners; other people regard the task of making beds to be about as pleasurable as a trip to the hospital. The responsibilities we assume as we move from childhood to adulthood—from dependence to independence—can be exhausting, frustrating, pleasing, and exhilarating. Find out what works for you, learn from your mistakes, and move on.

What Did We Learn?

A lot of information was contained in this chapter that could help protect you and your investments. Let's see how well you digested it.

1. Cite at least five expenses associated with moving.
2. Name three rights you have as a tenant.
3. Name seven responsibilities you must fulfill as a tenant.
4. What are three rights that a landlord can claim?
5. What are four responsibilities that a landlord must fulfill?
6. Name four fixed expenses associated with owning a car.
7. Name four flexible expenses that come with car ownership.
8. What is the *Kelley Blue Book*?
9. Name four different sources for used cars.
10. What are the four most critical ways to avoid a used car scam?
11. What is a Carfax Vehicle Report?
12. What steps should you take if you think you've bought a car that's a lemon?
13. What are the eight top tips for being an informed consumer?
14. Name three ways to protect your safety at home.
15. Name three ways to protect your safety while in your car.
16. Name three ways to protect your safety on the streets.

Bibliography

Jackson, M. (1998). *Car smarts: An easy-to-use guide to understanding your car and communicating with your mechanic.* Emeryville, CA: Avalon Travel Publishing.

Johnson, E., & Leamy, E. (2004). *The savvy consumer: how to avoid scams and ripoffs that cost you time and money.* Sterling, VA: Capital Books.

Lagatree, K. (1999). *Checklists for life: 104 lists to help you get organized, save time, and unclutter your life.* New York: Random House Reference.

Perkins, J., Ridenhour, A., & Kovsky, M. (2000). Attack *proof: The ultimate guide to personal protection.* Champaign, IL: Human Kinetics Publishers.

Portman, J., & Stewart M. (2002). *Every tenant's legal guide.* Berkeley, CA: Nolo.

Ross, J. R. (2001). *How to buy a car: A former car salesman tells all.* New York: St. Martin's Press.

Sacks, E. (1998). *The savvy renter's kit.* Chicago, IL: Dearborn Trade.

Sclar, D. (1998). *Buying a car for dummies.* Hoboken, NJ: John Wiley & Sons.

Links

CarBuyingTips.com. Retrieved December 9, 2005, from http://www.carbuyingtips.com/

Car maintenance basics from AAA. Retrieved December 9, 2005, from http://www.csaa.com/global/articleindexsubcat/0,1395,1004010300,00.html

General tips for consumers. Retrieved December 9, 2005, from http://www2.state.id.us/ag/consumer/tips/generaltips.htm

Personal safety tips for women. Retrieved December 9, 2005, from http://dede.essortment.com/personalsafety_rkbl.htm

Renting a house or apartment. Retrieved December 9, 2005, from http://www.consumeraffairs.com/rentals/how01.html

Word Smart

**Nail these vocabulary builders and use them
when you can:**

adversarial

aesthetic

complacent

dissuade

exult

primordial

restitution

CHARTING YOUR FUTURE

College can be such a completely consuming experience that sometimes you have to force yourself to think about what comes after it. In fact, what comes after comes relatively soon, so the time to start thinking about your future is now. As a well-known quotation from an anonymous source puts it, "When it comes to the future, there are three kinds of people: those who let it happen, those who make it happen, and those who wonder what happened." You, of course, want to be in that middle group, molding your future, as best you can, with careful thought, planning, and action. In this chapter, we'll be focusing on your career—how to figure out what you want to do and how to go about turning your dreams into realities. Hopefully, before long, any feelings of intimidation that you may be having will give way to a sense of excitement, possibility, and purpose.

You and Work

Why do some people succeed in their work lives while others flounder? Some would say it's all a matter of luck—being in the right place at the right time. Others would claim that success is available only to those who possess rare gifts or exceptional talents. Then there are those who believe that success runs in families and that if you're born with a silver spoon in your mouth, half the battle is won. The answer is that none of the above is true. Success is not principally determined by luck, talent, or heredity. More than anything, success is about effort.

Thomas A. Edison once said, "Genius is one percent inspiration, ninety-nine percent perspiration." You might say the same about success. Yes, luck helps, and, yes, extraordinary talent can count for a lot, but unless you're willing to do the work, then luck and talent will not count for much in the long run. Let's note, too, that many people who are born with silver spoons in their mouths wind up choking on them. The bottom line is that there is no substitute for hard work. You have to put in the time to reap the rewards.

While it may take a great deal of sweat equity to achieve success, the good news is that there is real satisfaction and even joy to be found in hard work. Professor Mihaly Cziksentmihalyi, Ph.D., of the Drucker School of Management at Claremont Graduate University, has coined a name for that special feeling that comes out of productive work: *flow*. Professor Cziksentmihalyi, named by President Clinton as one of his favorite authors, conducted a landmark study of adolescents in which he outfitted them with beepers that went off eight times a day over the course of one week each year. Every time the beepers signaled, the test group would report to Professor Cziksentmihalyi about what they were doing and how they felt about what they were doing. Cziksentmihalyi found that when people were involved in activities they enjoyed, they developed a sense of flow. This flow—the title of Cziksentmihalyi's best-selling book—can best be described as a very special feeling of energy that makes people want to continue doing what they're doing and return to it whenever possible.

Can you imagine what it would be like to experience that sense of flow on a regular basis—even daily perhaps? Many people enjoy exactly that experience on their jobs. They love what they do—helping people if they're a doctor, teacher, nurse, or firefighter; figuring out problems if they're an engineer, an architect, or a project manager; using their hands if they're carpenters, sculptors, or tailors; using their senses if they're cooks, florists, or musicians; using their quantitative intelligence if they're bankers, computer programmers, or accountants. Of course, there is much overlap between these skills and these careers, as well as so many other combinations and so many ways to enjoy your work. But that's exactly the point—there are so many ways to enjoy work. Your goal in college is to identify what interests you and what can sustain that interest over the long haul.

© 2005 Jupiterimages Corporation

271

What gives you that sense of "flow"? Have you ever felt it in a school setting? On a job? While pursuing a hobby or a special interest? Write down your thoughts on the subject of flow, asking yourself if, in fact, you've ever experienced it or under what conditions you can imagine experiencing it. At this point, fantasy is fine. If you think you would experience flow from being an astronaut, a ballet dancer, or a scuba diver, this is your chance to put it in writing.

FOOD FOR THOUGHT:
OCCUPATIONAL OUTLOOK HANDBOOK

What kinds of jobs are there? More than you could possibly imagine. Do you want to be a recreational therapist? A roofer? A rigger? A rabbi? There—we've just named four, and those are only from the R's. To explore occupations you've never even heard of, as well as those that have already piqued your interest, visit the Web site of the U.S. Department of Labor's Bureau of Labor Statistics at http://www.bls.gov/oco/home. htm and check out their *Occupational Outlook Handbook*. You'll find out about the many kinds of jobs that make up the labor market, as well as what kind of training is involved, the employment outlook, earnings potential, and sources for additional information.

JOBS VS. CAREERS

For some of you younger readers, the idea of finding a career that will feel good enough to last a lifetime seems way out of reach. You simply don't know what you want to be doing for the rest of your life, and that can make you feel lost, panicked, and unmotivated. But before you let your anxiety veer out of control, you should realize that your situation is hardly unique. In fact, your feelings are perfectly normal. Many people at your stage of life look toward career options with **trepidation** instead of enthusiasm.

The first thing you should realize is that choosing a career doesn't have to be forever. In an earlier era, people did have the expectation that jobs would last a lifetime and that they would ultimately retire with a gold watch or a nifty plaque. Well, welcome to America in the 21st century, where such ceremonial gold watches have gone the way of butter churners and manual typewriters. According to the Department of Labor, the average American in the 21st century will hold between 10 and 14 different jobs, with the average job lasting 3 to 5 years. **Flux** is the order of the day. The American worker is competing for jobs in a global arena now, and must continually stay ahead of the technological curve.

The idea of staying put in one place and having "The Company" take care of you may cast a rosy nostalgic glow, but that fantasy just doesn't make sense anymore. So it's important to figure out the things that you're good at and to understand how to go about getting and keeping the right job. In our next chapter, we will be focusing on the many tasks that will become a part of your job search. In this chapter, we'll be reviewing important general ways to prepare yourself for your career.

What Do You Want to Be When You Grow Up?

This is the question we all get asked when we're kids, and, for the most part, we parrot what our parents have told us. *Be a doctor. A lawyer. A teacher. A nurse.* Parents often advise children to pursue careers that are "safe," but what does "safe" mean? For the vast majority of people, it means a regular paycheck.

Some people are willing to forego that regular paycheck for what they think of as greater independence and freedom and may choose

trepidation fear or uneasiness about the future
flux constant change and instability

freelance work. Freelancing is a particularly popular avenue for creative types, like writers, graphic artists, and photographers, but it is also an option for paralegals, cosmetologists, practical nurses, and many other workers. As a freelancer, your time is your own. You get hired for jobs as they come along. Freelance work is exhilarating for some people, exhausting for others, and impossible for most.

Another kind of nontraditional route is the small business. Some people have a strong entrepreneurial bent and dream of owning a gift shop or a cookie outlet or a pet-grooming service. While such pursuits may sound intriguing, they are not for the faint at heart, as the overwhelming majority of small businesses fail in their first year. Business ventures should not be undertaken until one can claim some kind of sturdy foundation in business principles.

Let's assume for now that you're going to take the traditional route out of college and *get a job*. The problem is what do you want to do? You're at a crossroads and you're at a loss. One way to approach your problem is to get some testing—vocational testing as well as personality assessments.

TAKING INVENTORY

Vocational inventories, also called career inventories, and personality assessments can both be very useful. Vocational inventories are designed to help identify a range of careers that match a person's interests and skills. Personality assessments are intended to measure personal characteristics to see if they would be suited to a certain line of work or to determine if your personal "fit" goes with certain career possibilities.

These sorts of assessments can be very revealing. Keep in mind, however, that they are by no means **definitive**. No test has yet been designed—not the IQ, not the SAT, not the GRE—that can reveal everything about a person. All tests contain their share of *test error*—some flaw in the basic design of the test. Furthermore, different kinds of tests work for different kinds of people.

Some people don't like to take a test where they have to "pick one" because they don't see "one" that they like. Other people dislike tests that ask them to compare their answers to "how most people answered this question," because their self-esteem is shaky and they're afraid that they're not going to perform as well as others. We will be

definitive providing a final decision that will not be questioned or changed

© 2005 Jupiterimages Corporation

OPEN FOR DISCUSSION: CAREER CHOICES

What are you looking for in a career? Form a circle and exchange your thoughts on the subject. Are you looking for excitement? Security? Creativity? Companionship? Autonomy? What do you think your chances are of finding what you're looking for? If your feelings have a negative tilt to them, you may discover you're not alone. Try sharing your feelings and your ideas with your classmates. This could be a good opportunity to brainstorm on how to get what you're looking for.

discussing the characteristics of certain specific inventories and assessments as we go along, so you can get a sense of which ones might work best for you. You might want to take several different kinds of these evaluations until you find one that feels right.

Again, a test is just a test. If a test tells you that you should be a poultry farmer and you know that you have a tendency toward alektorophobia (fear of chickens—seriously), then you have to assume that there is some aspect of error in the test design. You may also fall through the cracks of a vocational test. Every person's destiny is, in a sense, unique, but yours might be even more so. Perhaps you're destined to be a glass blower, but that's not one of the fields that's going to be identified in the particular vocational test you're taking. If the results of a vocational inventory give you an answer that still doesn't feel like an answer, you'll just have to keep searching—by way of career counseling, networking, or other forms of job research.

Some of the more prevalent types of vocational inventories include the following:

- *Myers Briggs Type Indicator (MBTI)*. This indicator is designed to help you understand your personality type and how you relate to other people. It identifies your leadership potential, your capacity for teamwork, and other traits that count for a lot in the work world.
- *Strong Interest Inventory (SII)*. The SII takes about 25 minutes to complete and contains 317 items that measure your interest in a wide variety of occupations, hobbies, and leisure activities. Your inventory results are then compared to those of thousands of others who have taken the test and who report a high level of satisfaction in their career choices.
- *Self-Directed Search (SDS)*. This 15-minute inventory, which is self-administered and self-scored, helps you identify areas of interest that can translate into occupational paths. The inventory can be taken online at http://www.self-directed-search.com, and the results, in the form of a printable 8- to 16-page personalized report, can be ordered for a nominal fee.
- *Career Interest Inventory*. This popular inventory is made up of 60 questions and is a useful tool for helping with career exploration.
- *The Career Key*. This inventory, which measures your skills, values, talents, abilities, and interests, can help with your career choices as well as with your selection of a college major. This inventory can be found at http://www.careerkey.org.

Networking

You've probably heard quite a bit about networking—it's shaped up as a real 21st century buzzword—but, if you're not entirely sure what it means, it refers to the need to develop a broad range of contacts. These contacts, fostered both through work and social functions, can help immeasurably with your career goals.

Networking events go on all the time all over the country. People go to cocktail parties, wear badges to identify themselves, chat with each other over *hors d'oeuvres* and wine, and collect each other's business cards. Of course, all that may seem way ahead of you, but, as a student, you can—and should—network as well. It's never too early to get started.

Why would someone want to network? Principally, for the following two reasons:

- To gather information
- To make valuable connections that can lead to opportunities

In seeking employment, there are two types of interviews: a *formal* interview, which is part of the official application process, and an *informational* interview. When you ask people if they would be willing to sit for an informational interview with you, you're asking them contribute a certain amount of time, usually not very long, to help you fill in some of the blanks about the profession or industry that you're interested in. Such interviews can be very useful and can lay the groundwork for a job. After all, half the job of finding a job is getting into the same room with influential people, and these people are often willing to give earnest and ambitious people a few moments of their time.

© Image 100 Ltd.

Networking involves talking to strangers—a prospect that inspires pure dread in some people. In fact, very few of us are naturally drawn to such a situation. Most people who seem to handle this sort of thing well have *learned* to handle it well. You can too. Follow these tips to get a good grasp on the art of networking:

1) *Take a deep breath and jump in.* Don't be shy … or at least try not to be. Recognize that networking is an impulse that has its roots in basic human nature. People want to help other people, not necessarily out of a spirit of **altruism**, but because they think it can benefit them to do so. If they can help you get a good position, then maybe you'll help their son or daughter or niece or nephew or friend. That's the driving force behind networking—you scratch my back, I'll scratch yours.

2) *Talk to strangers.* Here we're suggesting that you do the opposite of what you were taught as a child. Learning to talk to people you don't know—which is something you'll want to become good at for the future, when you go to real networking events like cocktail parties—is another talent that few people are born with. You can practice talking to strangers whenever and wherever you want—on an elevator, on a bus, at a laundromat. Don't be afraid that people will think you're weird or out to pick them up. Just be friendly, pleasant, and brush up on your small talk skills. You'll see that conversing pleasantly with new people is a very nice way to experience the world.

3) *Understand boundaries.* If someone is kind enough to network with you, don't go overboard. For instance, don't ask to use that person as a reference—after all, you've only just met. Don't drop that person's name in some other context. You might come across someone who really does know that person, and the fact that your connection is so **tenuous** could prove embarrassing if the truth comes out.

4) *Don't take it personally.* Sometimes you'll try to network with someone, and you'll feel like you've come up against a brick wall. Don't take it to heart. For one thing, it may not be personal. The other person simply may not have time for you right now. Even if it

altruism an attitude or way of behaving marked by unselfish concern for the welfare of others
tenuous not based on anything significant or substantial

feels personal, don't take it personally. Other people's rudeness is their problem, not yours, and you mustn't allow it to damage your self-esteem.

5) *Always say thank you.* A follow-up note—or, when appropriate, an E-mail—is very much in order after someone has given you the gift of his or her time. Even if the note is very simple—and that's all it has to be—sending it can often make a big difference.

6) *Do unto others.* If you ever find yourself in the position where you can help other people as you were once helped, commit yourself to doing so. Remember how much it meant to you when you were in need?

Networking is a frame of mind. The more you do it, the more you improve. Start with friends and family and then move on to more challenging people—i.e., colleagues, neighbors, and then, ultimately, strangers. The idea is to expand your world, and to be excited, not fearful, in doing so.

THE WORKING LIFE

The best way to develop a profile that will present you as a good job candidate is by working. Every kind of work is worthwhile, whether it's babysitting or delivering newspapers or parking cars at the country club. Work is **intrinsically** valuable. It teaches you excellent life skills, like punctuality, ethical conduct, organization, teamwork, problem solving, and much, much more. In the next chapter, we will be discussing many aspects connected with the work world, like resumés, interviewing, salary negotiations, and more. In this chapter, we're going to continue to look at more general work-related topics, like internships, mentors, and volunteer work.

INTERNSHIPS

As we've said, all work is valuable, but certain kinds of work are more valuable than others. Successfully holding down a paper route is great, but working on a cruise ship if you want to become a travel agent is even better. One way to develop a resumé that will impress prospective employers in your chosen field is to hold an internship—an on-site work experience that is either directly related to your major field of study or that speaks to your career interest. Internships are usually tied to academic credit granted by the department in which you are majoring.

intrinsically by or in itself, rather than because of its associations or consequences

IN OTHER WORDS

"If A equals success, then the formula is A = X + Y + Z. X is work. Y is play. Z is keep your mouth shut."—Albert Einstein

While it is understood that internships are learning experiences, you will still be expected, as an intern, to make some kind of valuable contribution to the firm or organization you're working for. In other words, an internship is a real job—it just comes with a different set of rules than the "real" job you'll hold down the line. Internships can be paid or unpaid (although paid ones are obviously more difficult to get). They can be full-time or part-time. They can last for a month to a year or more.

In the increasing pressure these days for students to secure internships, a basic **disparity** becomes evident. Students who come from financially comfortable backgrounds are free to pursue their interests in unpaid internships; they don't need the money. Students from financially stretched backgrounds may not have the luxury to learn about banking or the music business or the fashion industry through an unpaid internship. They may need to work in a fast food restaurant or at the student cafeteria, earning money to meet their expenses. If you are one of those people who actually have to get paid for the work you do—welcome to the club. You might want to enhance your resumé by putting in a few hours a week, if you can afford it, doing some kind of volunteer work. We will be discussing this option in a few moments.

If you are planning to pursue an internship, follow these steps:

1) *Ask yourself the right questions*. Zero in on your goal by establishing your priorities. What are you looking to get out of an internship? What kind of organization do you want to work for? Government? Private sector? Not-for-profit? Large? Small? Are you interested in a particular industry or even a particular company?

2) *Be aware of hurdles*. It's one thing to stretch your pocketbook by taking an unpaid internship in the first place. It's another thing to intern in a city, like New York or L.A., where the housing can cost a small fortune, or to depend on something other than public transportation to take you to and from your place of work. Be clear about your needs and your limitations.

3) *Prepare yourself as if you're going for a real job*. Lining up a choice internship can be just as hard as landing a good job. The fact that you're not getting paid doesn't make it easy to secure an internship, particularly not the most sought-after ones. So you will

disparity lack of equality

need to have the usual job-search weapons at the ready—resumé, cover letter, references, etc. See Chapter 18 for useful tips on these matters.

4) *Synthesize the experience.* You'll want to get the very most out of your internship. That means that you should keep a record of the experience as it goes along, so that you can reflect on it when it's over. Keeping a log or journal of your experience is an excellent idea, as is writing a more extensive reflection at the end of the experience, which, if your internship is for academic credit, will most likely be mandatory.

Your internship can help you get a foot in the door and can serve as an entrée to your field of choice. If you're lucky, you might even find a mentor while you're interning.

MENTORING

Mentors are men and women who embody qualities—professional, personal, or both—that deserve to be emulated. Being lucky enough to find a mentor—or, eventually, to be one—can make an enormous difference in your life. Here are a few guidelines about the mentor-mentee relationship:

- *Don't confuse the relationship.* It's certainly possible that your mentor could become a significant person in your life, but he or she is not your father/mother, grandfather/grandmother, uncle/aunt, or anything of the sort. Your mentor occupies an important and unique position.

- *Be clear about your needs and your mentor's needs.* You are looking to your mentor for information and guidance. Your mentor wants to help, but doesn't want to do it all for you. Don't ask for "all." Simply ask for "some."

- *Use your networking skills to find a mentor.* It's not easy to find a mentor. You can't place an ad in the paper for one. You can ask around, however, and maybe someone will know someone who is open to hearing from an enterprising, ambitious person such as yourself. Let's say, for instance, that you want to learn something about filmmaking and you're willing to do any menial job in order to work with a filmmaker you admire. You might write that person, send a video you've shot, and hope that he or she will be persuaded by (a) your work and your talent; (b) your nerve/gumption/moxie; and (c) the way you interact with other people (namely, the person

you're pursuing). Hopefully, once you've made contact, you'll be able to impress that person with your perseverance, your potential, and what you have already been able to accomplish.

• *Understand that the mentor-mentee relationship is a two-way street.* Yes, you're looking to get something from the mentor. But guess what? The mentor is looking to get something from you, too. Your energy and spirit can be helpful in recharging a mentor's batteries, and your mentor may get a very good feeling from the time that he or she spends with you.

Finding a mentor is one of life's special "extras," and obviously you can survive and even prosper without one. The world of work is fiercely competitive, however, and any help you can get is welcome. Keep your eyes open, look around, and maybe you'll find someone who is ready, willing, and able to take on that mentoring role with you.

VOLUNTEERING AND COMMUNITY WORK

Lining up plum internships and influential mentors certainly can't hurt, but, as we've said, not everyone can afford to work in an internship and not everyone can find a mentor. The value of internships and mentors is that they expand your world, and, in doing so, they expose new opportunities and avenues for career development. Another valuable way to locate such opportunities is by contributing your time toward community and organizational work. Indeed, volunteering is every bit as valuable on your resumé as an internship or even a job.

Working with children, tutoring to advance literacy, working with the elderly, helping out in an animal shelter, manning a hotline, joining an organization like Habitat for Humanity or Meals on Wheels ... there are so many ways to contribute to your community and to the world. Sure, you say—nice idea. But show me the money. While it's true that volunteer work won't fatten your bank account, the fact is that devoting even a few hours of your time to a worthy cause can pay off in some very real long-term benefits. Some of these benefits include:

- *Experience*. If you're looking for a way to bulk up your resumé, volunteer work gives you some necessary ammunition. Usually, you won't need any real experience in order to get a volunteer job. After all, you're not getting paid so the organization that hires you is not going to put up a lot of roadblocks against free help. But, once you've got your foot in the door, you can really go places. You can be every bit as eager and hard working as you'd like. And, down the line, when potential employers consider you for *paying* jobs, they'll see that you're the sort of person who puts yourself out there. Your history with volunteer work will show that you're a self-starter, and that's music to an employer's ear.

- *Career information*. By working as a volunteer, you'll be able to get an inside look at careers. Let's say your dream is to be a veterinarian. You volunteer at a neighborhood animal shelter and you discover that you are violently allergic to cats and dogs. Time to find a new dream. You volunteer at a nursing home and you find out that you have a special rapport with elderly people. You enjoy the experience so much that you begin to think about a career as a geriatric social worker. Volunteering can help you research fields in a way that is meaningful and constructive and fluid. If a volunteer post shows you that a certain field is not right, you can just move on, with no harm done.

- *Connections*. Any kind of work expands your world of connections, and connections are a big factor in ultimately finding the job that's

"In my sophomore year in college, I started to volunteer, through my fraternity, working in an after school playground program in the neighborhood. I did it because everyone else I knew was doing something and it seemed easy—right here, outdoors, and I like kids. I went into college thinking I was going to be an accountant, but guess what? I fell in love with the playground. I don't know—in some ways, I guess I'm just a big kid myself, and this just felt so right. The great thing was that I found out that there was a whole major, and even a graduate degree, in Recreation. It's a really growing field and it seemed perfect for me. Now, as a senior, I'm planning to take more courses in Recreation, get a full-time job with the town recreation department when I graduate—they've already told me I can count on it—and do my graduate work while I'm in the job. What amazes me is that if I hadn't done the volunteer work, none of this would ever have happened."

—Cory Y., 20, Lansing, MI.

right for you. That's the whole point about networking. You might volunteer for Habitat for Humanity and find yourself driving nails into sheetrock alongside another volunteer, who turns out to be the president of a bank. He sees what kind of person you are—hard-working, curious, able to get along well with others—and he takes an interest in you. Suddenly, a powerful person is on your team, and who knows? Maybe you'll wind up in banking, which never would have happened if you hadn't picked up that hammer in the first place.

- *References*. When you ultimately apply for a paid position somewhere, you will be asked to provide references. The director of the day camp for disabled children where you have given your time generously over the years will have nothing but wonderful things to say about you. That will mean a lot to your prospective employer.

- *Self-esteem*. Doing good for others is doing good for yourself. It will make you feel like you're a fully contributing member of the human race, that you make a difference, and that you have strong and solid values. This benefit is probably the most valuable one of all. Your self-esteem will radiate as you make your way in the work world.

Keep in mind that your volunteer work shouldn't end once you land a paying job. Volunteer work is one way to get to the top of the pyramid, so plan on having it play a part in your life all through your life.

More School?

Right now, at this point in your life, it may be hard to imagine going on to graduate school. Of course, for many fields, graduate school is a must. Lawyers, physicians, teachers, architects, clergymen, social workers … all these professions require graduate study. For some students, the prospect of 2 to 8 more years of additional study feels utterly daunting. And why shouldn't it? Burnout is certainly as much a factor among students as it is for any segment of the work population. After all, at the point when you'll be ready to consider graduate school, you will have just spent 16 or more years as a student. That's a lot of books, tests, and homework. Before you commit to more school, you may need some time off to refresh yourself.

No matter what kind of graduate work you're considering, ask yourself the following questions to decide if the time is right:

- *Do I need a year off?* If you're exhausted, and segueing right into graduate school feels like more than you can handle, a year off is

© 2004 Stockbyte

not only justifiable on its own terms, but you could actually spend that time building up your profile, and thereby enhancing your chances of admission down the line. If, for instance, you're thinking of applying to medical school or law school, you could try to work for a year in the field, at a lab, or in a law office. Or you might take a prep-course for the GRE (Graduate Record Examination) or any of the other standardized tests that may be required for admission.

- *Do I need more convincing?* Graduate school is a big step—in terms of time, in terms of effort, in terms of money. Doing some kind of work in your area of interest *before* you go to graduate school may help you decide whether this is a world you really want to get involved in … or not.

- *Do I need real-world work experience?* Some fields, like business, for instance, expect students to have some significant real-world experience under their belts before making an application to graduate school. You should understand that if and when you do apply to graduate school, you'll be competing for admission against applicants who have held jobs, sometimes very impressive ones. Putting your time into a real job in the real world may be absolutely essential.

- *Am I financially up to this?* Maybe you need some pure infusion of capital before you can continue with the student life. There's nothing wrong with that. Stashing away some money will alleviate pressure once you get to graduate school.

- *Will I be motivated to return to school once I leave it?* Maybe yes, maybe no. If you're not feeling the urge, then it probably wouldn't

What Did We Learn?

Test your mettle on the following:

1. Define the concept of "flow."
2. What is the *Occupational Outlook Handbook?*
3. How many careers will the average 21st-century American hold in a lifetime?
4. What is the difference between vocational testing and personality assessments?
5. Define *networking.*
6. What are the two reasons why people network?
7. What is an informational interview?
8. What are the six top tips for improving your networking skills?
9. Define *internship.*
10. What is a mentor?
11. What are the four ground rules that apply to the mentor-mentee relationship?
12. What are the benefits of volunteer work?
13. When considering graduate studies, what are the six questions you should ask yourself?

Bibliography

Csikszentmihalyi, M. (1991). *Flow: The psychology of optimal experience.* New York: Harper Perennial.

Green, M. E. (1998). *Internship success.* New York: McGraw-Hill.

Lowe, N. (1998). *The pathfinder: How to choose or change your career for a lifetime of satisfaction and success.* New York: Fireside.

Martinent, J. (1992). *The art of mingling: Easy, proven techniques for mastering any room.* New York: St. Martin's Griffin.

Nierenberg, A. R. (2000). *Nonstop networking: How to improve your life, luck, and career.* Sterling, VA: Capital Books.

be a good idea to continue with graduate work right away. It's better to put off graduate school than to do it in a way that undercuts your chances for success.

- *Will I be too old if I wait?* Too old for what? Barring the unforeseen, most human beings can expect to enjoy a nice long life span. More than half of the students who attend graduate school in the United States are over the age of 30. It's never too late.

Many options open to you if you're interested in furthering your education beyond college. There are part-time and full-time programs, evening and day opportunities, online degrees, and more. It will be up to you to find out what's out there and what works best for your needs.

Moving Ahead

Søren Kierkegaard, the 19th-century Danish philosopher, wrote that, "Life can only be understood backwards, but it must be lived forwards."

That is your job right now—to live your life forward. In this chapter, we have looked at some of the "macro" aspects of your future career—deciding on the sort of work you want to do, networking with the people who can help you, finding the internship or the mentor that can make all the difference, figuring out when the time is right to pursue graduate studies. In our next and last chapter, we're going to be exploring some of the "micro" aspects of the work world—looking for jobs, developing a resumé, interviewing, salary negotiations, and more.

Shea, G. F. (1999). *Making the most of being mentored: How to grow from a mentoring partnership*. Stamford, CT: Crisp Publications.

Tieger, P. D., & Barron-Tieger, B. (2001). *Do what you are: Discover the perfect career for you through the secrets of personality type*. Boston: Little, Brown.

Links

Exploring career choices from the Bureau of Labor Statistics. Retrieved December 9, 2005, from http://www.bls.gov/k12/

Flow: The psychology of optimal experience by Mihalyi Czikszentmihalyi. Retrieved December 9, 2005, from http://www.butler-bowdon.com/flow.htm

Networking tips and pointers. Retrieved December 9, 2005, from http://www.rileyguide.com/nettips.html

Guides and Databases for Finding Internships

InternJobs.com. Retrieved December 9, 2005, from http://www.internjobs.com

National Internships Guide. Retrieved December 9, 2005, from http://www.internships.com

Rising Star Internships. Retrieved December 9, 2005, from http://www.rsinternships.com

Word Smart

Here is this chapter's crop:

altruism

intrinsic

definitive

disparity

flux

tenuous

trepidation

LANDING THE JOB

Looking for a job is no one's idea of fun. It is challenging work, demanding a high level of organization, motivation, and confidence. One of the unavoidable realities of looking for a job is that you may not get what you're looking for. Disappointment and frustration are natural by-products of this process. In this chapter, you'll find out what to anticipate and what steps to take so that the process can go more smoothly, and you'll also learn how to cope with the results, whatever they may be. There is a lot to review in this chapter, so let's get started.

Regarding Resumés

When it comes to a job search, your resumé is your most important tool. A resumé is a summary of your education, work experience, accomplishments, and objectives. Some people use the word *resumé* interchangeably with *curriculum vitae* (also known as CV or simply "vitae"). These are actually two different animals. A CV is more detailed than a resumé, and is most commonly used by people looking for jobs within the academic world. So, for our purposes, we will be focusing on the resumé.

In order to make your resumé as powerful as possible, you have to be clear about your qualifications and your objectives. As far as your qualifications go, perhaps you're a bit unsure of yourself or intimidated about touting your achievements. You might be wondering if you even *have* enough achievements to tout. Part of getting into the right frame of mind for your job search is being able to identify your strengths.

What do you see as your strengths? In order to identify them, you may have to do some brainstorming with friends and family. Let's imagine for the moment that you've been a serious athlete all your life—an active member of the hockey or basketball or baseball team. Teamwork is a much-prized value in the work world, and, as an athlete with a real track record, you have an authentic claim on that value. Teamwork, therefore, goes down as one of your strengths.

What about problem solving? That's another quality much valued in the work world. Let's say you worked as an assistant manager in the campus copy shop in your junior and senior years. Lots of problems came up and you were often the one who dealt with them, right? So, you can legitimately put down problem solving as one of your strengths.

Think about communication as another value in the work world. If you've developed your listening and speaking skills to a fairly advanced level, let your prospective employer see that on your resumé. Mention any major presentations that you've delivered to an audience. If you've put in time at the campus radio station, let that be known as well. Another big plus for employers is technological savvy. If you've had experience with computers, audiovisual equipment, or anything of the sort, that should be noted on your resumé. Do you get the idea? It's all about looking at your record of achievements and seeing how those achievements can be made relevant to the job you're going after.

As for your objectives, they should be tied to your strengths. Although you may not want to close any doors at this point, if you've been involved in the campus newspaper for four years and feel that writing is one of your primary skills, then it is reasonable to cite writing opportunities among your primary career objectives. If you've been selling cosmetics in a department store for the last two summers, and want to continue to work in the world of retail, then it makes good sense for you to write "sales position" as one of your objectives. Your objectives should always be keyed to your skills and your experience.

DECISIONS, DECISIONS …

As you craft your resumé, there will be choices to make and decisions to reach. One of the first things to consider is the way companies review resumés in this era of advanced technology. While many companies do

have Human Resources personnel that look over hard copies of resumés, companies today are increasingly turning to databases to process the resumés that they receive. When such a company receives a resumé—either on paper or via E-mail—it is entered into a database so that it can be searched and scanned electronically. Certain elements of the resumé, such as degrees (Associate, Bachelor, Masters) and skills (e.g., marketing, accounting, writing, word processing), show up as keywords in the scanning process, so think about how your resumé addresses this issue. Also, as scanners will not be able to handle fancy styling, like italics or bolds, your resumé should be formatted in a "text only" format. You should also have on hand a hard copy of your resumé, on good paper, with whatever visual stylings you choose. This can become part of your career portfolio, ready to be pulled out as needed.

The biggest decision you will have to make right at the start of the resumé process is whether you want your resumé to be *chronological* or *functional*. A chronological resumé lists your work experiences in the order in which they've occurred—actually, in reverse order, with the most recent accomplishments heading the list. On a chronological resumé, students generally list their educational accomplishments before their work experience. Job seekers who have been out of college for a while or older college students reverse that order, with work experience coming before educational attainments. A functional resumé, on the other hand, packages your work experience in terms of the various functions and skills that you have mastered in the course of your work life. You *analyzed, investigated, developed* … and so forth. Functional resumés are often the choice for people who have gaps in their careers or for career changers. When a recruiter sees a functional resumé instead of a chronological one, his or her antennae may go up, suspecting that the candidate is trying to cover for some problem or period of unemployment.

THE TOP 10 RESUMÉ RULES

When it comes to an actual job prospect, you should assume that you have one shot and one shot only to grab attention. The possibility of a second chance is remote. That said, here are 10 golden rules that will present your resumé in the best possible light:

1) *White paper only*. People who are attracted to "rainbow" colors may choose to reproduce their resumés on tangerine, violet, or shocking pink paper. Unfortunately, shocking pink could shock a prospective employer. Is it worth the risk? Obviously not. Stick with conservative shades only—white, buff, or gray.

FOOD FOR THOUGHT: RESUMÉ VERBS

There's nothing like a good verb to liven up a resumé. *MBA Style* magazine has a useful list of action verbs to consider. Among them are:

- adapted
- aided
- assisted
- audited
- collaborated
- conceived
- conceptualized
- consulted
- coordinated
- designed
- devised
- documented
- evaluated
- expanded
- formed
- gathered
- implemented
- initiated
- instituted
- led
- maintained
- managed
- negotiated
- operated
- organized
- originated
- planned
- produced
- reviewed
- spearheaded
- trained
- updated
- wrote

Check in at http://www.members.aol.com/mbastyle/web/verbs.html for more.

Source: MBA Style magazine's action verbs for MBA resumes. Copyright © 1996 *MBA Style* magazine. Retrieved December 9, 2005, from http://www.members.aol.com/mbastyle/web/verbs.html

2) *Keep it short.* Unless you're a Nobel Laureate or hold patents on hundreds of inventions, restrict your resumé to one page. You'd be surprised by how much you can pack into a single page (and chances are you don't have that much to pack yet).

3) *Proofread.* Your resumé must be *100 percent free* of errors. If a word is misspelled or out of sequence, that will be the first thing people focus on. Don't rely on your computer's spell-checker to catch your errors. Enlist your family, friends, teachers, your school's Career Guidance Office, and/or a professional resumé service to proof your resumé.

4) *Do not mention salary.* Salary requirements do not belong on a resumé. Reserve such discussion for when you actually get a job offer.

5) *Don't try to be funny.* We can't imagine life without a healthy dose of humor, but there's a time and a place for everything. A resumé is neither the time nor the place for humor. Not everyone is lucky enough to have a sense of humor, and your attempts to be **wry** could be misunderstood or unappreciated.

6) *Leave off personal references.* Do not include the names of any personal references. You may include the phrase "references on request" at the bottom of your resumé, if you wish, or you could dispense with references altogether. It is generally understood that we can all scratch up a few people in the world who have something good to say about us, and when the time comes that your prospective employer requests references, that's when you'll provide them.

7) *Don't forget your contact information.* Believe it or not, some people neglect to include their contact information on their resumé and only show it on the cover letter. Make sure the information appears on both.

8) *No photographs, please.* An amazing phenomenon occurs when you put a photograph on a resumé—it immediately takes on the look of those "Most Wanted" flyers you see at the post office.

9) *Do not use the title "Resumé" at the top of the page.* Everybody knows what it is—you don't have to announce it. Your name and contact information is quite enough.

wry somewhat perverse or ironic

STUDENT TALK:
RESUMÉ SERVICES

"After looking all over the Internet for information on resumé-writing, I decided I wasn't getting what I needed on my own, so I bit the bullet and paid a professional resumé service to help me pull it all together. It was expensive, but I think it was worth it. I came out with a really terrific-looking resumé that was very targeted and felt really dynamic. If you decide to go this route, make sure that you do a lot of comparison shopping. Look at four or five different services, ask to see their product, and check their prices against each other."

—Mary Ellen H., 27, Concord, NH.

Carmen Padilla

852 Madison Street
West Haven, CT 06516

860-229-3132
padillac@hotmail.com

Objective: Hotel Sales Manager

PROFESSIONAL SKILLS
Proficient in computers, including Leisureshopper, Microsoft Word, Excel, System One, and Apollo.

Experience
Travel Agent 2004–Present
AAA NORTHWAY, New Haven, CT
• Provides execptional customer service and bookings for air and train travel, cruises, packages, car rentals, and hotels.
• Maintains up-to-date information on various locations and attends regular customer service classes.

Administrative Assistant, Conferences 2003–2004
Services
PITNEY BOWES, Stanford, CT
• Competitvely selected as one of two interns to participate in the working experience at Pitney Bowes. Responsibilities included greeting and registering all visitors to Conference Center (98,000 annually), scheduling conference room facilities, indentifying and coordinating support services (audio/visual), assuring appropriate room arrangements as needed, coordinating and planning menus with clients and Canteen Food Service.
• Assisted visitors in arranging tranportation, lodging, and communications. Experienced in multiline telephones, e-mail, and scheduling through computer.

Walt Disney World College Program, 2003
Merchandise Hostess
WALT DISNEY WORLD COMPANY, Lake Buena Vista, FL
• Nationally selected from over 200 colleges and universities to be a participant in the living, working, and learning experience of the Walt Disney World College Program.
• Responsibilities included maintaining Disney standards in all aspects of job performance in order to provide quality service for over 100,000 guests from all over the world, as well as management responsibilities, philosophy, financial structures, corporate culture, employee etiquette, and protocol for "The Disney Success Formula."
• Lived with international students in a mulitcultural environment.

Bank Teller 2000–2002
FLEET BANK, New Haven, CT
• Promoted to assitant head teller.
• Provided cutomer service and monitored multicash transactions utilizing computerized banking system.

Waitress (Seasonal) 2003
WEST HAVEN MUNICIPAL GOLF COURSE, West Haven, CT

EDUCATION
President's List, published in National Dean's List; Ducktorate: a degree from Walt Disney World Company representing outstanding work performance given by the Disney University; selected for internships at Walt Disney World and Pitney Bowes.

A.A.S. Degree, Gateway Community College, 2003
New Haven, CT

CLUBS
Delta Phi Epsilon Sorority

10) *Never lie.* Some people cannot resist the impulse to embellish the truth, and so they pad their resumés with little white lies. Other people see the resumé as an opportunity to write fiction in a big way and tell outrageous lies. Either way, you can get into a lot of trouble by lying on your resumé. If your job search is restricted to a small town or even a small city and your deceptions have been exposed, word can travel fast and you may find yourself shut out of the local job market altogether.

The resumé is very, very important, but almost as important is the cover letter. Let's have a look at what constitutes a good cover letter.

The Cover Letter

Before a prospective employer even gets to your resumé, he or she is going to see your cover letter. If the cover letter is not as appealing as it should be, then it's unlikely that the employer is going to be sufficiently

motivated to turn to your resumé. Therefore, you have to find a way to make your cover letter into an invitation to read further, rather than a stumbling block to get around. Here are some good ideas with regard to cover letters:

- *Always personalize it.* Nothing turns people off faster than receiving a letter with an impersonal salutation. Such salutations as *Dear Sir or Madam* or *To whom this may concern* have no place in a cover letter. These anonymous salutations indicate that you haven't bothered to do the necessary legwork to uncover the exact name and title of the person receiving your letter. Do the work, and make sure you spell the person's name right!

- *Say not what the company can do for you, but what you can do for the company.* Some people write cover letters from the angle of what they can get out the company—"I feel that Sunrise Industries can help me achieve my full potential, etc...." The problem is that Sunrise Industries may have other matters on its mind than fulfilling your potential. A better take on the assignment is to put it in terms of what *you* can do for *them*. "I feel that my combination of bilingual fluency and public speaking prowess would make me an ideal representative of Sunrise Industries." Now that's something that might interest a prospective employer.

- *Color-coordinate with your resumé.* Match the color of your cover letter stationary with the color of your resumé paper. Also, if possible, keep the fonts of both the letter and the resumé the same.

- *Restrict yourself to one page.* There is absolutely no reason why your cover letter should extend beyond a page. It should essentially consist of three targeted paragraphs: (1) why you're writing (e.g., "I'm answering an ad that appeared in the 1/20/06 edition of the *Daily Gazette*" or "I'm writing at the suggestion of Mr. or Ms. Jones"); (2) what you have to offer (be specific about your skills and/or your knowledge of a certain sector of the industry); and (3) what your course of action will be (you will follow this letter with a phone call). End with a proactive statement. Don't sit back and expect to be called. The world doesn't work that way.

- *Let your E-mail serve as your cover letter.* If you are submitting a resumé electronically, your E-mail will suffice as a cover letter. There is no need to attach a separate cover letter.

- *Proofread.* The same rules apply here as with the resumé—don't trust your own eyes or your computer's spell-checker. Get a second and third reading from friends, family, teachers, or a professional service.

- *Avoid humor*. Again, this is neither the time nor the place for jokes. Stay serious.
- *Make a list*. Keep a checklist of things to remember about the cover letter. These include: (1) signing the letter (no one pays attention to unsigned letters); (2) ending with "Sincerely" (anything else is too familiar); (3) signing with blue or black ink; (4) using a conservative postage stamp, not one with Santa that's still hanging around from Christmas; and (5) typing or neatly printing the address on the envelope. Review your checklist before mailing.
- *Do not staple*. The resumé and the cover letter should never be stapled together.

If you follow these guidelines, you should be able to avoid the most **egregious** mistakes. Keep your tone friendly and to the point, and hope for the best.

The Interview

If your resumé and cover letter are well received, you may soon find yourself invited for an official job interview. We're hoping to put you in a positive frame of mind with some good solid information so that when the time comes, you'll be ready. Let's look at what you should be doing in the preparatory phase.

GETTING READY

As soon as your interview is scheduled, you may begin to feel an attack of nerves. Your main goal is to stay cool, calm, and collected. Is that possible? Certainly. Following these guidelines can help:

- *Be sure you know where you're going*. If at all possible, take a dry run ahead of time to the site where your interview will be taking place. You certainly don't want to wait for the appointed time to realize that you don't know how to get where you're going or to discover that there's no parking available when you get there. Go straight to your ultimate destination. Sometimes, if the interview is in one of those vast industrial parks, the layout can be extremely confusing and you can wind up in a sweat as you try to figure out where to go. Arriving at your interview in a sweat is not recommended.
- *Pull together all your relevant information*. When you go for an interview, bring along your Social Security card, your driver's license, the names and addresses of former employers, and the name and

egregious bad, blatant, or ridiculous

phone number of the nearest relative that does not live with you. Don't leave home without these, for you may be asked to provide this information as part of your employment application.

- *Bring along your resumé.* Even if you've mailed your resumé in advance of the interview, you should still print out another copy and bring it along on the appointed day.

- *Dress for success.* Again, there are no second chances when you try out for a job. First impressions count for everything. When you dress for an interview, the idea is to look professional and relatively conservative … unless, that is, you're applying for a job at the Hard Rock Café. Seriously though, you should look like you have some basic understanding of **decorum**. That means no platform shoes or sandals, no jeans, no halter tops, no bangle/spangle jewelry, no T-shirts, no sunglasses. Do not wear perfume or cologne—many people today find fragrances to be an unpleasant invasion of one's space. Clean, pressed clothing in muted colors and conservative styles is best.

- *Be absolutely punctual.* This is related to our first guideline—*Be sure you know where you're going*—but we thought it best to restate it so that the message sinks in. If you are even *1 minute* late, you can essentially bid this job farewell. Interviewers figure that if you're late on the day of the interview, you're going to be chronically late to the job.

- *Role-play with family and friends.* Rehearsing your interview with family and friends can be very useful, assuming that they take the

decorum dignity or correctness that is socially expected

FOOD FOR THOUGHT: WARDROBE HELP

Many people find it difficult, if not impossible, to afford the two or three outfits necessary to project a confident and professional image when going out into the workplace. Fortunately, there are some wonderful nonprofit organizations that have been formed to address this need. These organizations receive donations of clean and attractive outfits from individuals and manufacturers that are then passed along to the people who need them. For more information, check out these two Web sites:

- Wardrobe for Opportunity at http://www.wardrobe.org
- Dress for Success at http://www.dressforsuccess.org

role-playing seriously. Encourage them to ask you tough, probing questions. Have them assess your body language and the tone of your voice. Instruct them to be brutally honest, for that's the only way you're going to benefit from this exercise.

So much for the preliminaries. Now let's look at some do's and don'ts for when you're in the interview itself.

IN THE RING

Once you're in the interview, keep these considerations in mind:

- *Smile*. A smile is a universally acknowledged symbol that says, "Hello. I am glad to be here. I look forward to having this pleasant conversation with you." A smile goes a long way and is absolutely free, so why not start out with one?
- *Watch your habits*. You know all those bad habits that your parents are always criticizing you for—slouching in your chair, mumbling, playing with your hair, biting your nails? Well, your folks are right—such habits make a bad impression. Control them as best you can.
- *Eat not … drink not*. Never bring food or drink into an interview. Not a latté from Starbucks, not a bottled water for hydration purposes, not a stick of gum. This is a job interview, not a coffee break.
- *Hands off*. Don't lean on or touch the interviewer's desk. Some people are very territorial about their space—even irrationally so.
- *Don't air grievances*. A job interview is neither the time nor the place to start complaining about previous employers. There is no way you're going to look good by saying bad things about other people.

• *Always say "thank you."* Say it at the end of the interview, along with a handshake, and then follow-up with a thank you note or E-mail. Something simple—"I'd like to thank you for your time and I look forward to hearing from you"—is all that is necessary. The thank you note should not be viewed as an opportunity to restate your case for employment.

GOOD QUESTIONS, BAD QUESTIONS

At some point in the interview, you will be asked if you have any questions. This is not the time to sit there, looking pretty. Your interviewer wants to see if you're a genuinely curious, engaged, and thoughtful person who has prepared for this occasion. What are some good questions to ask the interviewer when it's your turn? Consider the following:

• Is this a new position?
• Who would be my supervisor?
• What is the company's culture? Formal? Relaxed? Flexible?
• How many people have held this position in the last 2 years?
• Are there any current plans for expansion or cutbacks?
• What opportunities are there for advancement in this department and/or company?
• What do you see as the most challenging aspects of this position?
• May I ask what attracted you to this company?

Note too that there are certain questions that interviewers are not permitted to ask. You should be clear about what these are. The following questions are off limits.

• Any question suggesting that the interviewer is trying to determine if you are over a certain age (like 40). The interviewer, however, may ask for proof of age to determine that you are old enough to meet the minimum job requirements.
• Any questions regarding arrests and convictions that are not relevant to the position being sought. You may be asked about arrests and convictions that have occurred *only within the last 7 years* and only about those that are relevant to job performance, like theft, robbery, embezzlement, or forgery. You cannot be asked about traffic offenses, drug convictions, and so on.
• Any questions regarding your weight or height.
• Any questions regarding marital status.
• Any questions regarding children, the employment or salary of your spouse, child care arrangements, or whether you have any other dependents.

FOOD FOR THOUGHT: DO THE RESEARCH

In order to compile good questions to ask your interviewer, you should do some research into the firm you're interviewing with in advance of your meeting. Let's say you're interviewing with Verizon. You'll do your research, and when the time comes that you get to ask a question, you'll be able to say something like, "I understand that Verizon has just acquired Acme Products [fictional name]. How do you think that will change the direction of the company?" Your interviewer will be most impressed with your preparation.

Some useful Web sites that can help you with this kind of research are:

• *American City Business Journals* (http://www.bizjournals.com). A collection of articles in business publications throughout the United States.
• *Annual Reports Gallery* (http://www.reportgallery.com). The largest collection of annual reports on the Internet.
• *CNN Money* (http://www.money.cnn.com). The news site with reports on all kinds of fascinating financial happenings.

- Any questions regarding your birthplace or ethnic background. In some situations, you may be asked to provide proof of citizenship or a visa or alien registration number.
- Any questions regarding military discharge.
- Any questions regarding race, skin color, or the color of your hair or eyes.
- Any questions regarding sexual conduct or sexual orientation.
- Any questions regarding your religious denomination or affiliations, or whether you observe any religious holidays.
- Any questions regarding handicaps that do not directly relate to one's capacity to perform the job, or any questions regarding pregnancy.
- Any questions pertaining to the names or relationships of persons with whom you reside, or whether you own or rent your home.

If you are asked any of these questions, simply state that you do not think the question is relevant to the position being filled, and that you would like to focus on those qualities and attributes that are relevant. The interviewer will get the point, and may very well be impressed with your presence of mind.

Negotiations

In the event that you are offered a job, your next step will be to negotiate terms. You'll be looking at salary, benefits, vacation time, and other factors. Pay close attention to the following pointers for help with this phase of the hiring process:

- *Do your homework.* Know the going rate in your geographical area for the kind of position you're being offered. A good Web site for researching such information is Salary.com (http://www.salary.com).
- *Operate from a position of good will.* Negotiating a salary is not like negotiating for a used car. If the hire goes through, you're going to be spending day after day, side by side with these people, so you want a good feeling to emanate out of your negotiations. Know when to negotiate and when to stop negotiating. Even if you accept a little less than you had hoped for, the amount of good will you can engender from not squeezing out every last cent is well worth the shortfall.
- *Understand the importance of benefits.* Benefits are factored into your total package and represent an important source of compensation. Some benefits include: health insurance; dental care; contributions to a pension plan or matching contributions to a 401(k) plan;

profit sharing; stock options; vision care; free or partially paid gym membership; paid vacation plus personal days; discounts on subscriptions to publications; life insurance; disability insurance; reimbursement for continuing education courses; and a company car or reimbursement for mileage or parking. You need to acquaint yourself with all of these "extras" because your overall salary negotiation may take these into account.

- *Let the interviewer do the talking.* If possible, let the person on the other side of the table bring up the subject of compensation. If he or she does not, make sure you do. If the interviewer asks what kind of salary you're looking for, a good response would be something like, "What is the range that the company pays for this position?" Feel free to cite some of the statistics you've uncovered regarding competitive salaries in your geographical area.

- *Don't plead poverty.* The fact that you're supporting your maiden aunt or that your house needs a new roof is not relevant to these discussions. Your salary negotiation should be based on merits, not hardships.

- *Keep selling yourself.* Whenever possible, promote your assets and the special qualities you would bring to the company. If the interviewer brings up the salary issue prematurely—i.e., before you've had an adequate chance to sell yourself—ask to defer the discussion for a little while longer. "I'd like to find out more about the position, please," is a good stalling tactic.

Sometimes a salary offer is made in the form of a letter, following your interview. If the salary happens to be what you're looking for, then congratulations. If it's lower than what you're looking for, ask to come by and discuss the situation in person. Face-to-face negotiations over salary are far more effective than negotiations by phone or E-mail.

REFERENCES

Most likely, you will be asked to submit references as part of your application—usually three. There is a **protocol** that you should follow when it comes to references. Here are the main points to consider:

- *Carefully choose your biggest fans.* Only ask people to serve as references if you are entirely sure that they can speak on your behalf *without reservation*. If there is any question in your mind, ask them

protocol the rules or conventions of correct behavior on official or ceremonial occasions

IN OTHER WORDS

"A date is a job interview that lasts all night. The only difference between a date and a job interview is that there are not many job interviews where there's a chance you'll end up naked at the end of it."—Jerry Seinfeld

outright about this. "Do you have any reservations about doing this for me?" Better to ask than to get a lukewarm endorsement.

- *Ask permission.* Make sure that your references *know* they've been asked to be references. Don't assume that just because somebody seems to like you, they're ready to provide a reference.
- *Take it outside the family.* Relatives should not be asked to write references. That would make you look like you have nobody else in the world to stand up for you.
- *Alert your references.* Your prospective employer will let you know when he or she is going to be contacting your references. That should be your green light to call your references and prepare them.
- *Keep your letters on file.* You should have letters of reference at the ready, in your career file. You don't want to be caught empty-handed if your references move to Australia or can't be easily reached by phone or E-mail.

Always remember to thank your references for the help they've provided. A follow-up phone call, note, or E-mail is a must.

Professional Behavior

Let's imagine that you've successfully gone through the whole process we've laid out in this chapter and you've been hired for the job. Hooray! It's a big and wonderful step in your life to land such a choice position and to start making your way in the world. The real work, however, lies ahead of you. Now that you have the job, you have to perform.

It's not a question of your talents or intelligence or likeability. Given the competitive job market today, you wouldn't have been hired if your employer did not see real potential in you. There's a difference between getting hired and *staying* hired, however. In order to hold on to a job, you have to behave professionally in the workplace.

What does it mean to behave professionally? Some of the hallmarks of professional behavior that will establish you in the eyes of your colleagues as a really valuable part of the organization include:

- *A positive attitude.* Are you even-keeled, upbeat, in control of your anger, and able to roll with the punches? Or are you moody, unpredictable, sour, and aloof? Your coworkers are looking for positive personalities that are easy to be around. Make sure you are such a person.
- *Staying ahead of the technology curve.* Technology is constantly evolving and, as a result, we must all continually educate ourselves about what's new and innovative. You don't want to be the one in the office who is always running to others for help with your computer.

© 2005 Jupiterimages Corporation

- *A capacity to listen*. Earlier in this book, we talked about the importance of listening. We're talking about it again … just in case you didn't hear us. If you don't listen, you can't communicate. If you can't communicate, you can't function as part of a team.
- *A talent for teamwork*. Most U.S. companies use the team as the model for their organization. You needn't have been a three-letter athlete in college to understand teamwork. (Although it certainly doesn't hurt to have played sports.) You can learn teamwork by working in groups on a variety of academic, community, and social projects, and in many other ways as well.
- *A willingness to change*. Flexibility and the capacity to go with the flow are very important in the work world. Change is always occurring, and those who grumble at change are often left behind.

© 2005 Jupiterimages Corporation

REFLECTIONS: *YOUR HISTORY*

Think about a time that you've been treated in a way that you felt was less than professional. Was it with a physician perhaps? With an attorney or an accountant? Was it with a teacher? Recapture that experience by writing about it now, and reflect on what professional behavior means to you.

What Did We Learn?

Learning about the job search has been a real job. Let's see how you did.

1. What is a resumé?
2. Explain the difference between a *chronological* resumé and a *functional* resumé.
3. What are the top 10 rules for creating a resumé?
4. Name nine important tips for writing a good cover letter.
5. What are some things you can do to prepare yourself for an interview?
6. What are some things you should do when you're in the actual interview situation?
7. Name five good questions to ask the interviewer when it's your turn to ask questions.
8. Name five areas that an interviewer is not permitted to question you about.
9. What should you say if you are asked a question in an interview that the interviewer is not permitted to ask?
10. What are the six rules to follow when you're negotiating your compensation?
11. What are the five main points you should remember with regard to references?
12. What are the eight qualities that best characterize professional behavior?

Bibliography

Angel, D. L. (1997). *No one is unemployable: Creative solutions to overcoming barriers to employment*. Hacienda Heights, CA: WorkNet Training Services.

DeLuca. M. J. (1996). *Best answers to the 201 most frequently asked interview questions*. New York: McGraw-Hill.

Greene, B. (2004). *Get the interview every time: Fortune 500 hiring professionals' tips for writing winning resumés and cover letters*. Chicago, IL: Dearborn Trade.

Kador, J. (2002). *201 best questions to ask on your interview*. New York: McGraw-Hill.

- *Dependability*. To really be viewed as a professional, you have to be the sort of person that others can count on. That means that you show up on time, with your assignments completed as they were supposed to be. There are no gray areas when it comes to this issue. You either are dependable or you're not. There's no such thing as "half-dependable."

- *An ear to the ground*. You must stay alert to and informed about what's going on around you and what's going on in the world. You should be aware of the political, social, and economic factors that affect our lives. You must not be adrift in "La-La Land," but, rather, should stay anchored to reality.

- *Adherence to ethics*. It is vital that you understand the ethical code of the profession you are working in. Some professions, like law and medicine, have very strict ethics around confidentiality, for instance. All jobs demand an ethical commitment to hard work and honesty.

Of course, there are other indicators of professional behavior, like openness to compromise, a commitment to excellence, and the courage to try new things. As you make your way in the work world, you will be surrounded by people who don't meet your standards and those whose standards you will aspire to. Learn from the latter.

A Final Word

Together, we have taken a long journey through this book. We hope that it has been helpful, and that it has given you a clear understanding of the skills and attributes you need in order to successfully navigate your college years.

You are at a time in your life that is full of promise, opportunity, and stimulation. We wish you much luck in making the most of it. You'll need more than luck, however. You'll need to be clear about what your goals are and what you have to do to accomplish them. Once you understand the need to balance the fun with the work and the freedom with the responsibility, you'll be able to go very far toward creating the kind of life you've always dreamed of.

Kasar, J. (2000). *Developing professional behaviors*. Clifton Park, NY: Thomson Delmar Learning.

Pinkley, R. L., & Northcraft, G. P. (2003). *Get paid what you're worth: The expert negotiator's guide to salary and compensation*. New York: St. Martin's Griffin.

Ryan, D. J. (2000). *Job search handbook for people with disabilities*. Indianapolis, IN: Jist Publishing.

Ryan, R. (2000). *60 seconds and you're hired*. New York: Penguin.

Links

Anatomy of a resume. Resume advice from Monster.com. Retrieved December 9, 2005, from http://resume.monster.com/articles/resumeanatomy/

Benefits of the job. Understanding fringe benefits. Retrieved December 9, 2005, from http://www.workshopsinc.com/manual/Ch4L2.2.html

Create interview rapport. Job interview advice from Monster.com. Retrieved December 9, 2005, from http://interview.monster.com

Research companies online. Retrieved December 9, 2005, from http://www.learnwebskills.com/company/

So you wanna write a cover letter? Retrieved December 9, 2005, from http://www.soyouwanna.com/site/syws/coverletter/coverletter.html

Web sources on salary negotiation. Retrieved December 9, 2005, from http://jobstar.org/tools/salary/negostrt.cfm#Web

Word Smart

Here you go—your last little batch.

decorum

egregious

protocol

wry

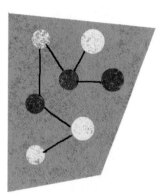

INDEX